Data Wrangling with SQL

Student Edition

Kimberly Seefeld, EdD

Table of contents

Data Wrangling with SQL

Student Edition

By Kimberly Seefeld, EdD

Published under **DataJoyAI** imprint

Companion resources for this book are available at:

DataJoyAI

https://datajoyai.com

Edition: First Edition
ISBN: 978-1-969233-42-5

Chapter 1

Introduction to Data Wrangling

1.1 Learning Outcomes

1-1: Define data wrangling and explain its critical role in preparing datasets for analysis

1-2: Identify the key stages of the data lifecycle and understand how data preparation impacts analysis quality

1-3: Compare the strengths of different data wrangling tools including Excel, SQL, R, and Python

1-4: Recognize common data quality challenges and understand systematic approaches to address them

1-5: Develop a framework for choosing appropriate tools based on data characteristics and project requirements

1.2 Introduction

Picture this: You're a marketing analyst at a growing e-commerce company, and your boss asks you to analyze customer purchasing patterns to improve the company's email marketing campaigns. You're excited—this is exactly the kind of project that could showcase your analytical skills and drive real business impact. The IT department provides you with three months of customer data, and you eagerly dive in.

Your excitement quickly turns to frustration. Customer names appear in dozens of different formats—some are "John Smith," others are "Smith, John," and still others are "J. Smith" or even "JOHN SMITH." Purchase dates range from perfectly reasonable to completely impossible, like orders placed on February 30th. Some customers have complete profiles with addresses, phone numbers, and purchase history, while others exist as little more than an email address. The product data is equally messy, with the same item appearing under multiple names and categories.

What seemed like a straightforward analysis project has suddenly become a complex puzzle of data detective work. You realize that before you can answer any business questions, you need to solve a more fundamental problem: transforming this messy, inconsistent data into something you can actually analyze.

Welcome to the world of data wrangling—the often unglamorous but absolutely essential process of cleaning, transforming, and preparing data for analysis. While it may not be the most exciting part of data analysis, it's arguably the most important. Every insight you generate, every recommendation you make, and every decision that flows from your analysis depends entirely on the quality of your data preparation.

1.3 The Reality of Real-World Data

1.3.1 Why Data Gets Messy

Data doesn't start life in perfect condition. In fact, the opposite is almost always true. Real-world data becomes messy through a combination of human error, system limitations, and the natural complexity of capturing information about the world around us.

Consider how customer information enters a typical business system. Sales representatives might enter names differently based on their personal preferences or training. Online forms might allow customers to enter information in various formats. Different systems might store the same information using different field names or data types. When a company grows through acquisitions, it inherits data from systems that were never designed to work together.

The problem compounds over time. A small inconsistency in how dates are formatted might seem trivial when you have a hundred records, but it becomes a major headache when you're dealing with hundreds of thousands of transactions. A missing field that affects only a few customers initially might represent a significant gap in your analysis when your customer base grows.

Understanding why data gets messy helps you approach data wrangling with the right mindset. You're not dealing with careless mistakes that could have been easily avoided—you're dealing with the inevitable result of complex systems, human behavior, and changing business requirements over time.

1.3.2 The Cost of Poor Data Quality

Poor data quality isn't just an inconvenience—it has real business consequences. Studies consistently show that organizations lose significant revenue due to data quality issues, with some estimates suggesting that poor data quality costs the average organization millions of dollars annually.

The costs manifest in multiple ways. Incorrect customer information leads to failed deliveries and frustrated customers. Inconsistent product data makes it difficult to track inventory accurately or analyze sales trends. Missing or inaccurate financial data can lead to poor business decisions or regulatory compliance issues.

Perhaps more importantly, poor data quality undermines confidence in analysis and decision-making. When business leaders can't trust the data, they're less likely to rely on data-driven insights, falling back on intuition and experience instead. This creates a vicious cycle where poor data quality leads to less data usage, which reduces investment in data quality improvement.

1.4 What Data Wrangling Really Means

1.4.1 Beyond Simple Cleaning

Data wrangling encompasses much more than just fixing obvious errors or filling in missing values. It's a comprehensive process that involves understanding your data's structure and limitations, making informed decisions about how to handle quality issues, and transforming data into formats that enable effective analysis.

Think of data wrangling as similar to preparing ingredients for a complex meal. A skilled chef doesn't just wash vegetables and hope for the best. They carefully select the best ingredients, understand how different preparation methods affect flavor and texture, and organize everything to create a cohesive final dish. Similarly, effective data wrangling requires understanding your data's characteristics, knowing how different transformation choices affect your analysis, and organizing information to support your analytical goals.

The "wrangling" metaphor captures the sometimes unpredictable and challenging nature of working with real-world data. Just as wrangling livestock requires patience, skill, and adaptability, working with messy data requires persistence, creativity, and the ability to adjust your approach as you discover new challenges.

1.4.2 The Art and Science of Data Preparation

Data wrangling combines technical skills with business judgment. The technical aspects involve knowing how to use tools effectively, understanding data formats and structures, and implementing transformations efficiently. The judgment aspects involve deciding how to handle ambiguous cases, determining what level of data quality is sufficient for your purposes, and balancing the time invested in data preparation against the value of improved data quality.

Consider the challenge of handling duplicate customer records. The technical aspect involves writing code or using tools to identify potential duplicates based on matching names, addresses, or other identifiers. The judgment aspect involves deciding what constitutes a "match"—should "John Smith" and "Jon Smith" be considered the same person? What about "John Smith" at "123 Main St" and "J. Smith" at "123 Main Street"?

These decisions require understanding your business context, the intended use of the data, and the trade-offs between different approaches. There's rarely a single "correct" way to handle data quality issues—instead, there are different approaches with different advantages and limitations.

1.5 The Data Wrangling Process

1.5.1 Discovery and Assessment

Every data wrangling project begins with discovery—understanding what data you have, where it came from, and what condition it's in. This exploration phase is crucial because it informs all subsequent decisions about how to clean and transform your data.

Discovery involves examining data structure, identifying patterns in missing values, understanding the range and distribution of different variables, and assessing the overall quality of your dataset. You might discover that certain fields are consistently missing for specific customer segments, that date fields contain impossible values, or that categorical variables have more unique values than expected.

This assessment phase often reveals surprises. Data that appeared clean in small samples might show significant quality issues when examined comprehensively. Fields that seemed straightforward might contain unexpected complexity. Understanding these issues early helps you plan an effective data preparation strategy.

1.5.2 Cleaning and Standardization

Once you understand your data's characteristics and limitations, you can begin the systematic process of cleaning and standardization. This involves correcting obvious errors, standardizing formats, and handling missing values in ways that support your analytical objectives.

Cleaning decisions should be guided by your understanding of the data's intended use. If you're preparing data for a customer segmentation analysis, ensuring consistent customer identifiers might be more important than having complete address information. If you're analyzing sales trends over time, having accurate and consistent date information becomes crucial.

Standardization involves establishing consistent formats and conventions across your dataset. This might mean converting all names to a standard case format, ensuring dates follow a consistent pattern, or establishing standard categories for products or services. The goal is creating consistency that enables effective analysis while preserving the meaningful information in your data.

1.5.3 Transformation and Enhancement

Beyond basic cleaning, data wrangling often involves transforming data to better support your analytical objectives. This might include creating new variables that combine information from multiple fields, aggregating data at different levels of detail, or restructuring data to match the requirements of your analysis tools.

Transformation decisions should be driven by your analytical goals rather than technical convenience. If your analysis requires understanding customer behavior over time, you might need to transform transaction-level data into customer-level summaries. If you're comparing performance across different regions, you might need to standardize geographic information and create regional groupings.

Enhancement involves adding value to your data through external sources or derived calculations. This might include adding demographic information based on zip codes, calculating customer lifetime value from transaction history, or creating seasonal indicators from date information.

1.6 The Multi-Tool Reality

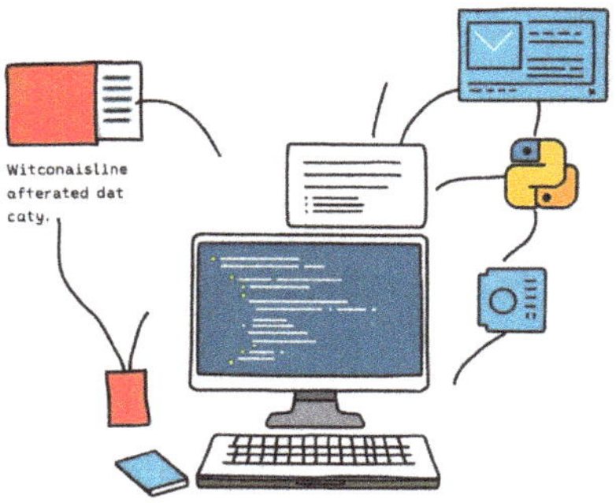

1.6.1 Why No Single Tool Rules

Modern data wrangling rarely involves using just one tool from start to finish. Instead, effective data preparation typically combines multiple tools, each optimized for different aspects of the process. Understanding when and how to use different tools is a key skill for effective data wrangling.

Different tools excel at different tasks. Spreadsheet software provides intuitive interfaces for data exploration and manual cleaning tasks. Database query languages like SQL offer powerful capabilities for working with large, structured datasets. Programming languages like R and Python provide flexibility for complex transformations and automated processing.

The choice of tools often depends on factors like data size, complexity, team skills, and integration requirements. A project involving a few thousand records might be handled entirely in Excel, while a project involving millions of records might require SQL for initial processing and Python for complex transformations.

1.6.2 Excel: The Universal Explorer

Despite the emergence of sophisticated programming tools, Excel remains a crucial component of most data wrangling workflows. Its visual interface makes it ideal for initial data exploration, quality assessment, and manual cleaning tasks that require human judgment.

Excel excels at helping you understand your data quickly. You can sort columns to see value ranges, use conditional formatting to highlight unusual values, and create simple charts to visualize data distributions. For many data wrangling tasks, this visual approach is more efficient than writing code.

Excel's limitations become apparent as data size and complexity increase. It struggles with datasets larger than a million rows and lacks the automation capabilities needed for complex, repeatable data preparation processes. However, even in projects that primarily use other tools, Excel often plays a valuable role in exploration and validation.

1.6.3 SQL: The Structured Data Specialist

Structured Query Language (SQL) provides unmatched capabilities for working with large, structured datasets stored in databases. SQL's declarative approach makes it relatively easy to express complex data manipulation logic, and its optimization for database operations makes it efficient for processing large volumes of data.

SQL is particularly valuable for initial data extraction and basic cleaning operations. When your source data lives in databases—as it often does in business environments—SQL provides the most efficient way to select relevant records, filter out unwanted data, and perform initial aggregations.

SQL's limitations become apparent when dealing with unstructured data, complex statistical operations, or advanced text processing. While modern SQL implementations include some support for these tasks, they're generally better handled by programming languages designed for flexible data manipulation.

1.6.4 R: The Statistical Powerhouse

R was designed specifically for statistical analysis and data manipulation, making it particularly well-suited for data wrangling tasks that require statistical sophistication. R's extensive library ecosystem includes specialized packages for virtually every aspect of data preparation.

R excels at tasks that require statistical thinking, such as identifying and handling outliers, imputing missing values using advanced techniques, or transforming data to meet analytical assumptions. For projects that involve complex statistical analysis, using R for data preparation creates natural workflow integration.

R's functional programming approach and vectorized operations make it efficient for applying complex transformations across large datasets. The language's emphasis on reproducible research also aligns well with the need for documented, repeatable data preparation processes.

1.6.5 Python: The Versatile Integrator

Python has emerged as one of the most popular languages for data analysis, making it a natural choice for data wrangling workflows. Python's pandas library provides powerful data manipulation capabilities that rival specialized tools, while its integration with other libraries creates seamless workflows from data preparation through analysis and visualization.

Python's strength lies in its versatility and ecosystem integration. You can use Python to extract data from APIs, process unstructured text, manipulate images, and perform complex transformations—all within a single environment. This integration capability makes Python particularly valuable for projects that involve diverse data types and complex preparation workflows.

The programming nature of Python also makes it excellent for automating data preparation processes. When you need to process new data regularly or apply consistent transformations across multiple datasets, Python's scripting capabilities enable robust, repeatable workflows.

1.7 Common Data Quality Challenges

1.7.1 The Missing Data Dilemma

Missing data represents one of the most common and challenging aspects of data wrangling. Data can be missing for many reasons—system failures, user choices, privacy concerns, or simple oversight. Understanding why data is missing helps you choose appropriate strategies for handling it.

Missing data isn't always random. Customers with higher incomes might be less likely to provide salary information. Older customers might be less likely to provide email addresses. Understanding these patterns helps you assess whether missing data might bias your analysis and choose appropriate handling strategies.

The impact of missing data depends on how much is missing, which variables are affected, and how you plan to use the data. A small amount of missing data in non-critical fields might have minimal impact, while extensive missing data in key variables might require significant attention or even additional data collection.

1.7.2 Format Inconsistencies

Real-world data rarely follows consistent formats, especially when it comes from multiple sources or has been collected over time. Names might appear in different orders, dates might follow different conventions, and categorical values might use different terminology for the same concepts.

Format inconsistencies can prevent you from properly analyzing relationships in your data. If the same customer appears with different name formats, you might count them multiple times. If dates follow different formats, you might not be able to properly sort or filter temporal data.

Addressing format inconsistencies requires understanding the business context behind your data. Sometimes apparent inconsistencies reflect meaningful differences that should be preserved. Other times, they represent arbitrary variations that should be standardized.

1.7.3 Duplicate Records and Identity Resolution

Duplicate records occur when the same entity appears multiple times in your dataset, often with slight variations that make exact matching difficult. This is particularly common with customer data, where the same person might appear with different spellings of their name, different addresses, or different contact information.

Identifying duplicates requires balancing precision and recall. Too strict matching criteria might miss legitimate duplicates, while too loose criteria might incorrectly merge distinct entities. The optimal approach depends on your data characteristics and the consequences of different types of errors.

Identity resolution—determining when different records refer to the same entity—often requires combining multiple pieces of information and applying business rules. This process typically involves both automated matching algorithms and human review of ambiguous cases.

1.8 Building Your Data Wrangling Toolkit

1.8.1 Developing a Systematic Approach

Effective data wrangling requires a systematic approach that combines technical skills with analytical thinking. This involves developing standard processes for assessing data quality, choosing appropriate tools for different tasks, and documenting your decisions for future reference.

Start by developing a consistent approach to data exploration. Create checklists for assessing data quality, standard queries for identifying common issues, and templates for documenting your findings. This systematic approach helps ensure you don't miss important issues and makes it easier to communicate your findings to others.

Document your data wrangling decisions and their rationale. This documentation serves multiple purposes—it helps you remember why you made certain choices, enables others to understand and validate your work, and provides a foundation for handling similar issues in future projects.

1.8.2 Balancing Perfection and Practicality

One of the biggest challenges in data wrangling is knowing when to stop. Data can always be cleaned further, formats can always be more consistent, and missing values can always be handled more sophisticatedly. The key is finding the right balance between data quality and project timelines.

This balance depends on your analytical objectives and the consequences of data quality issues. If you're conducting exploratory analysis to identify general trends, a moderate level of data cleaning might be sufficient. If you're building models that will drive important business decisions, more extensive data preparation might be justified.

Consider the law of diminishing returns in data wrangling. The first 80% of data quality improvement often requires 20% of the effort, while the remaining 20% of improvement might require 80% of the effort. Understanding where you are on this curve helps you make informed decisions about how much time to invest in data preparation.

1.9 Conclusion

Data wrangling forms the foundation of effective data analysis. While it may not be the most glamorous aspect of working with data, it's arguably the most important. The quality of your data preparation directly impacts the reliability of your analysis, the accuracy of your insights, and the value of your recommendations.

Effective data wrangling requires combining technical skills with business judgment, understanding the strengths and limitations of different tools, and developing systematic approaches to common data quality challenges. It's both an art and a science—requiring creativity and problem-solving skills alongside technical proficiency.

As you develop your data wrangling skills, remember that perfection isn't always the goal. The objective is preparing data that's fit for your intended purpose, balancing quality improvements against time constraints and project requirements. With practice and experience, you'll develop the judgment needed to make these trade-offs effectively.

The investment you make in learning data wrangling skills will pay dividends throughout your career. In our increasingly data-driven world, the ability to transform messy, real-world data into clean, analyzable datasets is one of the most valuable skills you can develop. Whether you're working in marketing, finance, operations, or any other business function, these skills will help you extract maximum value from the data at your disposal.

1.10 Key Terms

Data Wrangling – The process of cleaning, transforming, and preparing messy, real-world data so it can be accurately analyzed.

Data Lifecycle – The stages data goes through, from creation and collection to storage, preparation, analysis, and use in decision-making.

Data Quality – A measure of how accurate, complete, consistent, and reliable data is for analysis.

Real-World Data – Data collected from business systems, people, and processes that is often incomplete, inconsistent, or messy.

Messy Data – Data containing errors, inconsistencies, duplicates, missing values, or formatting problems.

Data Preparation – The broader process of getting data analysis-ready, including wrangling, cleaning, structuring, and organizing.

Cleaning and Standardization – Correcting errors, fixing formats, aligning values, and ensuring consistency across datasets.

Transformation – Changing the structure or format of data to support analysis, such as aggregating, reshaping, or creating new variables.

Enhancement – Improving a dataset by adding new information or derived fields that increase its value and insight.

Missing Data – Values that are not recorded or available, which can bias or weaken analysis if not handled carefully.

Format Inconsistencies – Differences in how similar information is recorded, such as different date formats, name structures, or category labels.

Duplicate Records – Multiple entries representing the same person, product, or entity, often with slight variations that require identity resolution.

Identity Resolution – Determining when separate records refer to the same real-world entity and deciding how to merge or manage them.

Discovery and Assessment – The initial step of exploring data, identifying problems, and understanding its condition before cleaning begins.

Systematic Approach – A structured, repeatable method for assessing, cleaning, and preparing data rather than handling problems randomly.

Excel – A spreadsheet tool useful for visual exploration, quick fixes, and smaller datasets.

SQL – A database language for querying, filtering, and managing large structured datasets efficiently.

R – A programming language specialized for statistical analysis and sophisticated data preparation tasks.

Python – A versatile programming language used for automation, complex transformations, integration across systems, and repeatable workflows.

Art and Science of Data Wrangling – The idea that data wrangling requires both technical skills (science) and judgment-based decision-making (art).

Balance of Perfection and Practicality – The need to clean data enough to meet project goals without wasting excessive time chasing unnecessary perfection.

1.11 Review Questions

1. What is data wrangling, and why is it considered a critical step before performing any meaningful data analysis?
2. How does data wrangling fit into the broader data lifecycle, and in what ways does the quality of data preparation influence analysis outcomes and decision-making?
3. Compare Excel, SQL, R, and Python as data wrangling tools. What types of wrangling tasks is each tool generally best suited for, and why?
4. Identify at least three common data quality challenges discussed in the chapter (for example, missing data, inconsistent formats, or duplicate records). How can each of these challenges affect analysis results?
5. Explain why real-world data often becomes messy over time. What organizational, technical, and human factors contribute to poor data quality?
6. Why is data wrangling described as both an "art" and a "science"? Provide an example of a technical decision and a judgment-based decision that a data wrangler might need to make.
7. Describe the major phases of the data wrangling process (discovery, cleaning/standardization, transformation/enhancement). What is the primary purpose of each stage?
8. Why is it important to balance "perfection" with practicality in data wrangling? Describe a situation where "good enough" data preparation might be appropriate and a situation where near-perfect data quality is essential.

1.12 Lab 1 Setup

Welcome to your first lab! Before diving into data analysis with R, you need to set up a proper development environment. This guide will walk you through multiple IDE (Integrated Development Environment) options, giving you the flexibility to choose what works best for your learning style and technical setup.

1.12.1 Overview

Having the right development environment will make these tasks much more manageable and enjoyable. This lab provides you with multiple options so you can choose the setup that best fits your needs, technical constraints, and preferences.

1.12.1.1 IDE Options Overview

You have several excellent options for your R development environment. Each has its own strengths, and the choice depends on your preferences, technical setup, and learning goals. Here's a comprehensive overview of the most popular options:

1.12.1.1.1 RStudio Desktop (Recommended)

RStudio Desktop is the most popular and feature-rich IDE for R development. It's specifically designed for data science workflows and provides an intuitive interface that makes R programming more accessible.

Key Features:

- Integrated script editor with syntax highlighting and auto-completion
- Interactive console for immediate code execution
- Environment pane showing variables and data objects
- Integrated help system and documentation viewer
- Built-in package management and installation tools
- Plot viewer for data visualizations
- Project management capabilities

Best For: Students who want the most comprehensive R experience, those planning to do extensive data analysis, and learners who prefer a dedicated R environment.

Pros:

- Purpose-built for R and data science
- Excellent documentation and community support
- Intuitive interface for beginners
- Powerful debugging and profiling tools

Cons:

- Requires local installation and setup
- Can be resource-intensive on older machines
- Limited to R programming (not multi-language)

1.12.1.1.2 RStudio Cloud/Posit Cloud

RStudio Cloud (now called Posit Cloud) provides the full RStudio experience through your web browser. This cloud-based solution eliminates installation hassles and ensures everyone has the same environment.

Key Features:

- Full RStudio IDE accessible through any web browser
- Pre-installed R packages and common libraries
- Automatic saving and cloud storage
- Easy sharing and collaboration features
- No local installation required

Best For: Students with limited local storage, those using shared computers, learners who want to get started immediately without installation, and situations requiring consistent environments across different machines.

Pros:

- Zero installation - works immediately
- Access from any device with internet
- Automatic updates and maintenance
- Built-in collaboration tools

Cons:

- Requires stable internet connection
- Free tier has usage limitations
- Less control over environment configuration

1.12.1.1.3 VS Code with R Extension

Visual Studio Code is a powerful, general-purpose code editor that can be configured for R development through extensions. This option is ideal for students who want to learn a versatile editor that supports multiple programming languages.

Key Features:

- Lightweight and fast code editor
- Extensive extension ecosystem
- Integrated terminal and Git support
- Customizable interface and themes

- Multi-language support (R, Python, SQL, etc.)

Best For: Students who plan to work with multiple programming languages, those who prefer a more general-purpose editor, and learners who want to develop broader coding skills beyond R.

Pros:

- Supports many programming languages
- Highly customizable and extensible
- Excellent Git integration
- Free and open source

Cons:

- Requires more setup and configuration
- Less R-specific features than RStudio
- Steeper learning curve for beginners

1.12.1.2 Installation Instructions

Follow the instructions for your chosen IDE. Remember, you only need to install ONE of these options to complete the course labs.

Option A: RStudio Desktop (Recommended)

1. **Install R first:**

• Visit https://cran.r-project.org/

• Download R for your operating system

• Run the installer with default settings

2. **Install RStudio Desktop:**

• Visit https://posit.co/download/rstudio-desktop/

• Download the free version for your OS

• Install with default settings

3. **Launch RStudio and verify installation**

Option B: RStudio Cloud/Posit Cloud

4. Visit https://posit.cloud/
5. Create a free account
6. Start a new project

7. Begin coding immediately - no installation needed!

Option C: VS Code with R Extension

8. **Install R (same as Option A step 1)**
9. **Install VS Code:**

- Visit https://code.visualstudio.com/
- Download and install for your OS

10. **Install R Extension:**

- Open VS Code
- Go to Extensions (Ctrl+Shift+X)
- Search for ”R” and install the R extension by REditorSupport

11. **Configure R path if needed**

1.12.1.3 Essential R Packages

What are R Packages?

R packages are collections of functions, data, and documentation that extend R's capabilities. Think of them as specialized toolkits - base R gives you basic tools, but packages provide powerful specialized functions for specific tasks like data manipulation, visualization, and statistical analysis.

Regardless of which IDE you choose, you'll need to install several R packages for the upcoming labs. These packages provide the functions and tools you'll use for data manipulation, analysis, and visualization.

Important Notes:

- Package installation requires an internet connection and may take several minutes
- You only need to **install** packages once, but you must **load** them in each R session using library()
- If a future lab uses a package you don't have, simply run install.packages(”package_name”) first

What if I encounter a missing package in future labs?

Don't worry! If you see an error like ”there is no package called 'xyz'”, simply install it:

install.packages(”xyz”)

Then load it:

library(xyz)

This is normal - R has thousands of packages, and we only install the most essential ones upfront.

1.12.1.4 Testing Your Setup

Once you've installed your chosen IDE and the required packages, it's important to test everything is working correctly. Follow these steps to verify your setup:

Step 1: Basic R Functionality

Open your IDE and run these basic commands in the R console:

```
# Test basic arithmetic

2 + 2

# Create a simple vector

numbers <- c(1, 2, 3, 4, 5)

print(numbers)
```

Step 2: Test Package Loading

Load each required package to ensure they installed correctly:

```
library(dplyr)

library(lubridate)

library(stringr)

library(ggplot2)

library(tidyr)
```

If any package fails to load, you may need to reinstall it using the install.packages() command.

Step 3: Create Sample Data

Test data manipulation functions with this sample dataset:

```
# Create sample data similar to Lab 2

test_data <- data.frame(

ID = 1:5,

Age = c(25, 34, 45, 29, 38),

Income = c(45000, 62000, 85000, 51000, 73000)

)

# View the data
```

```
print(test_data)

str(test_data)
```

Expected Output: You should see a data frame with 5 rows and 3 columns, and the structure should show the data types for each column.

Chapter 2

Data Sources, Structures, and Formats

2.1 Learning Outcomes

2-1: Identify and classify the five main data types (numeric, categorical, text, image, timestamp)

2-2: Distinguish between structured and unstructured data formats and know when to use CSV, JSON, SQL databases, and log files

2-3: Understand AI-enhanced and synthetic data concepts and their role in modern data science workflows

2-4: Apply basic data profiling techniques using multiple tools to assess data quality before analysis

2-5: Make informed decisions about data format selection based on project requirements and tool capabilities

2.2 Introduction

Imagine you're starting a new job as a data analyst at a healthcare company. On your first day, you're handed five different files: a CSV spreadsheet with patient demographics, a JSON file from the company's mobile app, a database connection to electronic health records, image files from medical scans, and log files from the hospital's monitoring systems. Each contains valuable information, but they're all organized differently and require different approaches to work with effectively.

This scenario illustrates the modern data landscape—information comes in many forms, each with its own characteristics and requirements. Understanding these different data types and structures is essential for anyone working with data, especially as artificial intelligence applications become more common in business and research.

The goal of this module isn't to make you an expert in every data format, but to help you recognize what you're working with and choose appropriate tools and approaches. Think of it as learning to identify different types of building materials before you start construction—you need to know whether you're working with wood, metal, or concrete before you can choose the right tools and techniques.

As AI applications become more prevalent, the variety of data sources continues to expand. Traditional business data from spreadsheets and databases now combines with social media posts, sensor readings, images, and artificially generated data. Understanding these different types helps you make informed decisions about how to collect, store, and prepare data for analysis and AI applications.

2.3 Data Types and Their Characteristics

2.3.1 The Five Essential Data Types

Every piece of information you'll encounter in data analysis falls into one of five fundamental categories. Understanding these categories helps you choose appropriate tools, apply correct analysis techniques, and avoid common mistakes that can derail your projects.

2.3.2 Numeric Data

Numeric data represents quantities and measurements—ages, prices, temperatures, counts, and percentages. This is often the easiest type for both humans and computers to work with because mathematical operations have clear meanings.

Numeric data comes in two varieties: continuous and discrete. Continuous data can take any value within a range (like temperature: 98.6°F, 98.7°F, 98.65°F), while discrete data represents countable items (like number of customers: 5, 6, 7, but never 5.5 customers).

For AI applications, numeric data often provides the clearest signals for machine learning algorithms. A recommendation system can easily understand that a customer who rates movies 4.5 stars prefers them to movies rated 2.1 stars. However, the scale and distribution of numeric data can significantly affect analysis results, which is why data preparation techniques like scaling and normalization become important.

Different tools handle numeric data with varying sophistication. Excel excels at basic calculations and visualizations. SQL databases efficiently store and aggregate large amounts of numeric data. R provides advanced statistical analysis capabilities, while Python offers flexible preprocessing for machine learning applications.

2.3.3 Categorical Data

Categorical data represents discrete choices or classifications—product categories, customer segments, geographic regions, or yes/no responses. Unlike numeric data, categorical data doesn't have inherent mathematical relationships between values.

Understanding the difference between nominal and ordinal categories is crucial. Nominal categories have no natural order (like colors: red, blue, green), while ordinal categories have meaningful sequence (like satisfaction ratings: poor, fair, good, excellent). This distinction affects how you can analyze and process the data.

For AI applications, categorical data requires special handling because most machine learning algorithms expect numeric inputs. Converting categories to numbers while preserving their meaning is a key skill in data preparation. A customer segment labeled ”premium” contains valuable information, but an AI model needs this converted to a numeric representation to use it effectively.

Each tool provides different approaches for working with categorical data. Excel can create basic summary tables and charts. SQL excels at grouping and counting categories. R provides sophisticated factor handling, while Python offers comprehensive encoding techniques for machine learning workflows.

2.3.4 Text Data

Text data includes everything from customer reviews and social media posts to email content and survey responses. This type contains rich information but requires specialized techniques to extract meaningful insights.

Text data presents unique challenges because human language is complex, ambiguous, and constantly evolving. The same concept can be expressed in countless ways—"excellent product," "love it," and "five stars" all convey positive sentiment but use completely different words.

For AI applications, text data has become increasingly valuable as natural language processing techniques have improved. Customer reviews can reveal product issues, social media posts can indicate brand sentiment, and support tickets can identify common problems. However, converting text into formats that algorithms can process requires careful preprocessing and feature engineering.

Tool capabilities for text processing vary significantly. Excel provides basic text functions for simple cleaning tasks. SQL includes string functions for pattern matching and basic text manipulation. R offers comprehensive text analysis packages, while Python provides the most extensive ecosystem for natural language processing and text analytics.

2.3.5 Image Data

Image data includes photographs, scans, diagrams, charts, and any other visual content. While humans process images intuitively, computers require sophisticated techniques to extract meaningful information from visual data.

Image data characteristics vary dramatically based on source and purpose. Medical imaging requires different handling than social media photos. High-resolution professional images have different storage and processing requirements than smartphone snapshots. Understanding these variations helps you choose appropriate tools and techniques.

For AI applications, image data has become increasingly important as computer vision techniques have advanced. AI systems can now identify objects in photos, detect anomalies in medical scans, and analyze satellite imagery for environmental monitoring. However, image processing requires significant computational resources and specialized tools.

Most traditional data analysis tools have limited image processing capabilities. Excel can display images but offers minimal analysis features. SQL databases can store image files but typically don't process their content. Specialized tools and programming languages like Python with computer vision libraries become essential for serious image analysis work.

2.3.6 Timestamp Data

Timestamp data records when events occur, enabling analysis of trends, patterns, and sequences over time. This includes transaction timestamps, sensor readings, log entries, and any data that includes temporal information.

Time data comes in various formats and granularities—from precise millisecond timestamps to simple date fields. Understanding these different formats and their implications helps you choose appropriate storage and analysis approaches. Some analyses require precise timing, while others work with daily or monthly aggregations.

For AI applications, temporal patterns often provide crucial insights. Customer behavior changes over time, equipment performance degrades gradually, and market conditions evolve continuously. AI models that can identify and learn from these temporal patterns often outperform those that ignore time-based information.

Different tools provide varying capabilities for time-based analysis. Excel offers basic date functions and simple trend analysis. SQL provides powerful time-based filtering and aggregation capabilities. R excels at time series analysis and temporal modeling, while Python offers flexible time-based processing integrated with machine learning workflows.

2.3.7 Understanding Data Type Implications

The data type you're working with fundamentally affects every aspect of your analysis—from storage requirements and tool selection to analysis techniques and interpretation of results. Recognizing these implications early in your project helps you make informed decisions and avoid common pitfalls.

2.3.7.1 Storage and Performance Considerations

Different data types have vastly different storage requirements and performance characteristics. Numeric data typically requires minimal storage and processes quickly. Text data requires more storage and processing time, especially for large documents. Image data can require enormous storage space and significant computational resources for processing.

These differences become particularly important as datasets grow larger. A database with millions of numeric records might perform well, while the same database with millions of high-resolution images could become unusably slow. Understanding these trade-offs helps you design data architectures that support your analysis goals.

2.3.7.2 Tool Selection and Workflow Design

Your data types significantly influence which tools are most appropriate for your project. A project working primarily with numeric data might use Excel for exploration and SQL for processing. A project involving text analysis would likely require R or Python. Image analysis almost certainly requires specialized programming tools.

Understanding these tool requirements early helps you plan your workflow and ensure you have the necessary skills and resources. It's much easier to learn appropriate tools at the beginning of a project than to discover halfway through that your current tools can't handle your data types effectively.

2.4 Structured vs. Unstructured Data

2.4.1 Understanding Data Organization

The way data is organized fundamentally affects how you can work with it. Structured data follows predictable patterns that make it easy to process with standard tools, while unstructured data requires more sophisticated techniques to extract meaningful information.

2.4.2 Structured Data: Organized and Predictable

Structured data follows a consistent, predefined format where each piece of information has a designated place and meaning. Think of it like a well-organized filing cabinet where every document goes in a specific folder, and every folder follows the same labeling system.

The most common example of structured data is a spreadsheet or database table where each row represents a record (like a customer) and each column represents an attribute (like age, income, or purchase history). This organization makes it easy to perform calculations, create summaries, and identify patterns.

For AI applications, structured data often provides the foundation for machine learning models. The consistent format makes it straightforward to prepare data for algorithms, and the clear relationships between different attributes help models learn meaningful patterns. Customer databases, transaction records, and sensor measurements typically fall into this category.

2.4.2.1 CSV Files: Universal Data Exchange

CSV (Comma-Separated Values) files represent the most universal format for structured data. Almost every data tool can read and write CSV files, making them ideal for sharing data between different systems and applications.

CSV files store data in a simple text format where each row represents a record and commas separate the different fields. This simplicity makes CSV files easy to understand and work with, but it also means they lack advanced features like data type information or multiple worksheets.

For AI projects, CSV files often serve as the common denominator for data exchange. You might extract data from a database into CSV format for analysis in Python, or export results from R into CSV format for presentation in Excel. Understanding how to work effectively with CSV files is essential for most data analysis workflows.

2.4.2.2 SQL Databases: Structured Data at Scale

SQL databases provide robust, scalable storage for structured data that exceeds the capabilities of spreadsheets. They excel at handling large datasets, maintaining data integrity, and supporting multiple users accessing the same data simultaneously.

The key advantage of SQL databases is their ability to efficiently store and retrieve related information. Customer information, order details, and product catalogs can be stored in separate tables but linked together when needed. This approach reduces data duplication and ensures consistency across the system.

For AI applications, SQL databases often serve as the primary data source for machine learning projects. The ability to join related tables and perform complex queries makes it easy to create comprehensive datasets that combine information from multiple sources. Understanding basic SQL concepts helps you work effectively with enterprise data systems.

2.4.3 Unstructured Data: Flexible but Complex

Unstructured data doesn't follow a predefined format, making it more flexible but also more challenging to process. Examples include email messages, social media posts, images, audio files, and web pages. This data often contains valuable information, but extracting it requires specialized techniques.

The challenge with unstructured data is that each piece of information might be organized differently. One customer review might be a single sentence, while another might be several paragraphs with bullet points and ratings. This variability makes it difficult to apply standard analysis techniques.

For AI applications, unstructured data has become increasingly valuable as processing techniques have improved. Natural language processing can extract insights from text, computer vision can analyze images, and audio processing can transcribe and analyze speech. However, working with unstructured data typically requires more advanced tools and techniques.

2.4.3.1 JSON: Semi-Structured Flexibility

JSON (JavaScript Object Notation) provides a middle ground between structured and unstructured data. It allows for flexible, nested structures while maintaining enough organization to be processed systematically.

JSON files can represent complex, hierarchical information in a readable format. A customer record might include basic information like name and address, but also nested information like order history, preferences, and interaction logs. This flexibility makes JSON popular for web applications and APIs.

For AI applications, JSON data often requires preprocessing to extract and flatten the information into formats suitable for machine learning algorithms. Understanding how to work with JSON structures helps you integrate data from web services and modern applications into your analysis workflows.

2.4.3.2 Log Files: Structured Patterns in Unstructured Format

Log files represent a special category that combines elements of both structured and unstructured data. They typically follow consistent patterns (like timestamp, user ID, action) but contain free-form text that requires parsing to extract meaningful information.

Server logs, application logs, and system monitoring files often contain valuable information about user behavior, system performance, and error patterns. However, extracting this information requires understanding the log format and applying appropriate parsing techniques.

For AI applications, log data can provide insights into user behavior, system performance, and anomaly detection. Web server logs can reveal usage patterns, application logs can identify common errors, and security logs can detect suspicious activities. Understanding how to process log data opens up valuable data sources for analysis.

2.4.4 Choosing the Right Format

The choice between different data formats depends on your specific requirements, including the tools you're using, the size of your data, the complexity of your information, and your performance requirements.

2.4.4.1 Project Requirements and Tool Compatibility

Your project requirements significantly influence format choice. If you're working primarily in Excel, CSV files provide the most straightforward option. If you're building a web application, JSON might be more appropriate. If you're working with large datasets that require complex queries, a SQL database becomes essential.

Consider also who else needs to access your data. CSV files are universally readable, making them ideal for sharing with stakeholders who use different tools. JSON files work well for technical teams but might be challenging for business users. SQL databases provide robust access control but require technical expertise to use effectively.

2.4.4.2 Scale and Performance Considerations

Data size and performance requirements also affect format choice. Small datasets (thousands of records) work well in CSV files or Excel spreadsheets. Medium datasets (hundreds of thousands of records) might benefit from database storage. Large datasets (millions of records) typically require specialized storage and processing approaches.

Consider also how frequently your data changes. Static datasets work well in CSV files, while frequently updated data benefits from database storage. Real-time data streams might require specialized formats and processing approaches.

2.5 AI-Enhanced and Synthetic Data

2.5.1 The Evolution of Data Sources

Traditional data analysis relied primarily on data collected through business operations, surveys, and experiments. Modern AI applications increasingly use enhanced and artificially generated data to improve model performance, address data scarcity, and overcome privacy constraints.

2.5.2 AI-Enhanced Data: Augmenting Reality

AI-enhanced data involves using artificial intelligence techniques to improve, expand, or enrich existing datasets. This might include using AI to clean and standardize data, generate additional features, or fill in missing information.

One common application is using AI to enhance image datasets. Computer vision algorithms can automatically crop, resize, and normalize images to create consistent datasets for machine learning. Natural language processing can standardize text data by correcting spelling, expanding abbreviations, and identifying key concepts.

For business applications, AI enhancement might involve using machine learning to predict missing values, identify and correct errors, or generate additional features that improve model performance. Customer data might be enhanced with predicted preferences, transaction data might be enriched with seasonal patterns, and sensor data might be augmented with derived measurements.

Understanding AI-enhanced data helps you recognize opportunities to improve your datasets and understand the limitations and assumptions involved in enhancement processes. Enhanced data can significantly improve analysis results, but it's important to understand what has been modified and how those modifications might affect your conclusions.

2.5.3 Synthetic Data: Creating Artificial Information

Synthetic data is artificially generated information that mimics the statistical properties of real data without containing actual personal or sensitive information. This approach addresses privacy concerns while providing realistic datasets for analysis and model development.

Synthetic data generation uses statistical models or machine learning algorithms to learn the patterns in real data and then generate new data points that follow similar patterns. A synthetic customer dataset might have the same age distributions, income patterns, and purchase behaviors as real customers, but without containing any actual customer information.

For AI applications, synthetic data provides several advantages. It can generate unlimited training examples, create balanced datasets that address bias issues, and provide data for testing without privacy concerns. Financial institutions use synthetic transaction data for fraud detection testing, healthcare organizations use synthetic patient data for research, and technology companies use synthetic user data for product development.

However, synthetic data also has limitations. It can only reproduce patterns that exist in the original data, might not capture rare but important events, and could perpetuate biases present in the source data. Understanding these trade-offs helps you use synthetic data effectively while recognizing its limitations.

2.5.4 Data Augmentation Techniques

Data augmentation involves creating variations of existing data to increase dataset size and improve model robustness. This is particularly common in image analysis, where techniques like rotation, scaling, and color adjustment can create multiple versions of each image.

For text data, augmentation might involve synonym replacement, sentence restructuring, or translation to other languages and back. For numeric data, augmentation might involve adding small amounts of noise or creating interpolated values between existing data points.

Understanding augmentation techniques helps you recognize when your datasets might benefit from expansion and how to apply appropriate techniques for different data types. Augmentation can significantly improve model performance, especially when working with limited datasets.

2.5.5 Implications for Data Analysis

AI-enhanced and synthetic data create new opportunities and challenges for data analysis. Understanding these implications helps you work effectively with modern datasets and make informed decisions about data sources and preparation techniques.

2.5.5.1 Quality and Validation Considerations

Enhanced and synthetic data require careful validation to ensure they maintain the essential characteristics of the original data while providing the intended benefits. This might involve comparing statistical properties, testing model performance, and validating business logic.

For enhanced data, it's important to understand what modifications have been made and how they might affect your analysis. If missing values have been predicted, you need to understand the accuracy and assumptions of those predictions. If features have been generated, you need to understand their relationship to the original data.

For synthetic data, validation involves ensuring that the generated data maintains the important patterns and relationships from the original data while successfully protecting privacy. This might involve statistical tests, expert review, and performance validation on downstream tasks.

2.5.5.2 Ethical and Legal Considerations

The use of AI-enhanced and synthetic data raises important ethical and legal questions. Enhanced data might introduce biases or make assumptions that affect fairness. Synthetic data might not adequately represent minority groups or rare but important cases.

Understanding these considerations helps you use enhanced and synthetic data responsibly. This might involve documenting enhancement processes, testing for bias, ensuring appropriate representation, and maintaining transparency about data modifications.

2.6 Data Profiling and Quality Assessment

2.6.1 Understanding Your Data Before Analysis

Data profiling involves systematically examining your data to understand its characteristics, quality, and suitability for analysis. This process helps you identify potential issues before they affect your results and make informed decisions about data preparation and analysis approaches.

2.6.2 Basic Data Profiling Techniques

Data profiling starts with understanding the basic characteristics of your dataset—how many records it contains, what variables are included, what data types are present, and how the data is distributed. This foundational understanding guides all subsequent analysis decisions.

For each variable in your dataset, you want to understand its range, distribution, and patterns. Numeric variables might have minimum and maximum values, average and median values, and information about skewness or outliers. Categorical variables might have counts for each category and information about the most and least common values.

Missing data patterns provide crucial information about data quality and collection processes. Understanding which variables have missing values, how much data is missing, and whether missingness follows patterns helps you choose appropriate handling strategies.

Different tools provide varying capabilities for data profiling. Excel offers basic statistical functions and visualization capabilities that help you understand data distribution. SQL provides efficient aggregation capabilities for summarizing large datasets. R excels at statistical analysis and distribution visualization, while Python offers comprehensive profiling tools designed for data science workflows.

2.6.3 Quality Assessment Dimensions

Data quality encompasses several dimensions that each affect analysis results in different ways. Understanding these dimensions helps you prioritize quality improvement efforts and make informed decisions about data preparation.

Accuracy refers to how well your data reflects reality. This might involve checking for logical inconsistencies (like negative ages), validating against external sources, or identifying outliers that might indicate errors. Accuracy issues can significantly affect analysis results, especially for variables that are central to your analysis goals.

Completeness refers to how much of the expected data is actually present. Missing data can bias results, reduce statistical power, and limit the applicability of your findings. Understanding completeness patterns helps you choose appropriate analysis techniques and interpret results correctly.

Consistency refers to whether the same information is represented the same way throughout your dataset. Inconsistent formatting, spelling variations, and different coding schemes can create artificial patterns that confuse analysis results.

Timeliness refers to whether your data is current enough for your analysis purposes. Outdated data might not reflect current conditions, while data that's too recent might not include important seasonal or cyclical patterns.

2.6.4 Tool-Agnostic Profiling Approaches

Effective data profiling uses multiple tools and approaches to build a comprehensive understanding of your data. Each tool provides different perspectives and capabilities, and combining their strengths gives you the most complete picture.

Visual profiling uses charts and graphs to reveal patterns that might not be apparent in statistical summaries. Histograms show distribution shapes, scatter plots reveal relationships between variables, and box plots identify outliers and skewness. These visual approaches work across all tools and provide intuitive understanding of data characteristics.

Statistical profiling uses numerical summaries to quantify data characteristics. Measures of central tendency (mean, median, mode) describe typical values, while measures of variability (standard deviation, range, interquartile range) describe data spread. These statistical approaches provide precise, comparable measures across different datasets.

Pattern-based profiling looks for systematic relationships and anomalies in your data. This might involve checking for duplicate records, identifying unusual value combinations, or detecting systematic biases in data collection. These approaches help identify quality issues that might not be apparent through basic statistical analysis.

2.6.5 Building Quality into Your Workflow

Rather than treating data profiling as a separate step, effective data analysis integrates quality assessment throughout the entire workflow. This approach helps prevent quality issues from affecting results and creates sustainable processes for maintaining data quality over time.

Early profiling during data collection helps identify issues before they become embedded in your analysis. Understanding data characteristics as you collect it enables you to make adjustments to collection processes and address quality issues proactively.

Ongoing profiling during analysis helps you understand how data preparation steps affect data characteristics and quality. Monitoring data quality as you clean, transform, and analyze it ensures that your preparation steps improve rather than degrade data quality.

Documentation and communication of profiling results helps team members understand data characteristics and quality considerations. Clear documentation of data quality issues and improvement efforts supports reproducible analysis and informed decision-making.

2.6.6 Practical Profiling Strategies

Developing systematic approaches to data profiling helps you consistently assess data quality across different projects and datasets. These systematic approaches ensure that you don't overlook important quality considerations and provide frameworks for communicating quality issues to stakeholders.

2.6.6.1 Automated Profiling Tools and Techniques

Many tools provide automated profiling capabilities that can quickly generate comprehensive summaries of data characteristics and quality issues. These automated approaches provide efficient starting points for quality assessment, though they typically require human interpretation and follow-up investigation.

Excel's data analysis tools can generate basic statistical summaries and identify some quality issues automatically. SQL queries can efficiently calculate summary statistics and identify patterns across large datasets. R and Python provide comprehensive profiling packages that can generate detailed reports with minimal code.

Understanding the capabilities and limitations of automated profiling tools helps you use them effectively while recognizing when manual investigation is needed. Automated tools excel at identifying obvious quality issues and generating comprehensive summaries, but they might miss subtle patterns or domain-specific quality concerns.

2.6.6.2 Manual Investigation and Domain Expertise

While automated tools provide efficient starting points, effective data profiling often requires manual investigation guided by domain expertise. Understanding the business context, data collection processes, and intended use cases helps you identify quality issues that automated tools might miss.

Domain expertise helps you recognize when data patterns make sense and when they might indicate quality issues. A sudden spike in customer ages might indicate a data entry error, or it might reflect a legitimate change in customer demographics. Understanding the business context helps you distinguish between real patterns and data quality issues.

Manual investigation also helps you understand the implications of quality issues for your specific analysis goals. Some quality problems might be critical for certain analyses but irrelevant for others. Understanding these relationships helps you prioritize quality improvement efforts and make informed decisions about data preparation.

2.7 Conclusion

This module has shown that modern data work requires more than simply receiving a dataset and running analyses; it requires understanding what kind of data you are dealing with, how it is structured, and what that means for tools, storage, and workflows. By exploring numeric, categorical, text, image, and timestamp data, as well as the differences between structured, unstructured, and semi-structured formats like CSV, SQL databases, JSON, and log files, you gained a practical framework for recognizing data characteristics and their implications. You also learned how data types influence everything from performance and scalability to analysis techniques and AI readiness.

Beyond formats and data types, the module emphasized how AI-enhanced, synthetic, and augmented data are reshaping modern analytics while introducing new responsibilities around validation, ethics, and transparency. Finally, the discussion of data profiling and quality assessment reinforced that understanding your data—its completeness, accuracy, structure, and reliability—is not optional but essential. Together, these concepts prepare you to approach real-world datasets with greater confidence, make smarter decisions about tools and methods, and build analyses that are both technically sound and trustworthy.

2.8 Key Terms

Numeric Data – Quantitative information that represents measurable values such as age, price, temperature, or counts; used heavily in statistics and machine learning.

Continuous Data – Numeric data that can take any value within a range, such as height or temperature.

Discrete Data – Numeric data that consists of whole, countable values such as number of customers or items sold.

Categorical Data – Data that represents labels, groups, or classifications such as gender, product category, or region.

Nominal Data – Categorical data with no natural order, such as colors or types of products.

Ordinal Data – Categorical data with a meaningful order, such as rating scales (poor, fair, good, excellent).

Text Data – Information stored as written language, such as reviews, emails, comments, and documents.

Image Data – Visual data in the form of photos, scans, diagrams, and other graphical formats.

Timestamp Data – Data that records when events occur, enabling trend analysis, sequencing, and time-based insights.

Structured Data – Data organized in a fixed, tabular format such as spreadsheets or database tables, making it easy to query and analyze.

Unstructured Data – Data without a predefined organization, such as emails, images, audio, or social media posts.

Semi-Structured Data – Data that has some organization but allows flexibility, such as JSON files.

CSV (Comma-Separated Values) – A widely used simple text format for structured data where each row is a record and each value is separated by commas.

SQL Database – A structured data storage system that supports efficient querying, relational organization, and data integrity at scale.

JSON (JavaScript Object Notation) – A flexible, hierarchical data format commonly used in web applications and APIs.

Log Files – System or application records that track events over time, often containing timestamps and event details.

AI-Enhanced Data – Real-world data improved or enriched using AI techniques such as cleaning, predicting missing values, or generating new features.

Synthetic Data – Artificially created data that imitates real datasets while protecting privacy and supporting model development.

Data Augmentation – Techniques that create modified versions of existing data to expand dataset size and improve AI model robustness.

Data Profiling – The systematic process of examining datasets to understand content, quality, distribution, and potential issues.

Data Quality – The measure of how accurate, complete, consistent, and reliable a dataset is for analysis.

Distribution – The way values of a dataset are spread, helping analysts understand patterns, variation, and outliers.

Tool Compatibility – The alignment between the data format and the tools required to access, analyze, or process that data.

2.9 Review Questions

1. What are the five major data types, and how does each one influence the kinds of analyses or AI applications you can perform?
2. Explain the difference between continuous and discrete numeric data. Provide one real-world example of each.
3. How do nominal and ordinal categorical data differ, and why does that difference matter in AI and analytics?
4. Why is text data both powerful and challenging to use in AI systems?
5. What makes image data computationally demanding, and why is it increasingly important?
6. Why is timestamp data critical for understanding patterns and trends over time?
7. Define structured, unstructured, and semi-structured data. Provide an example of each.
8. When would a CSV file be a better choice than a SQL database, and when would a SQL database be preferable?
9. What makes JSON useful in modern data workflows, especially for AI and web-based systems?

10. Why are log files valuable sources of insight, and what challenges do they present?
11. What is AI-enhanced data, and how can it improve business analytics or AI model performance?
12. What is synthetic data, and what are its key benefits and limitations?
13. What is data augmentation, and why is it especially useful in image and text analysis?
14. What is the purpose of data profiling, and why should it occur before analysis?
15. How do storage, performance, and tool compatibility influence decisions about data formats?

2.10 References

[1] Anaconda. (2024). 2024 State of Data Science Report: Data Preparation Trends. Anaconda Data Science Survey. https://www.anaconda.com/state-of-data-science-2024

[2] MIT Technology Review. (2024). Synthetic Data Generation for AI Applications. MIT Technology Review AI Section. https://www.technologyreview.com/2024/synthetic-data-ai-applications/

[3] Harvard Business Review. (2024). Data Quality Management in the AI Era. Harvard Business Review Data & Analytics. https://hbr.org/2024/data-quality-management-ai-era

[4] O'Reilly Media. (2024). Modern Data Formats and Structures: A Practical Guide. O'Reilly Data Newsletter. https://www.oreilly.com/radar/modern-data-formats-structures-2024/

[5] DataCamp. (2024). Understanding Data Types for Machine Learning. DataCamp Learn Platform. https://www.datacamp.com/blog/data-types-machine-learning-2024

2.11 Lab 2-1 Working with Essential Data Types

Every piece of data can be classified into one of five essential data types: numeric, categorical, text, image, and timestamp. Numeric data includes measurable values such as age, income, or temperature, and can be used in calculations and statistical analysis. Categorical data represents groups or labels, such as gender, region, or product type, and is typically used for grouping or comparison. Text data consists of unstructured or semi-structured language-based information like comments, descriptions, or reviews. Image data includes visual information such as photographs or scanned documents, which often require specialized tools for analysis. Timestamp data captures points in time, such as dates and events, and is essential for time-series analysis and tracking change over time.

These data types may be either structured—organized in a predefined format like tables—or unstructured, such as free text or images that do not follow a fixed schema. In R, different functions are used depending on the data type to ensure correct handling and analysis, and AI tools can further assist by validating data types and suggesting appropriate analytical methods.

2.11.1 Demonstration

In this demonstration, we load the required R packages (**dplyr**, **lubridate**, and **stringr**) and create a sample dataset that includes a essential data types: numeric, categorical, text, and timestamp data. The dataset represents simple customer information such as ID, age, income, segment, review text, and purchase date.

We use data.frame() to construct the dataset with 20 observations. Numeric data is represented by Age and Income, categorical data by Segment, text data by Review, and timestamp data by Purchase date. After creating the dataset, we check the structure and confirm that each variable is stored in the correct format. We then use head(data) to preview the first few rows of the dataset.

2.11.1.1 Setup

```
library(dplyr)
library(lubridate)
library(stringr)

# Sample dataset with all 5 types
data <- data.frame(
  ID = 1:20,

  Age = c(
    25, 34, 45, 29, 38,
    52, 31, 27, 41, 33,
    28, 39, 46, 32, 37,
    44, 30, 35, 42, 26
  ),

  Income = c(
    45000, 62000, 85000, 51000, 73000,
    95000, 58000, 49000, 78000, 64000,
    53000, 71000, 89000, 60000, 75000,
    82000, 56000, 67000, 80000, 48000
  ),

  Segment = c(
```

```
    "Budget", "Standard", "Premium", "Budget", "Standard",
    "Premium", "Standard", "Budget", "Premium", "Standard",
    "Budget", "Standard", "Premium", "Standard", "Standard",
    "Premium", "Budget", "Standard", "Premium", "Budget"
  ),

  Review = c(
    "Great product!", "Good value", "Excellent quality", "Not
    ↪  satisfied",
    "Amazing service", "Poor quality", "Perfect for me", "Overpriced",
    "Highly recommend", "Good experience", "Disappointed", "Great
    ↪  quality",
    "Excellent", "Fair price", "Good product", "Outstanding",
    "Not worth it", "Very satisfied", "Excellent service", "Good value"
  ),

  Purchase = as.Date(c(
    "2024-01-15", "2024-02-20", "2024-01-08", "2024-03-12",
    "2024-02-28", "2024-01-22", "2024-03-05", "2024-02-14",
    "2024-01-30", "2024-03-18", "2024-02-10", "2024-01-25",
    "2024-03-22", "2024-02-05", "2024-01-18", "2024-03-08",
    "2024-02-25", "2024-01-12", "2024-03-15", "2024-02-18"
  ))
)
```

```
head(data)
```

```
  ID Age Income  Segment            Review   Purchase
1  1  25  45000   Budget    Great product! 2024-01-15
2  2  34  62000 Standard        Good value 2024-02-20
3  3  45  85000  Premium Excellent quality 2024-01-08
4  4  29  51000   Budget     Not satisfied 2024-03-12
5  5  38  73000 Standard   Amazing service 2024-02-28
6  6  52  95000  Premium      Poor quality 2024-01-22
```

2.11.1.2 Step 1: Numeric Data

Numeric Data refers to quantities and measurements such as ages, prices, temperatures, counts, and percentages. It is one of the easiest data types to work with because it can be directly used in mathematical operations like addition, subtraction, averages, and comparisons.

2.11.1.2.1 Continuous vs Discrete

Continuous data refers to numerical values that can take any value within a given range, including decimals and fractions. Examples include temperature (98.6°F, 98.65°F, 98.7°F) or income measured to the nearest cent. These values are measured rather than counted, meaning there are infinitely many possible values between any two points.

Discrete data, on the other hand, represents countable values that can only take specific whole numbers. Examples include the number of customers (5, 6, 7) or number of items purchased, where fractional values are not meaningful.

In analysis, numeric data can be summarized using functions such as summary() to describe central tendency and spread. Distributions can be visualized using histograms, while quantile() helps identify data spread across percentiles. Relationships between numeric variables can be measured using correlation, and potential outliers can be detected using standard deviation rules or visual inspection. Numeric data can also be grouped into categories (such as age groups) to compare averages across segments using aggregation methods.

```
# Analyze numeric columns

print("=== NUMERIC DATA ANALYSIS ===")
```

```
[1] "=== NUMERIC DATA ANALYSIS ==="
```

```
summary(data[c("Age", "Income")])
```

```
      Age            Income     
 Min.   :25.00   Min.   :45000  
 1st Qu.:29.75   1st Qu.:55250  
 Median :34.50   Median :65500  
 Mean   :35.70   Mean   :67050  
 3rd Qu.:41.25   3rd Qu.:78500  
 Max.   :52.00   Max.   :95000  
```

```
# Check if discrete or continuous
print(
  paste(
    "Age - Unique values:",
    length(unique(data$Age)),
    "(discrete)"
  )
)
```

```
[1] "Age - Unique values: 20 (discrete)"
```

```
print(
  paste(
    "Income - Unique values:",
    length(unique(data$Income)),
    "(continuous)"
  )
)
```

```
[1] "Income - Unique values: 20 (continuous)"
```

```
# Distribution analysis
print("Age distribution:")
```

```
[1] "Age distribution:"
```

```
hist(
  data$Age,
  main = "Age Distribution",
  breaks = 5
)
```

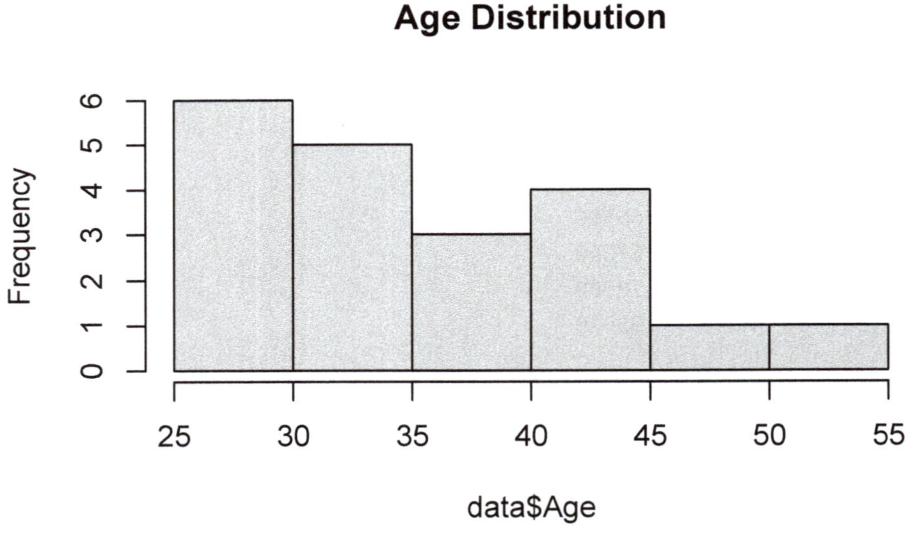


```
print("Income quartiles:")
```

```
[1] "Income quartiles:"
```

```
quantile(data$Income)
```

```
   0%   25%   50%   75%  100%
45000 55250 65500 78500 95000
```

```
# Relationships between numeric variables
correlation <- cor(data$Age, data$Income)

print(
  paste(
    "Age-Income correlation:",
    round(correlation, 3)
  )
)
```

```
[1] "Age-Income correlation: 0.99"
```

```
# Outlier detection
age_outliers <- data$Age[
  data$Age > (mean(data$Age) + 2 * sd(data$Age)) |
  data$Age < (mean(data$Age) - 2 * sd(data$Age))
]

print(
  paste(
    "Age outliers:",
    paste(age_outliers, collapse = ", ")
  )
)
```

```
[1] "Age outliers: 52"
```

```
# Income analysis by age groups
data$AgeGroup <- cut(
  data$Age,
  breaks = c(0, 30, 45, 100),
  labels = c("Young", "Middle", "Senior")
)

print("Average income by age group:")
```

```
[1] "Average income by age group:"
```

```
aggregate(
  Income ~ AgeGroup,
```

```
  data = data,
  FUN = mean
)
```

```
  AgeGroup   Income
1    Young 50333.33
2   Middle 71250.00
3   Senior 92000.00
```

2.11.1.2.2 AI Applications for Numeric Data

AI applications for numeric data are based on the fact that most machine learning systems operate on numbers rather than raw labels or text. Numeric variables such as age, income, and counts allow models to detect patterns, learn relationships, and make predictions. In real AI systems, numeric data is not only described but actively used to train algorithms that can forecast outcomes, identify anomalies, and support decision-making. Before numeric data can be used effectively in AI models, it often needs to be standardized so that variables measured on different scales, such as age and income, do not distort the results. This process is typically called scaling or normalization.

In practice, AI can assist with numeric data analysis by helping determine which methods are most appropriate for a given dataset and by identifying patterns that may not be obvious through manual inspection. For example, when detecting outliers in income or age data, traditional statistical methods such as the interquartile range or z-scores apply fixed mathematical rules. AI-based approaches extend this idea by learning what "normal" patterns look like in the data and flagging values that deviate based on learned structure rather than a single fixed threshold. More advanced AI models may use anomaly detection techniques such as isolation-based methods or neural network reconstruction error to identify unusual observations.

The key distinction is that traditional methods rely on predefined rules, while AI systems learn from the data itself to make adaptive decisions about what is normal or unusual.

2.11.1.3 2. Categorical Data

Categorical data represents data that is organized into distinct groups or labels rather than measured numerically. These values describe characteristics such as product categories, customer segments, geographic regions, or yes/no responses. Unlike numeric data, categorical values cannot be meaningfully added, subtracted, or averaged because they do not represent quantities.

2.11.1.3.1 Nominal vs Ordinal Categories

This section demonstrates how categorical data is analyzed and summarized in R, with a focus on understanding both frequency patterns and relationships between categories.First, a frequency table is created using table(data$Segment) to show how many customers fall into each segment. This is followed by converting those counts into percentages using prop.table(), which makes it easier to compare category proportions.

Next, the Segment variable is converted into an ordered factor with factor(), defining a meaningful hierarchy from Budget to Premium. This allows R to treat the categories as ordinal data rather than simple labels. The code then creates a cross-tabulation between Segment and Age Group to examine how customer segments vary across different age categories. A chi-square test is applied to determine whether there is a statistically significant relationship between the two variables.

Finally, the most common category (the mode) is calculated by identifying the segment with the highest frequency.

```
print("=== CATEGORICAL DATA ANALYSIS ===")
```

```
[1] "=== CATEGORICAL DATA ANALYSIS ==="
```

```
# Basic frequency analysis
print("Customer Segment distribution:")
```

```
[1] "Customer Segment distribution:"
```

```
segment_table <- table(data$Segment)
print(segment_table)
```

```

  Budget  Premium Standard 
       6        6        8 
```

```
# Convert to percentages
print("Customer Segment percentages:")
```

```
[1] "Customer Segment percentages:"
```

```
segment_percent <- round(prop.table(segment_table) * 100, 1)
print(segment_percent)
```

```

  Budget  Premium Standard 
      30       30       40 
```

```
# Properly order the categorical variable (ordinal)
data$Segment <- factor(data$Segment,
  levels = c("Budget", "Standard", "Premium"), ordered = TRUE)
print("Ordered segments:")
```

```
[1] "Ordered segments:"
```

```r
levels(data$Segment)
```

```
[1] "Budget"   "Standard" "Premium"
```

```r
# Cross-tabulation with other variables
print("Segment by Age Group:")
```

```
[1] "Segment by Age Group:"
```

```r
segment_age_table <- table(data$Segment, data$AgeGroup)
print(segment_age_table)
```

```
          Young Middle Senior
  Budget       6      0      0
  Standard     0      8      0
  Premium      0      4      2
```

```r
# Chi-square test for independence
chi_test <- chisq.test(segment_age_table)
print(paste("Chi-square p-value:", round(chi_test$p.value, 4)))
```

```
[1] "Chi-square p-value: 1e-04"
```

```r
# Mode (most frequent category)
mode_segment <- names(sort(table(data$Segment), decreasing=TRUE))[1]
print(paste("Most common segment:", mode_segment))
```

```
[1] "Most common segment: Standard"
```

2.11.1.3.2 AI Applications for Categorical Data

One-hot encoding is a method used in machine learning to convert categorical variables into a numeric format so that algorithms can process them. Instead of assigning categories arbitrary numbers, one-hot encoding creates a separate binary column for each category. Each row is marked with a 1 in the column that matches its category and 0 in all others. This preserves the meaning of the original categories without implying any order or ranking.

In this dataset, the variable Segment contains three categories: Budget, Standard, and Premium. To apply one-hot encoding in R, we create new columns that represent each category as a separate binary feature.

```r
create_dummy_vars <- function(data, column) {

  categories <- unique(data[[column]])
```

```
  for (cat in categories) {

    data[[paste0(column, "_", cat)]] <-
      as.numeric(data[[column]] == cat)

  }

  return(data)

}

data_encoded <- create_dummy_vars(data, "Segment")

data_encoded[
  c(
    "Segment_Budget",
    "Segment_Standard",
    "Segment_Premium"
  )
][1:10, ]
```

```
   Segment_Budget Segment_Standard Segment_Premium
1               1                0               0
2               0                1               0
3               0                0               1
4               1                0               0
5               0                1               0
6               0                0               1
7               0                1               0
8               1                0               0
9               0                0               1
10              0                1               0
```

After running this code, the original Segment column is expanded into three new columns. For each row, only one column contains a value of 1 (indicating the customer's segment), while the others contain 0. For example, a customer in the Premium segment will have Segment_Premium = 1 and all other segment columns set to 0. This transformation allows machine learning models to interpret categorical data as numeric inputs without losing meaning or introducing false ordering between categories.

2.11.1.4 3. Text Data

Text data refers to unstructured information written in natural language, such as customer reviews, social media posts, emails, and survey responses. Unlike numeric or categorical data, text data does not follow a fixed structure and must be processed before it can be analyzed. It contains rich meaning, but that meaning is often hidden in word choice, context, and phrasing.

Text data analysis focuses on transforming raw language into measurable features. This includes calculating basic statistics such as the length of each review in characters and words, identifying frequently used words, and detecting patterns in how customers express feedback. Common words and repeated phrases can reveal overall sentiment or recurring themes.

Because text is highly variable, one of the key challenges is that the same idea can be expressed in many different ways. For example, phrases like "excellent product," "love it," and "very satisfied" may all communicate similar positive sentiment, even though they use completely different words. This makes structured analysis more complex and often requires techniques such as tokenization, pattern matching, and sentiment classification.

2.11.1.4.1 Text Data Challenges

In this example, R is used to measure review length, count words, identify reviews containing specific terms, and calculate word frequency. A simple sentiment classification function is also applied to label each review as positive, negative, or neutral based on the presence of predefined keywords. The results are then summarized overall and compared across customer segments to show how sentiment varies between groups.

```
print("=== TEXT DATA ANALYSIS ===")
```

```
[1] "=== TEXT DATA ANALYSIS ==="
```

```
# Basic text statistics
data$ReviewLength <- nchar(data$Review)

data$WordCount <- str_count(
  data$Review,
  "\\S+"
)

print("Text statistics:")
```

```
[1] "Text statistics:"
```

```
print(
  paste(
```

```
    "Average review length:",
    round(mean(data$ReviewLength), 1),
    "characters"
  )
)
```

```
[1] "Average review length: 12.8 characters"
```

```
print(
  paste(
    "Average word count:",
    round(mean(data$WordCount), 1),
    "words"
  )
)
```

```
[1] "Average word count: 1.9 words"
```

```
print(
  paste(
    "Shortest review:",
    min(data$ReviewLength),
    "characters"
  )
)
```

```
[1] "Shortest review: 9 characters"
```

```
print(
  paste(
    "Longest review:",
    max(data$ReviewLength),
    "characters"
  )
)
```

```
[1] "Longest review: 17 characters"
```

```
# Text patterns
print("Reviews containing 'excellent':")
```

```
[1] "Reviews containing 'excellent':"
```

```
excellent_reviews <- data$Review[
  grepl(
    "excellent",
```

```
    data$Review,
    ignore.case = TRUE
  )
]

print(excellent_reviews)

[1] "Excellent quality" "Excellent"         "Excellent service"

# Word frequency analysis
all_words <- unlist(
  strsplit(
    tolower(data$Review),
    "\\s+"
  )
)

word_freq <- table(all_words)

print("Most common words:")

[1] "Most common words:"

print(
  sort(word_freq, decreasing = TRUE)[1:5]
)

all_words
     good excellent   quality     great       not
        4         3         3         2         2

# Simple sentiment analysis
classify_sentiment <- function(text) {

  text_lower <- tolower(text)

  positive_words <- c(
    "great",
    "excellent",
    "amazing",
    "perfect",
    "good",
    "outstanding",
    "love"
  )
```

```
  negative_words <- c(
    "poor",
    "bad",
    "terrible",
    "awful",
    "disappointed",
    "overpriced",
    "not worth"
  )

  pos_count <- sum(
    sapply(
      positive_words,
      function(x) grepl(x, text_lower)
    )
  )

  neg_count <- sum(
    sapply(
      negative_words,
      function(x) grepl(x, text_lower)
    )
  )

  if (pos_count > neg_count) {
    return("Positive")
  }

  if (neg_count > pos_count) {
    return("Negative")
  }

  return("Neutral")
}

data$Sentiment <- sapply(
  data$Review,
  classify_sentiment
)

print("Sentiment distribution:")
```

```
[1] "Sentiment distribution:"
```

```
print(table(data$Sentiment))
```

```
Negative  Neutral Positive
       4        4       12
```

```
# Sentiment by customer segment
print("Sentiment by customer segment:")
```

```
[1] "Sentiment by customer segment:"
```

```
sentiment_segment <- table(
  data$Segment,
  data$Sentiment
)

print(sentiment_segment)
```

```
           Negative Neutral Positive
  Budget          3       1        2
  Standard        0       2        6
  Premium         1       1        4
```

2.11.1.5 4. Timestamp Data

Timestamp data records when events occur and is used to analyze how behavior, activity, or performance changes over time. This type of data is essential for understanding sequences, trends, and timing patterns in real-world systems such as customer purchases, system logs, or sensor readings. Unlike static data types, timestamp data introduces a temporal dimension that allows analysis to move beyond what is happening to also include when it is happening.

Time data can be stored in different formats and levels of detail, ranging from simple dates to precise timestamps that include hours, minutes, and seconds. Understanding this structure is important because it determines how the data can be grouped, summarized, or compared over time.

2.11.1.5.1 Time Data Formats and Granularities

In this example, R is used to explore purchase dates by identifying the earliest and most recent transactions and calculating the overall time span of the dataset. The data is then broken down into temporal components such as year, month, weekday, and quarter to reveal seasonal and cyclical patterns. Additional calculations measure how many days have passed since each purchase, allowing customers to be grouped by recency. These time-based features are then used to summarize trends such as purchase frequency by month and variations in income across time periods.

```
print("=== TIMESTAMP DATA ANALYSIS ===")
```

```
[1] "=== TIMESTAMP DATA ANALYSIS ==="
```

```
# Basic date analysis
print("Purchase date range:")
```

```
[1] "Purchase date range:"
```

```
print(paste("Earliest purchase:", min(data$Purchase)))
```

```
[1] "Earliest purchase: 2024-01-08"
```

```
print(paste("Most recent purchase:", max(data$Purchase)))
```

```
[1] "Most recent purchase: 2024-03-22"
```

```
print(paste("Date span:", as.numeric(max(data$Purchase) -
↪  min(data$Purchase)), "days"))
```

```
[1] "Date span: 74 days"
```

```
# Extract temporal components
data$Year <- year(data$Purchase)
data$Month <- month(data$Purchase, label = TRUE)
data$Weekday <- weekdays(data$Purchase)
data$Quarter <- quarter(data$Purchase)

# Temporal patterns
print("Purchases by month:")
```

```
[1] "Purchases by month:"
```

```
month_table <- table(data$Month)
print(month_table)
```

```
Jan Feb Mar Apr May Jun Jul Aug Sep Oct Nov Dec
  7   7   6   0   0   0   0   0   0   0   0   0
```

```
print("Purchases by weekday:")
```

```
[1] "Purchases by weekday:"
```

```
weekday_table <- table(data$Weekday)
print(weekday_table)
```

```
   Friday    Monday  Saturday    Sunday  Thursday   Tuesday Wednesday 
        4         5         1         2         2         4         2 
```

```
print("Purchases by quarter:")
```

```
[1] "Purchases by quarter:"
```

```
quarter_table <- table(data$Quarter)
print(quarter_table)
```

```
 1 
20 
```

```
# Time-based calculations
current_date <- as.Date("2024-04-01")
data$DaysAgo <- as.numeric(current_date - data$Purchase)
data$WeeksAgo <- data$DaysAgo / 7

print("Time since purchase statistics:")
```

```
[1] "Time since purchase statistics:"
```

```
print(summary(data$DaysAgo))
```

```
   Min. 1st Qu.  Median    Mean 3rd Qu.    Max. 
  10.00   26.25   45.00   46.65   67.75   84.00 
```

```
# Recency analysis
data$Recency <- cut(data$DaysAgo,
                   breaks = c(0, 30, 60, 90, Inf),
                   labels = c("Recent", "Moderate", "Old", "Very
                    ↪  Old"))
print("Customer recency distribution:")
```

```
[1] "Customer recency distribution:"
```

```
print(table(data$Recency))
```

```
  Recent Moderate      Old Very Old 
       6        7        7        0 
```

```
# Seasonal patterns
print("Average income by purchase month:")
```

```
[1] "Average income by purchase month:"
```

```
income_by_month <- aggregate(Income ~ Month, data = data, FUN =
↪ mean)
print(income_by_month)
```

```
  Month   Income
1   Jan 73714.29
2   Feb 57285.71
3   Mar 70666.67
```

```
# Time series preparation
monthly_purchases <- data %>%
  group_by(Year, Month) %>%
  summarise(Count = n(), AvgIncome = mean(Income), .groups =
   ↪ 'drop')
print("Monthly purchase summary:")
```

```
[1] "Monthly purchase summary:"
```

```
print(monthly_purchases)
```

```
# A tibble: 3 x 4
   Year Month Count AvgIncome
  <dbl> <ord> <int>     <dbl>
1  2024 Jan       7    73714.
2  2024 Feb       7    57286.
3  2024 Mar       6    70667.
```

2.11.1.5.2 AI Applications for Temporal Data

Temporal data refers to information that includes a time element, such as dates or timestamps. This type of data is important because it allows us to understand not only what happened, but also when it happened. In many real-world problems, timing is just as important as the values themselves. For example, customer behavior can change depending on the time of year, day of the week, or how long it has been since their last purchase.

Instead of using raw dates directly, we convert timestamps into simpler, more useful variables called features. A feature is just a new column that helps explain patterns in the data. For temporal data, these features help describe behavior over time in a way that machine learning models can understand.

Common time-based features include how many days have passed since a purchase, whether an event happened on a weekend, which month or quarter it occurred in, and how often events happen over time. These features make it easier to identify patterns such as repeat buying behavior, seasonal trends, or changes in activity levels.

In this example, R is used to transform raw purchase dates into useful time-based variables. The data is first ordered by customer and date so that events are in the correct sequence. New variables are then created to measure time gaps between purchases, identify weekend activity, and detect month-end or quarter-end behavior. Additional calculations measure how far each purchase is from the start of the dataset. These new variables help summarize customer behavior in a way that can be used for prediction and analysis.

By converting raw timestamps into structured time-based features, we make it possible for AI and machine learning models to learn patterns in behavior over time, rather than just working with isolated dates.

```
# AI-suggested temporal feature engineering
engineer_temporal_features <- function(data) {
  # Sort by customer and date
  data <- data[order(data$ID, data$Purchase), ]

  # Calculate purchase intervals (for customers with multiple
   ↪ purchases)
  data$PurchaseInterval <- NA
  for(customer in unique(data$ID)) {
    customer_data <- data[data$ID == customer, ]
    if(nrow(customer_data) > 1) {
      intervals <- diff(customer_data$Purchase)
      data$PurchaseInterval[data$ID == customer][-1] <-
↪ as.numeric(intervals)
    }
  }

  # Seasonal indicators
  data$IsWeekend <- weekdays(data$Purchase) %in% c("Saturday",
↪ "Sunday")
  data$IsMonthEnd <- day(data$Purchase) > 25
  data$IsQuarterEnd <- month(data$Purchase) %in% c(3, 6, 9, 12)

  # Time-based aggregations
  data$MonthsSinceStart <- as.numeric(data$Purchase -
↪ min(data$Purchase)) / 30.44

  return(data)
```

```r
}

data_with_temporal <- engineer_temporal_features(data)
print("Temporal features created:")
```

```
[1] "Temporal features created:"
```

```r
cat(
  paste(
    names(data_with_temporal)[grep(
      "Purchase|Weekend|Month|Quarter",
      names(data_with_temporal)
    )],
    collapse = "\n"
  )
)
```

```
Purchase
Month
Quarter
PurchaseInterval
IsWeekend
IsMonthEnd
IsQuarterEnd
MonthsSinceStart
```

```r
# Weekend vs weekday analysis
print("Weekend purchase analysis:")
```

```
[1] "Weekend purchase analysis:"
```

```r
weekend_analysis <- aggregate(Income ~ IsWeekend, data =
↪ data_with_temporal, FUN = mean)
print(weekend_analysis)
```

```
  IsWeekend   Income
1     FALSE 69647.06
2      TRUE 52333.33
```

2.11.2 Practice

```r
library(dplyr)
library(lubridate)
library(stringr)
```

```r
practice <- data.frame(
  ID = 1:15,
  Age = c(22, 35, 41, 29, 33, 27, 50, 38, 26, 44, 31, 36, 28,
          45, 39),
  Income = c(42000, 68000, 79000, 52000, 61000, 48000, 90000,
             75000,  46000, 82000, 57000, 66000, 50000,
             85000, 72000),
  Segment = c("Budget", "Standard", "Premium", "Budget",
              "Standard", "Budget", "Premium", "Standard",
              "Budget", "Premium","Standard", "Standard",
              "Budget", "Premium", "Standard"),
  Review = c(
    "Great service", "Good value", "Excellent experience",
    "Not satisfied",  "Very good", "Poor quality",
    "Outstanding product", "Fair price","Amazing support",
    "Highly recommend", "Good experience","Excellent service",
    "Okay product", "Perfect quality", "Good value"
  ),
  Purchase = as.Date(c(
    "2024-01-05","2024-01-10","2024-01-12","2024-01-18",
    ↪  "2024-01-22",
    "2024-02-01","2024-02-05","2024-02-10","2024-02-14",
    ↪  "2024-02-18",
    "2024-02-22","2024-03-01","2024-03-05","2024-03-10",
    ↪  "2024-03-15"
  ))
)

head(practice)
```

```
  ID Age Income  Segment               Review   Purchase
1  1  22  42000   Budget        Great service 2024-01-05
2  2  35  68000 Standard           Good value 2024-01-10
3  3  41  79000  Premium Excellent experience 2024-01-12
4  4  29  52000   Budget        Not satisfied 2024-01-18
5  5  33  61000 Standard            Very good 2024-01-22
6  6  27  48000   Budget         Poor quality 2024-02-01
```

2.11.2.1 Questions

1. Run str(practice) and identify the four data types used in this dataset.
2. Compute a summary of Age and Income using summary().

3. What is the mean Income across all customers?
4. Create a histogram of Age. What does the distribution look like?
5. Find the correlation between Age and Income.
6. Identify the highest and lowest Income values.
7. Create a frequency table of Segment.
8. Convert Segment into percentages. Which segment is most common?
9. Identify all reviews that contain the word "good".
10. Count how many characters are in each Review.
11. Extract the earliest and latest Purchase dates.
12. Find how many total days span the dataset (latest minus earliest Purchase).

2.12 Lab 2-2 Data Profiling

Data profiling is the systematic examination of data to understand its structure, content, relationships, and quality. Think of it as conducting a thorough health checkup on your dataset before analysis—just as a doctor runs tests to understand your overall health, data profiling examines your data to identify potential problems that could affect your conclusions.

In this lab, you'll first master traditional data profiling fundamentals using statistical methods and R functions. Then you'll learn how modern data scientists enhance these traditional approaches by using AI tools. This two-phase approach mirrors professional practice: solid statistical foundations enhanced by AI-powered insights for more thorough and intelligent data quality assessment.

2.12.1 Demonstration

2.12.1.1 Step 1: Dataset Creation and Initial Examination

You're a data analyst at RetailCorp, and the marketing team has provided a customer database for analysis. Before running any analytics, you must systematically profile this data to assess its quality and reliability.

Let's create a realistic customer dataset with intentional quality issues that mirror real-world problems:

```
# Load required packages
library(dplyr)
library(ggplot2)
library(lubridate)
```

```
library(tidyr)

# Create customer dataset with realistic quality issues
set.seed(42)
customer_data <- data.frame(
  CustomerID = c(paste0("CUST", sprintf("%03d", 1:18)),
                 "CUST019", "CUST019"), # Duplicate ID
  Age = c(25, 34, NA, 29, 150, 52, 31, 27, 41, 33, 28, 39, 46, 32,
          37, 44, 30, 35, 42, 26), # Invalid age
  Income = c(
    45000, 62000, 85000, 51000, 73000, -5000, 58000, 49000, 78000,
    64000,  53000, 71000, 89000, 60000, 75000, 82000, 56000,
    67000, 80000, 48000
  ), # Negative income
  PurchaseAmount = c(
    120, 250, 180, 90, 320, 450, 200, 110, 380, 220,
    130, 290, 410, 190, 310, 390, 170, 260, 350, 140
  ),
  CustomerType = c(
    "Budget", "Premium", "Standard", "Budget", "Premium", "Budget",
    "Standard", "Budget", "Premium", "Standard", "Budget", "Standard",
    "Premium", "Standard", "Standard", "Premium", "Budget", "Standard",
    "Premium", "Budget"
  ),
  LastPurchaseDate = c(
    "2024-01-15", "2024-02-20", "2024-01-08", "invalid-date",
    "2024-02-28", "2024-01-22", "2024-03-05", "2024-02-14",
    "2024-01-30", "2024-03-18", "2024-02-10", "2024-01-25",
    "2024-03-22", "2024-02-05", "2024-01-18", "2024-03-08",
    "2024-02-25", "2024-01-12", "2024-03-15", "2024-02-18"
  ),
  Email = c(
    "john@email.com", "jane@email.com", "bob@email.com",
     ↪ "invalid-email",
    "mary@email.com", "tom@email.com", "lisa@email.com",
     ↪ "mike@email.com",
    "sarah@email.com", "david@email.com", "emma@email.com",
     ↪ "james@email.com",
    "anna@email.com", "peter@email.com", "lucy@email.com",
     ↪ "mark@email.com",
    "kate@email.com", "paul@email.com", "nina@email.com",
     ↪ "alex@email.com"
  )
```

```
)

# Display basic dataset information
print("=== DATASET OVERVIEW ===")
```

```
[1] "=== DATASET OVERVIEW ==="
```

```
print(paste("Dataset dimensions:", nrow(customer_data), "rows",
↪  ncol(customer_data), "columns"))
```

```
[1] "Dataset dimensions: 20 rows, 7 columns"
```

```
print("First 6 records:")
```

```
[1] "First 6 records:"
```

```
head(customer_data)
```

```
  CustomerID Age Income PurchaseAmount CustomerType LastPurchaseDate
1    CUST001  25  45000            120       Budget       2024-01-15
2    CUST002  34  62000            250      Premium       2024-02-20
3    CUST003  NA  85000            180     Standard       2024-01-08
4    CUST004  29  51000             90       Budget     invalid-date
5    CUST005 150  73000            320      Premium       2024-02-28
6    CUST006  52  -5000            450       Budget       2024-01-22
           Email
1 john@email.com
2 jane@email.com
3  bob@email.com
4  invalid-email
5 mary@email.com
6  tom@email.com
```

2.12.1.2 Step 2: Completeness Analysis

Completeness refers to the extent to which a dataset contains all required values without missing entries. In real-world data, missing values are common and can affect the reliability of results by introducing bias, reducing statistical power, or limiting the types of analysis that can be performed. This step evaluates the amount and pattern of missing data in the dataset to determine whether any variables or records require cleaning or imputation before further analysis.

```
print("=== COMPLETENESS ANALYSIS ===")
```

```
[1] "=== COMPLETENESS ANALYSIS ==="
```

```
# Method 1: Count missing values per column
missing_counts <- customer_data %>%
  summarise_all(~sum(is.na(.)))
print("Missing value counts by column:")
```

```
[1] "Missing value counts by column:"
```

```
print(missing_counts[,1:4])
```

```
  CustomerID Age Income PurchaseAmount
1          0   1      0              0
```

```
print(missing_counts[,5:7])
```

```
  CustomerType LastPurchaseDate Email
1            0                0     0
```

```
# Method 2: Calculate missing percentages
missing_percentages <- customer_data %>%
  summarise_all(~round(sum(is.na(.)) / length(.) * 100, 1))
print("Missing value percentages by column:")
```

```
[1] "Missing value percentages by column:"
```

```
print(missing_percentages[,1:4])
```

```
  CustomerID Age Income PurchaseAmount
1          0   5      0              0
```

```
print(missing_percentages[,5:7])
```

```
  CustomerType LastPurchaseDate Email
1            0                0     0
```

```
# Method 3: Create completeness summary table
completeness_summary <- data.frame(
  Column = names(customer_data),
  Total_Records = nrow(customer_data),
  Missing_Count = as.numeric(missing_counts),
  Missing_Percentage = as.numeric(missing_percentages),
  Complete_Records = nrow(customer_data) - as.numeric(missing_counts)
)
print("Completeness Summary Table:")
```

```
[1] "Completeness Summary Table:"
```

```
print(completeness_summary)
```

```
             Column Total_Records Missing_Count Missing_Percentage
1        CustomerID            20             0                  0
2               Age            20             1                  5
3            Income            20             0                  0
4    PurchaseAmount            20             0                  0
5      CustomerType            20             0                  0
6  LastPurchaseDate            20             0                  0
7             Email            20             0                  0
  Complete_Records
1               20
2               19
3               20
4               20
5               20
6               20
7               20
```

2.12.1.3 Step 3: Consistency Analysis

Consistency analysis evaluates whether data values follow logical relationships, expected patterns, and defined rules across variables. Even when data is complete, it may still contain inconsistencies such as mismatched categories, illogical numeric relationships, or incorrectly formatted values. This step helps identify structural errors in the dataset by examining relationships between variables (e.g., income and customer type), expected correlations, and formatting standards such as date structures.

```
print("=== CONSISTENCY ANALYSIS ===")
```

```
[1] "=== CONSISTENCY ANALYSIS ==="
```

```
# Check 1: CustomerType vs Income/Purchase alignment
consistency_check <- customer_data %>%
  filter(!is.na(Age), Income > 0) %>% # Remove invalid records for
   ↪ analysis
  group_by(CustomerType) %>%
  summarise(
    Count = n(),
    Avg_Income = round(mean(Income), 0),
    Avg_Purchase = round(mean(PurchaseAmount), 0),
    Min_Income = min(Income),
    Max_Income = max(Income),
    .groups = "drop"
```

```
  )
print("CustomerType vs Income/Purchase Consistency:")
```

```
[1] "CustomerType vs Income/Purchase Consistency:"
```

```
print(consistency_check)
```

```
# A tibble: 3 x 6
  CustomerType Count Avg_Income Avg_Purchase Min_Income Max_Income
  <chr>        <int>      <dbl>        <dbl>      <dbl>      <dbl>
1 Budget           6      50333          127      45000      56000
2 Premium          6      77333          350      62000      89000
3 Standard         6      65833          245      58000      75000
```

```
# Check 2: Age vs Income correlation (should be positive)
valid_data <- customer_data %>% filter(!is.na(Age), Income > 0, Age <=
  ↪ 100)
age_income_correlation <- cor(valid_data$Age, valid_data$Income)
print(paste("Age-Income Correlation:", round(age_income_correlation,
  ↪ 3)))
```

```
[1] "Age-Income Correlation: 0.989"
```

```
# Check 3: Date format consistency
date_formats <- customer_data %>%
  mutate(
    date_valid = !is.na(as.Date(LastPurchaseDate, format =
      ↪ "%Y-%m-%d")),
    date_format_check = ifelse(grepl("^\\d{4}-\\d{2}-\\d{2}$",
      ↪ LastPurchaseDate), "Valid Format", "Invalid Format")
  )
print("Date Format Consistency:")
```

```
[1] "Date Format Consistency:"
```

```
table(date_formats$date_format_check)
```

```

Invalid Format   Valid Format
             1             19
```

2.12.1.4 Step 4: Validity Analysis

Validity analysis evaluates whether data values conform to defined business rules, acceptable ranges, and required formats. Unlike completeness or consistency checks, validity focuses on whether individual values are acceptable in isolation—for example, whether numeric fields fall within realistic limits, whether text fields follow required patterns, and whether identifiers remain unique. This step ensures that the dataset not only contains values, but that those values are meaningful and usable for analysis.

```
print("=== VALIDITY ANALYSIS ===")
```

```
[1] "=== VALIDITY ANALYSIS ==="
```

```
# Define business rules for valid ranges
validity_rules <- list(
  age_min = 18, age_max = 100,
  income_min = 0, income_max = 200000,
  purchase_min = 0, purchase_max = 1000
)

# Check 1: Age validity
age_validity <- customer_data %>%
  filter(!is.na(Age)) %>%
  summarise(
    total_records = n(),
    valid_ages = sum(Age >= validity_rules$age_min & Age <=
     ↪ validity_rules$age_max),
    invalid_ages = sum(Age < validity_rules$age_min | Age >
     ↪ validity_rules$age_max),
    invalid_percentage = round(invalid_ages / total_records * 100,
     ↪ 1)
  )
print("Age Validity Check:")
```

```
[1] "Age Validity Check:"
```

```
print(age_validity)
```

```
  total_records valid_ages invalid_ages invalid_percentage
1            19         18            1                5.3
```

```
# Check 2: Income validity
income_validity <- customer_data %>%
  summarise(
    total_records = n(),
    valid_incomes = sum(Income >= validity_rules$income_min &
     ↪ Income <= validity_rules$income_max, na.rm = TRUE),
    invalid_incomes = sum(Income < validity_rules$income_min |
     ↪ Income > validity_rules$income_max, na.rm = TRUE),
    invalid_percentage = round(invalid_incomes / total_records *
     ↪ 100, 1)
```

```
  )
print("Income Validity Check:")
```

```
[1] "Income Validity Check:"
```

```
print(income_validity)
```

```
  total_records valid_incomes invalid_incomes invalid_percentage
1            20            19               1                  5
```

```
# Check 3: Email format validity
email_validity <- customer_data %>%
  mutate(
    valid_email =
    ↪  grepl("^[A-Za-z0-9._%+-]+@[A-Za-z0-9.-]+\\.[A-Za-z]{2,}$",
    ↪  Email)
  ) %>%
  summarise(
    total_records = n(),
    valid_emails = sum(valid_email),
    invalid_emails = sum(!valid_email),
    invalid_percentage = round(invalid_emails / total_records *
    ↪  100, 1)
  )
print("Email Validity Check:")
```

```
[1] "Email Validity Check:"
```

```
print(email_validity)
```

```
  total_records valid_emails invalid_emails invalid_percentage
1            20           19              1                  5
```

```
# Check 4: Duplicate ID detection
duplicate_check <- customer_data %>%
  summarise(
    total_records = n(),
    unique_ids = n_distinct(CustomerID),
    duplicate_count = total_records - unique_ids
  )
print("Duplicate ID Check:")
```

```
[1] "Duplicate ID Check:"
```

```
print(duplicate_check)
```

```
  total_records unique_ids duplicate_count
1            20         19               1
```

2.12.1.5 Step 5: Statistical Anomaly Detection

Statistical anomaly detection identifies unusual or extreme values that deviate significantly from the overall distribution of the data. These outliers may indicate data entry errors, measurement issues, or genuinely rare but important observations. By applying statistical techniques such as Z-scores and interquartile range (IQR), this step helps distinguish between typical values and potential anomalies, allowing analysts to decide whether to investigate, correct, or retain these records in the dataset.

```
print("=== STATISTICAL ANOMALY DETECTION ===")
```

```
[1] "=== STATISTICAL ANOMALY DETECTION ==="
```

```
# Prepare clean data for analysis
clean_data <- customer_data %>%
  filter(!is.na(Age), Income > 0, Age <= 100)

# Method 1: Z-Score Analysis (values >3 standard deviations from mean)
clean_data <- clean_data %>%
  mutate(
    Income_ZScore = abs(scale(Income)[, 1]),
    Purchase_ZScore = abs(scale(PurchaseAmount)[, 1]),
    Age_ZScore = abs(scale(Age)[, 1])
  )

# Identify statistical outliers
statistical_outliers <- clean_data %>%
  filter(Income_ZScore > 2 | Purchase_ZScore > 2 | Age_ZScore > 2) %>%
  select(
    CustomerID, Age, Income, PurchaseAmount, CustomerType,
    Income_ZScore, Purchase_ZScore, Age_ZScore
  )

print("Statistical Outliers (Z-score > 2):")
```

```
[1] "Statistical Outliers (Z-score > 2):"
```

```
print(statistical_outliers)
```

```
[1] CustomerID      Age             Income          PurchaseAmount
[5] CustomerType    Income_ZScore   Purchase_ZScore Age_ZScore
<0 rows> (or 0-length row.names)
```

```
# Method 2: Interquartile Range (IQR) Method
calculate_outliers_iqr <- function(x) {
  Q1 <- quantile(x, 0.25, na.rm = TRUE)
  Q3 <- quantile(x, 0.75, na.rm = TRUE)
  IQR <- Q3 - Q1
  lower_bound <- Q1 - 1.5 * IQR
  upper_bound <- Q3 + 1.5 * IQR
  return(x < lower_bound | x > upper_bound)
}

iqr_outliers <- clean_data %>%
  mutate(
    Income_Outlier = calculate_outliers_iqr(Income),
    Purchase_Outlier = calculate_outliers_iqr(PurchaseAmount),
    Age_Outlier = calculate_outliers_iqr(Age)
  ) %>%
  filter(Income_Outlier | Purchase_Outlier | Age_Outlier)

print("IQR Method Outliers:")
```

```
[1] "IQR Method Outliers:"
```

2.12.1.6 Step 6: AI Insight Layer

Traditional data profiling helps identify errors and issues within a dataset, but it does not always indicate which problems matter most. In practice, not all data issues have the same impact. Some, such as duplicate identifiers or invalid numeric values, can significantly distort analysis results, while others, like missing values, may be less critical or easier to address. This is where AI adds an important layer of value.

The AI insight layer enhances data profiling by helping analysts interpret their findings and prioritize actions. Rather than writing additional code, analysts can use AI tools to summarize results, identify patterns, and suggest next steps. For example, after completing profiling, an analyst might ask an AI system which issues should be addressed first. The AI can evaluate the findings and highlight the most critical problems, such as duplicate customer IDs that affect data integrity, while also noting that some unusual records may represent legitimate edge cases rather than errors.

This shifts the workflow from simply identifying and fixing all issues to making more informed decisions about what to address first. Instead of treating every problem equally, analysts can focus on the issues that have the greatest impact on analysis and business outcomes. In this way, AI does not replace traditional data profiling, but strengthens it by adding interpretation, prioritization, and context to the results.

2.12.2 Practice

Run the code below to generate the dataset, then answer the questions using R and brief responses.

```
library(dplyr)

set.seed(123)

practice_data <- data.frame(
  CustomerID = c(paste0("ID", 101:115), "ID110", "ID116", "ID117"),
  Age = c(22, 45, 31, NA, 28, 135, 40, 29, 33, 27, 38, 41,
          36, 30, 25, 50, NA, 34),
  Income = c(48000, 72000, 61000, 55000, -2000, 68000, 75000,
             52000, 58000,  60000, 64000, 71000, 69000, 73000,
             56000, 80000, 62000, 59000),
  PurchaseAmount = c(100, 220, 180, 150, 90, 300, 350, 120, 200,
                     210, 230, 260, 240, 270, 160, 400, 190, 205),
  CustomerType = c("Budget", "Premium", "Standard", "Budget", "Budget",
                   "Premium", "Premium", "Standard", "Standard",
                   "Budget", "Standard", "Premium", "Standard",
                   "Premium", "Budget", "Premium", "Standard",
                   "Budget"),
  LastPurchaseDate = c("2024-01-10", "2024-02-15", "bad-date",
                       "2024-01-20", "2024-03-01", "2024-02-28",
                       "2024-01-30", "2024-02-12", "2024-03-05",
                       "2024-01-18", "2024-02-22", "2024-03-10",
                       "2024-01-25", "invalid", "2024-02-05",
                       "2024-03-15",
                       "2024-02-18", "2024-01-12"),
  Email = c("a@email.com", "b@email.com", "c@email.com", "invalid",
            "e@email.com", "f@email.com", "g@email.com", "h@email.com",
            "i@email.com", "j@email.com", "k@email.com", "l@email.com",
            "m@email.com", "n@email.com", "o@email.com", "p@email.com",
            "q@email.com", "wrong-email")
)

practice_data
```

```
  CustomerID Age Income PurchaseAmount CustomerType LastPurchaseDate
1      ID101  22  48000            100       Budget       2024-01-10
2      ID102  45  72000            220      Premium       2024-02-15
3      ID103  31  61000            180     Standard         bad-date
4      ID104  NA  55000            150       Budget       2024-01-20
5      ID105  28  -2000             90       Budget       2024-03-01
```

```
6       ID106 135  68000            300      Premium      2024-02-28
7       ID107  40  75000            350      Premium      2024-01-30
8       ID108  29  52000            120     Standard      2024-02-12
9       ID109  33  58000            200     Standard      2024-03-05
10      ID110  27  60000            210       Budget      2024-01-18
11      ID111  38  64000            230     Standard      2024-02-22
12      ID112  41  71000            260      Premium      2024-03-10
13      ID113  36  69000            240     Standard      2024-01-25
14      ID114  30  73000            270      Premium         invalid
15      ID115  25  56000            160       Budget      2024-02-05
16      ID110  50  80000            400      Premium      2024-03-15
17      ID116  NA  62000            190     Standard      2024-02-18
18      ID117  34  59000            205       Budget      2024-01-12
          Email
1   a@email.com
2   b@email.com
3   c@email.com
4       invalid
5   e@email.com
6   f@email.com
7   g@email.com
8   h@email.com
9   i@email.com
10  j@email.com
11  k@email.com
12  l@email.com
13  m@email.com
14  n@email.com
15  o@email.com
16  p@email.com
17  q@email.com
18  wrong-email
```

2.12.2.1 Questions

1. How many missing values are in each column? Which column has the most?
2. What percentage of Age values are missing?
3. Calculate average Income by CustomerType. Does it make sense?
4. What is the correlation between Age and Income?
5. How many records contain invalid date formats?
6. How many Age values are outside 18–100?

7. How many Income values are invalid (e.g., negative)?
8. How many invalid Email values are present?
9. Are there duplicate CustomerID values? How many?
10. Identify any outliers in Income or PurchaseAmount.
11. Find one customer that looks unusual across multiple variables. Explain briefly.
12. Which data issue should be fixed first? Why?
13. Which issue is least important? Why?
14. Are any unusual records likely valid (not errors)? Explain.
15. In 3–4 sentences, describe the overall data quality of this dataset.

Chapter 3

Cleaning Messy Data

3.1 Learning Outcomes

3-1: Detect missing values and anomalous data points using systematic approaches across different tools

3-2: Apply AI-assisted imputation techniques and correction suggestions to improve data quality

3-3: Normalize text and date formats to create consistent data representations

3-4: Perform de-duplication and record consistency checks using SQL and other tools

3-5: Design effective data cleaning workflows that combine multiple techniques appropriately

3.2 Introduction

Imagine receiving a customer database that looks like this:

Name	Age	Phone	Join_Date
John Smith	25	555-1234	2023-01-15
JANE DOE		(555) 234-5678	Jan 20, 2023
Bob Johnson	150	5552345678	1/25/23
Jane Doe	28	555-234-5678	2023-01-20

Even this small sample reveals multiple data quality issues: missing values, impossible ages, inconsistent formatting, and potential duplicates. These problems are typical of real-world data and can seriously impact analysis results and AI model performance.

Data cleaning is the systematic process of identifying and correcting these quality issues. It's often the most time-consuming part of any data project, but it's also one of the most critical. Poor data quality leads to unreliable analysis, biased AI models, and incorrect business decisions.

This module teaches you how to systematically detect and correct common data quality problems using appropriate tools and techniques. You'll learn to identify what needs fixing, choose the right approach for each problem, and validate that your cleaning actually improves the data.

3.3 Detecting Missing and Anomalous Values

3.3.1 Understanding Missing Data Patterns

Missing data occurs when expected information is absent from your dataset. However, not all missing data is the same, and understanding the different types helps you choose appropriate handling strategies.

3.3.1.1 Types of Missing Data

Missing Completely At Random (MCAR) occurs when the absence of data has no relationship to any other variables. This might happen due to random technical failures or data collection errors. For example, if a survey system randomly fails to record some responses due to server issues.

Missing At Random (MAR) occurs when the probability of missing data depends on observed variables but not on the missing values themselves. For instance, younger customers might be less likely to provide phone numbers, but among customers of the same age, phone number availability is random.

Missing Not At Random (MNAR) occurs when the probability of missing data depends on the unobserved values themselves. High-income customers might deliberately skip income questions, or dissatisfied customers might be less likely to complete satisfaction surveys.

Understanding these patterns is crucial because they require different handling approaches. MCAR data can often be safely ignored or imputed using simple methods. MAR data might require more sophisticated techniques that consider relationships with other variables. MNAR data requires careful consideration of the underlying causes.

3.3.1.2 Common Forms of Missing Data

Missing data doesn't always appear as empty cells. You need to recognize various forms:

- Empty cells or NULL values in databases
- Placeholder text like "N/A," "Unknown," or "TBD"
- Default values like 0, 999, or 01/01/1900 used as placeholders
- Impossible values that indicate missing data (age = -1)
- Inconsistent coding schemes across different data sources

3.3.2 Systematic Detection Approaches

Rather than manually scanning for problems, systematic detection helps you quickly identify patterns and prioritize cleaning efforts.

3.3.2.1 Basic Detection Methods

Start by calculating missing value percentages for each variable to understand the scope of the problem. Variables with high percentages of missing data might require different handling than those with occasional missing values.

Pattern analysis reveals whether missing data occurs randomly or follows systematic patterns. If missing values cluster in certain time periods, geographic regions, or customer segments, this suggests underlying causes that need investigation.

Visual analysis using charts and graphs can reveal missing data patterns that aren't apparent in statistical summaries. Missing data plots show patterns across multiple variables simultaneously, while time series plots can reveal whether missing data increases or decreases over time.

3.3.2.2 Tool-Specific Approaches

Excel provides accessible tools for initial missing data detection. Conditional formatting can highlight empty cells, while simple formulas like COUNTBLANK() can count missing values. Pivot tables can summarize missing data patterns across different categories.

SQL offers powerful capabilities for systematic analysis of large datasets. Aggregate functions can efficiently calculate missing value statistics, while WHERE clauses can filter records with missing data for detailed examination.

R and Python provide comprehensive packages for missing data analysis and visualization. These tools excel at pattern detection and can generate detailed reports about missing data characteristics.

3.3.3 Identifying Anomalous Values

Anomalous values, or outliers, represent data points that differ significantly from typical patterns in your dataset. These might indicate data entry errors, measurement problems, or genuinely unusual cases that require special attention.

3.3.3.1 Statistical Approaches

Statistical methods provide systematic approaches to identifying values that fall outside expected ranges. The simplest approach uses standard deviations to identify values that fall far from the mean. Values more than two or three standard deviations from the mean are often considered potential outliers.

Interquartile range (IQR) methods provide more robust outlier detection by identifying values that fall below the first quartile minus 1.5 times the IQR or above the third quartile plus 1.5 times the IQR. This approach works better for skewed distributions than standard deviation methods.

Z-scores normalize values relative to the mean and standard deviation, making it easier to compare outliers across different variables. Modified z-scores use median and median absolute deviation instead of mean and standard deviation, providing more robust detection for skewed distributions.

3.3.3.2 Business Rule Validation

Statistical methods provide starting points, but domain knowledge is crucial for distinguishing between errors and legitimate unusual values. A customer age of 150 years is almost certainly an error, while a customer age of 95 might be unusual but legitimate.

Business rules help identify values that are logically impossible or highly unlikely, ensuring that data remains realistic and trustworthy. For example, age values are typically validated to fall within reasonable human limits, such as between 0 and 120 years. Historical datasets should not contain dates that occur in the future, since that would indicate an entry or system error. Phone numbers are often checked to ensure they contain the correct number of digits, while email addresses are validated to confirm they include required elements such as an "@" symbol. In addition, zip codes are compared against known geographic patterns to verify that they match valid locations. These kinds of rules help organizations quickly detect and correct errors before they affect analysis and decision-making.

Cross-variable validation checks for consistency between related fields. If a customer's state is "California" but their zip code corresponds to New York, this inconsistency suggests a data quality issue.

3.4 AI-Assisted Imputation and Correction

3.4.1 Understanding Modern Imputation Methods

Traditional imputation methods like mean substitution or forward filling often oversimplify complex relationships in data. AI-assisted techniques can learn sophisticated patterns and use multiple variables to predict missing values more accurately.

3.4.1.1 Evolution from Simple to Smart Imputation

Simple imputation methods replace missing values with basic statistics like means, medians, or modes. While easy to implement, these methods can distort relationships between variables and create unrealistic data patterns.

Smart imputation methods use machine learning algorithms to learn patterns from existing data and predict missing values based on relationships with other variables. For example, missing customer ages might be predicted based on purchase history, geographic location, and other demographic information.

The choice between simple and sophisticated methods depends on your data characteristics, the amount of missing data, and the importance of preserving relationships between variables. Simple methods might be sufficient for small amounts of randomly missing data, while complex methods become valuable when missing data follows patterns or when accuracy is critical.

3.4.1.2 Machine Learning-Based Approaches

Regression-based imputation uses statistical models to predict missing values based on other variables in the dataset. Linear regression works well for continuous variables with linear relationships, while logistic regression can handle categorical variables.

Tree-based methods like Random Forest can handle complex, non-linear relationships and interactions between variables. These methods automatically identify which variables are most predictive of missing values and can handle both numerical and categorical data effectively.

Deep learning approaches can learn very complex patterns for imputation, especially when dealing with high-dimensional data or complex relationships. However, these methods require larger datasets and more computational resources than simpler approaches.

3.4.1.3 Validation and Quality Assurance

AI-assisted cleaning requires careful validation to ensure that automated corrections improve rather than degrade data quality. Cross-validation techniques can test imputation accuracy by hiding known values and checking how well the AI system predicts them.

Comparison with domain expertise helps validate that AI suggestions make sense in the business context. While AI systems excel at identifying statistical patterns, human experts understand business rules and contextual factors that might not be apparent in the data.

Documentation of AI-assisted changes is crucial for transparency and reproducibility. Understanding what changes were made, why they were made, and how confident the system was in its suggestions helps evaluate the reliability of cleaned data.

3.4.2 Practical Implementation Strategies

Implementing AI-assisted cleaning requires balancing automation with human oversight. The goal is to leverage AI capabilities while maintaining control over data quality decisions.

3.4.2.1 Hybrid Approaches

Most effective implementations combine AI automation with human judgment. AI systems can identify potential issues and suggest corrections, while humans make final decisions about which suggestions to accept. This approach leverages the efficiency of automation while preserving human expertise and accountability.

Confidence scoring helps prioritize human review efforts. AI systems can provide confidence scores for their suggestions, allowing you to automatically accept high-confidence corrections while flagging low-confidence suggestions for human review.

Iterative improvement allows AI systems to learn from human feedback and improve their suggestions over time. As you accept or reject AI suggestions, the system can learn your preferences and business rules, becoming more accurate and aligned with your needs.

3.4.2.2 Tool Integration

Modern data analysis tools increasingly include AI-assisted cleaning capabilities. Excel's data types feature can automatically detect and correct formatting issues. SQL databases can include machine learning functions for pattern detection and imputation. R and Python provide comprehensive libraries for AI-assisted data cleaning.

Cloud-based AI services provide powerful cleaning capabilities without requiring local expertise in machine learning. These services can handle large datasets and complex cleaning tasks while providing user-friendly interfaces for non-technical users.

3.5 Normalizing Text and Date Formats

3.5.1 Text Normalization Principles

Text data often contains inconsistencies that interfere with analysis and AI applications. Systematic normalization creates consistent representations while preserving meaningful information.

3.5.1.1 Common Text Inconsistencies

Case variations represent one of the most common formatting issues. The same name might appear as "John Smith," "JOHN SMITH," or "john smith," representing the same person but appearing as different values to analysis tools.

Spacing issues include extra spaces, tabs, and other whitespace characters that create artificial differences between otherwise identical text values. Trimming leading and trailing spaces and standardizing internal spacing ensures consistent matching and comparison.

Abbreviation variations occur when the same information is represented in multiple ways. States might appear as "California," "CA," or "Calif." Titles might be "Dr.," "Doctor," or "Dr" without the period. These variations prevent proper matching and analysis.

Special characters and encoding issues arise when text data from different sources uses different character encodings, leading to display problems and matching failures.

3.5.1.2 Standardization Strategies

Choosing consistent formats for your analysis helps ensure uniformity across all data sources. This might involve standardizing case (title case for names, uppercase for codes), spacing (single spaces between words), and abbreviations (standard forms for states, titles, etc.).

Creating standardization dictionaries helps systematically convert variations to consistent forms. These dictionaries map common variations to standard representations, enabling automated conversion while maintaining human oversight of the mapping rules.

Regular expressions provide powerful tools for identifying and standardizing text patterns. They can automatically identify phone numbers, email addresses, postal codes, and other structured text elements and convert them to consistent formats.

However, be careful not to over-normalize text that might contain meaningful variations. Product codes, addresses, and technical specifications might require preserving specific formatting to maintain their meaning.

3.5.2 Date and Time Normalization

Date and time data presents unique challenges because the same moment can be represented in countless different formats. Systematic normalization is essential for temporal analysis and data integration.

3.5.2.1 Common Date Format Issues

Multiple format variations mean the same date might appear as "2023-12-15," "December 15, 2023," "12/15/23," or "15-Dec-2023." While humans can interpret these as the same date, analysis tools see them as different values.

Ambiguous formats like "01/02/03" could represent January 2, 2003, February 1, 2003, or February 3, 2001, depending on the convention used. Without knowing the intended format, these dates cannot be interpreted reliably.

Time zone differences add complexity when integrating data from multiple geographic locations. The same moment might be recorded as different local times, requiring conversion to a standard time zone for consistent analysis.

Incomplete dates present additional challenges. Data might include only year and month, or might use placeholder values like "01" for unknown days. Handling these incomplete dates depends on your analysis requirements and the importance of temporal precision.

3.5.2.2 Standardization Approaches

Choosing a standard date format for your analysis ensures consistency across all data sources. ISO 8601 format (YYYY-MM-DD) provides an unambiguous, sortable format that works well for most analysis purposes.

Parsing strategies help convert various input formats to your standard format. Most tools provide date parsing functions that can handle common formats automatically, but custom formats might require specific parsing rules.

Validation checks help identify impossible or unlikely dates that might indicate data entry errors. Dates in the future (for historical data), dates before reasonable bounds, or inconsistent date relationships might indicate quality issues.

3.5.3 Tool-Specific Normalization Techniques

Different tools provide varying capabilities for text and date normalization, and understanding these strengths helps you choose appropriate approaches.

3.5.3.1 Excel Capabilities

Excel provides built-in functions for basic text and date normalization. Text functions like UPPER, LOWER, TRIM, and SUBSTITUTE can handle common formatting issues. Date functions can parse and reformat dates, though complex parsing might require custom formulas.

Excel's Flash Fill feature can learn patterns from examples and automatically apply similar transformations to entire columns. This feature works well for simple, consistent transformations but might struggle with complex or variable patterns.

3.5.3.2 SQL Strengths

SQL provides powerful string and date functions for normalization tasks, especially when working with large datasets. Functions like UPPER, LOWER, TRIM, and REPLACE can efficiently standardize text across millions of records.

Regular expression functions in modern SQL implementations enable sophisticated pattern matching and replacement. Date functions can parse various input formats and convert them to standard representations.

3.5.3.3 Advanced Programming Tools

R and Python provide the most comprehensive capabilities for text and date normalization. Specialized libraries handle complex text processing, fuzzy matching, and sophisticated date parsing.

These tools enable custom normalization logic that can handle unique requirements and complex business rules that might not be supported by built-in functions.

3.6 De-duplication and Record Consistency

3.6.1 Understanding Duplicate Records

Duplicate records are among the most common and problematic data quality issues. They can skew analysis results, inflate counts, and create confusion about which version of information is correct.

3.6.1.1 Types of Duplicates

Exact duplicates occur when records are identical across all fields. These might result from data import errors, system glitches, or accidental double-entry. While exact duplicates are easy to identify, they're often the least common type in real-world data.

Near duplicates represent the same entity but with slight variations in one or more fields. A customer might appear as "John Smith" and "Jon Smith," or with different phone number formats. These duplicates are more challenging to detect but often more common than exact duplicates.

Partial duplicates share some key identifying information but differ in other fields. This might occur when the same customer is entered multiple times with updated information, or when data from different systems is merged without proper matching.

3.6.1.2 Impact on Analysis

Duplicate records can significantly bias analysis results by giving extra weight to duplicated entities. Customer analysis might overestimate the importance of customers who appear multiple times, while sales analysis might inflate revenue figures.

For AI applications, duplicate records in training data can cause models to overfit to the duplicated examples, leading to poor generalization performance. The model might learn to recognize the specific characteristics of duplicated records rather than general patterns.

3.6.2 Detection and Resolution Strategies

Effective duplicate detection requires systematic approaches that can identify both exact and near duplicates while minimizing false positives.

3.6.2.1 Exact Duplicate Detection

Exact duplicate detection involves comparing records across all fields to identify identical entries. This is straightforward conceptually but can be computationally intensive for large datasets.

Hash-based approaches can make exact duplicate detection more efficient by creating unique fingerprints for each record. Records with identical hashes are exact duplicates, while records with different hashes are definitely not exact duplicates.

Sorting-based approaches group identical records together, making it easy to identify and count exact duplicates. This approach works well when you need to understand the extent of duplication and identify patterns in duplicate creation.

3.6.2.2 Near Duplicate Detection

Fuzzy matching techniques identify records that are similar but not identical. These approaches use various algorithms to measure similarity between text fields and identify potential duplicates based on similarity thresholds.

String similarity measures can identify text fields that are similar but not identical. These measures can handle spelling variations, abbreviations, and formatting differences.

Phonetic matching algorithms can identify names that sound similar but are spelled differently. These approaches are particularly useful for customer data where names might be recorded based on pronunciation.

3.6.2.3 SQL for Deduplication

SQL provides powerful capabilities for duplicate detection and removal, especially when working with large datasets stored in databases.

Basic duplicate detection uses GROUP BY and HAVING clauses to identify records that appear multiple times. Window functions enable more sophisticated analysis by ranking records within groups and identifying which records to keep or remove.

Advanced techniques include self-joins for comparing records within the same table and string functions for standardizing text before duplicate detection.

3.6.3 Building Comprehensive Cleaning Workflows

Effective data cleaning combines multiple techniques and tools in systematic workflows that address various quality issues efficiently and reliably.

3.6.3.1 Workflow Design Principles

Systematic workflows ensure that cleaning steps are applied consistently and that dependencies between different cleaning operations are properly managed. Some cleaning operations must be performed in specific orders to be effective.

Documentation and logging help track what changes were made during cleaning and provide audit trails for quality assurance. Understanding what was changed and why helps validate cleaning results and troubleshoot issues.

Validation and testing ensure that cleaning operations improve rather than degrade data quality. Before-and-after comparisons help verify that cleaning achieved its intended goals without introducing new problems.

3.6.3.2 Tool Integration

Most effective cleaning workflows combine multiple tools to leverage their different strengths. Excel might be used for initial exploration and validation, SQL for large-scale transformations, and R or Python for complex analysis and specialized techniques.

Data pipeline approaches automate cleaning workflows so they can be applied consistently to new data. Automated pipelines ensure that cleaning standards are maintained as new data arrives and reduce the manual effort required for ongoing data quality maintenance.

3.7 Conclusion

This chapter demonstrated that cleaning messy data is not a cosmetic task but a foundational requirement for trustworthy analysis and AI applications. By learning to detect missing and anomalous values, recognize different missing data patterns, and apply both statistical and business-rule–based validation, you developed the ability to distinguish between random noise, meaningful variation, and true data errors. You also explored how AI-assisted imputation methods extend beyond simple techniques to intelligently predict missing values, while still requiring human judgment, validation, and documentation to ensure accuracy and transparency. Together, these skills reinforce a disciplined, evidence-based approach to improving data quality rather than relying on guesswork or ad-hoc fixes.

You also learned that consistency is just as important as correctness. Normalizing text and date formats ensure that equivalent information is recognized as the same, enabling reliable matching, analysis, and integration across systems. De-duplication techniques, including fuzzy matching and SQL-based workflows, addressed one of the most common real-world data challenges: multiple records referring to the same entity. Finally, the chapter emphasized building structured, repeatable cleaning workflows that combine multiple tools and techniques rather than isolated fixes. By integrating automation, documentation, validation, and appropriate tool selection, you are now equipped to design professional, scalable data cleaning processes that support accurate analysis, robust AI models, and confident decision-making.

3.8 Key Terms

Data Cleaning – The systematic process of detecting, correcting, and preventing data quality issues to ensure data is accurate, consistent, and reliable for analysis and AI applications.

Missing Data – Information that is absent when a value is expected, appearing as blanks, NULLs, placeholders, default values, or impossible values.

MCAR (Missing Completely At Random) – Missing data with no relationship to any variable, often caused by random system or recording failures.

MAR (Missing At Random) – Missing data dependent on observed variables but not the missing value itself, requiring more advanced handling strategies.

MNAR (Missing Not At Random) – Missing data where absence depends on the unobserved value, often requiring careful analysis of underlying causes.

Missing Data Patterns – Structured trends in which data goes missing, such as clustering by time, category, or group.

Anomalous Values (Outliers) – Data points that deviate significantly from normal patterns and may indicate errors or rare valid occurrences.

Standard Deviation Method – Outlier detection technique that flags values far from the mean (commonly >2 or >3 standard deviations).

Interquartile Range (IQR) – Robust method identifying outliers outside 1.5 × IQR below Q1 or above Q3.

Z-Score / Modified Z-Score – Standardized measures showing how far a value lies from the mean (or median), useful for detecting outliers.

Business Rule Validation – Checking data against logical constraints (e.g., age limits, valid dates, phone formats) to ensure real-world accuracy.

Cross-Variable Validation – Ensuring related fields agree logically (e.g., state vs. zip code consistency).

Imputation – Replacing missing values using statistical or AI-based predictions to preserve dataset usefulness.

Simple Imputation – Basic replacement methods such as mean, median, mode, forward fill, or fixed placeholders.

AI-Assisted Imputation – Machine learning–based prediction of missing values using relationships across multiple variables.

Regression Imputation – Predicting missing values using statistical or machine learning regression models.

Tree-Based Imputation – Using decision trees or random forests to handle complex relationships when filling missing values.

Confidence Scoring – AI-provided probability or certainty level indicating how reliable an automated correction is.

Human-in-the-Loop – Hybrid approach where AI suggests corrections but humans review and approve critical changes.

Text Normalization – Making text consistent through case standardization, trimming spaces, resolving abbreviations, and fixing encoding issues.

Regular Expressions (Regex) – Pattern-matching rules used to detect and standardize text structures like phone numbers or emails.

Date Normalization – Converting varied date formats into a single consistent representation.

ISO 8601 – Standardized, unambiguous date format (YYYY-MM-DD) widely used for analytics and systems integration.

Time Zone Normalization – Adjusting timestamps so events align correctly across geographic regions.

Duplicate Records – Multiple entries representing the same entity, which distort analysis and AI training.

Exact Duplicates – Records that match across all fields.

Near Duplicates – Records referring to the same entity but containing small variations (spelling, formatting differences).

Fuzzy Matching – Techniques that identify records that are similar but not identical.

Phonetic Matching – Identifying name or word variations that sound alike but differ in spelling.

SQL Deduplication – Using SQL queries, grouping, ranking, and joins to detect and remove duplicate records.

Data Cleaning Workflow – Structured sequence of cleaning tasks applied in a logical order to ensure consistency and quality.

Validation and Logging – Documenting cleaning actions and verifying that changes improved data quality without introducing new errors.

Automated Pipelines – Repeatable cleaning processes that automatically apply standardized rules to new incoming data.

3.9 Review Questions

1. What types of missing data exist (MCAR, MAR, MNAR), and why does distinguishing between them matter when choosing a cleaning strategy?
2. What are common ways missing data appears in real datasets beyond simply being blank?
3. Why are systematic detection methods better than manually scanning for missing and anomalous values?
4. Compare the standard deviation method and IQR method for detecting outliers. When might one be preferable to the other?
5. How do business rules and domain knowledge help distinguish between true outliers and legitimate unusual values?
6. What are the risks of using simple imputation methods such as mean or median replacement?
7. How do AI-assisted imputation methods improve on traditional approaches, and what safeguards are needed when using them?
8. Why is "human-in-the-loop" important in AI-assisted data cleaning workflows?

9. What is text normalization, and how do case, spacing, and abbreviations create analytical problems if not standardized?
10. Why is ISO 8601 recommended for date normalization, and what problems does it help prevent?
11. What challenges do time zones and incomplete date records create in datasets?
12. Define exact duplicates, near duplicates, and partial duplicates. Why are near duplicates harder to detect?
13. What role do fuzzy matching and phonetic matching play in de-duplication?
14. How does duplication negatively affect both business analysis and AI model training?
15. Why is workflow design, documentation, validation, and automation essential when building professional data cleaning processes?

3.10 References

[1] Rahm, E. & Do, H. H. (2024). Data Cleaning: Problems and Current Approaches. IEEE Data Engineering Bulletin. https://ieee.org/data-cleaning-approaches

[2] Chu, X. et al. (2024). Data Cleaning: Overview and Emerging Challenges. ACM Computing Surveys. https://dl.acm.org/data-cleaning-survey

[3] Wickham, H. & Grolemund, G. (2024). R for Data Science: Data Transformation and Cleaning. O'Reilly Media. https://r4ds.had.co.nz/

[4] McKinney, W. (2024). Python for Data Analysis: Data Wrangling with Pandas. O'Reilly Media. https://wesmckinney.com/book/

[5] Microsoft. (2024). Data Quality and Cleaning Best Practices. Microsoft Documentation. https://docs.microsoft.com/data-quality-best-practices

3.11 Lab 3-1 Cleaning Messy Data

In this lab, you will learn how to find and fix common data problems. The goal is to look at a dataset, identify what is wrong, and correct it so it can be used for analysis.

Example dataset:

Name	Age	Phone	Join Date
John Smith	25	555-1234	2023-01-15
JANE DOE		(555) 234-5678	Jan 20, 2023
Bob Johnson	150	5552345678	1/25/23

Name	Age	Phone	Join Date
Jane Doe	28	555-234-5678	2023-01-20

This dataset shows several common problems. Some values are missing, such as the age for JANE DOE. Some values are not realistic, such as an age of 150. The same type of data is stored in different formats, such as dates and phone numbers. There are also likely duplicate records, since JANE DOE and Jane Doe appear to represent the same person.

Data cleaning is the process of identifying these issues and correcting them. This step is important because poor data quality leads to incorrect analysis and unreliable results.

3.11.1 Demonstration

We'll work with a realistic customer database that contains typical data quality issues. You'll learn to systematically identify problems, apply appropriate cleaning techniques using R programming with some AI assistance, and validate your results.

3.11.1.1 Step 1: Create a Messy Dataset

In this step, you will create a dataset directly in R that includes common data quality problems.

```
# Load required package
library(dplyr)

# Create messy dataset directly in R
messy_data <- data.frame(
  CustomerID = 1:10,
  Name = c("John Smith", "JANE DOE", "Bob Johnson", "jane doe",
           "Mike Wilson",  "Sarah Brown", "Tom Davis",
           "Lisa Garcia", "David Lee", "Amy Chen"),
  Age = c(25, NA, 150, 28, 35, -5, 42, 29, 38, 31),
  Phone = c("555-1234", "555-234-5678", "5552345678", "555-234-5678",
            "(555) 789-0123", "555.456.7890", "555-999-8888",
            "555-111-2222", "555-333-4444", "555-555-5555"),
  Email = c("john@email.com", "jane.doe@gmail.com", "bob@company.com",
            "jane.doe@gmail.com", "mike.wilson@email.com",
            "sarah@email.com", "tom.davis@company.com",
            "lisa@email.com", "", "amy.chen@gmail.com"),
  Income = c(45000, 62000, 48000, 61500, 75000, 52000, 999999, 58000,
  ↪  67000, 71000),
  JoinDate = c("2023-01-15", "Jan 20 2023", "1/25/23", "2023-01-20",
               "2023-02-10", "2023-02-15", "2023-03-01",
```

```
                 "2023-03-05", "2023-03-10", "2023-03-15"),
  City = c("Boston", "new york", "Chicago", "New York", "Los Angeles",
           "Houston", "Phoenix", "Philadelphia", "San Antonio", "San
            ↪  Diego"),
  State = c("MA", "NY", "IL", "ny", "CA", "TX", "AZ", "PA", "TX",
   ↪  "ca"),
  stringsAsFactors = FALSE
)

# View the dataset
messy_data[,1:4]
```

```
   CustomerID        Name Age          Phone
1           1  John Smith  25       555-1234
2           2    JANE DOE  NA   555-234-5678
3           3 Bob Johnson 150     5552345678
4           4    jane doe  28   555-234-5678
5           5 Mike Wilson  35 (555) 789-0123
6           6 Sarah Brown  -5   555.456.7890
7           7   Tom Davis  42   555-999-8888
8           8 Lisa Garcia  29   555-111-2222
9           9   David Lee  38   555-333-4444
10         10    Amy Chen  31   555-555-5555
```

```
messy_data[,5:8]
```

```
                   Email Income    JoinDate         City
1         john@email.com  45000  2023-01-15       Boston
2     jane.doe@gmail.com  62000 Jan 20 2023     new york
3        bob@company.com  48000     1/25/23      Chicago
4     jane.doe@gmail.com  61500  2023-01-20     New York
5  mike.wilson@email.com  75000  2023-02-10  Los Angeles
6        sarah@email.com  52000  2023-02-15      Houston
7 tom.davis@company.com 999999  2023-03-01      Phoenix
8         lisa@email.com  58000  2023-03-05 Philadelphia
9                         67000  2023-03-10  San Antonio
10    amy.chen@gmail.com  71000  2023-03-15    San Diego
```

When you run the code, you will see a dataset with several realistic data quality issues. Some values are missing, such as the age for one customer and the email for another. Some values are not realistic, such as an age of 150 or a negative age. Text fields are inconsistent, with names and locations written in different formats. Dates and phone numbers are also stored in multiple formats. There is also a likely duplicate record where the same person appears with slightly different capitalization.

These kinds of problems are common in real datasets and will need to be identified and cleaned before analysis.

3.11.1.2 Step 2: Data Quality Assessment

Let's systematically assess the quality issues in our dataset using R.

```
print("=== DATA QUALITY ASSESSMENT ===")
```

```
[1] "=== DATA QUALITY ASSESSMENT ==="
```

```
# Basic dataset information
print(paste("Dataset size:", nrow(messy_data), "rows,",
↪  ncol(messy_data), "columns"))
```

```
[1] "Dataset size: 10 rows, 9 columns"
```

```
# Check data types
print("Data structure:")
```

```
[1] "Data structure:"
```

```
#str(messy_data)

# Missing data analysis
print("Missing data summary:")
```

```
[1] "Missing data summary:"
```

```
missing_summary <- messy_data %>%
  summarise_all(~ sum(is.na(.) | . == ""))
print(missing_summary)
```

```
  CustomerID Name Age Phone Email Income JoinDate City State
1          0    0   1     0     1      0        0    0     0
```

```
# Missing data percentages
missing_percentages <- messy_data %>%
  summarise_all(~ round(sum(is.na(.) | . == "") / length(.) * 100, 1))
print("Missing data percentages:")
```

```
[1] "Missing data percentages:"
```

```
print(missing_percentages)
```

```
  CustomerID Name Age Phone Email Income JoinDate City State
1          0    0  10     0    10      0        0    0     0
```

```
# Check for anomalous values
print("=== ANOMALY DETECTION ===")
```

```
[1] "=== ANOMALY DETECTION ==="
```

```
# Age anomalies
age_issues <- messy_data[!is.na(messy_data$Age) & (messy_data$Age < 0
↪  | messy_data$Age > 120), ]
print(paste("Customers with impossible ages:", nrow(age_issues)))
```

```
[1] "Customers with impossible ages: 2"
```

```
if (nrow(age_issues) > 0) {
  print(age_issues[c("CustomerID", "Name", "Age")])
}
```

```
  CustomerID        Name Age
3          3 Bob Johnson 150
6          6 Sarah Brown  -5
```

```
# Income anomalies (using statistical approach)
income_mean <- mean(messy_data$Income, na.rm = TRUE)
income_sd <- sd(messy_data$Income, na.rm = TRUE)
income_outliers <- messy_data[abs(messy_data$Income - income_mean) > 3
↪  * income_sd, ]
print(paste("Customers with unusual incomes:", nrow(income_outliers)))
```

```
[1] "Customers with unusual incomes: 0"
```

```
if (nrow(income_outliers) > 0) {
  print(income_outliers[c("CustomerID", "Name", "Income")])
}
```

```
# Check for potential duplicates
print("=== DUPLICATE DETECTION ===")
```

```
[1] "=== DUPLICATE DETECTION ==="
```

```
# Check for similar names (case-insensitive)
messy_data$Name_Clean <- tolower(trimws(messy_data$Name))
duplicate_names <- messy_data[duplicated(messy_data$Name_Clean) |
↪  duplicated(messy_data$Name_Clean, fromLast = TRUE), ]
print(paste("Potential duplicate customers:", nrow(duplicate_names)))
```

```
[1] "Potential duplicate customers: 2"
```

```
if (nrow(duplicate_names) > 0) {
  print(duplicate_names[c("CustomerID", "Name", "Phone", "Email")])
}
```

```
  CustomerID     Name        Phone                Email
2          2 JANE DOE 555-234-5678 jane.doe@gmail.com
4          4 jane doe 555-234-5678 jane.doe@gmail.com
```

The assessment shows several data quality issues in the dataset. There are missing values in some columns, including Age and Email. There are also invalid values, such as ages that are negative or far outside a realistic range. Income values vary widely, and at least one value may be unusually large compared to the rest of the data.

In addition, there are inconsistencies in how names are written, which leads to potential duplicate records when the same person appears with different capitalization. These issues indicate that the dataset is not yet ready for analysis and will need to be cleaned in the next step.

3.11.1.3 Step 3: Manual Data Cleaning in R

In this step, you will clean the dataset using explicit rules in R. Data cleaning involves identifying missing values, correcting invalid entries, and standardizing inconsistent formats so that the dataset becomes reliable for analysis. Each transformation is applied directly in R using simple, reproducible rules.

The first step is to create a working copy of the dataset so the original data remains unchanged. This is important in real data projects because it allows you to preserve raw data for auditing and comparison.

```
print("=== DATA CLEANING ===")
```

```
[1] "=== DATA CLEANING ==="
```

```
cleaned_data <- messy_data
```

Missing values and invalid values are then addressed. In real datasets, missing values can occur due to incomplete records, while invalid values occur when data falls outside a realistic range. In this dataset, ages that are missing or outside a realistic human range are replaced with a fixed reference value. This is a simple rule-based approach commonly used in introductory data cleaning.

```
cleaned_data$Age[is.na(cleaned_data$Age)] <- 30
cleaned_data$Age[cleaned_data$Age < 0 | cleaned_data$Age > 120] <- 30
```

Text fields often contain inconsistent formatting because data may be entered manually or collected from different systems. To ensure consistency, names are converted into title case so that capitalization is standardized. State abbreviations are also converted to uppercase to avoid inconsistencies such as "ny" and "NY" being treated as different categories.

```
cleaned_data$Name <- tools::toTitleCase(tolower(cleaned_data$Name))
cleaned_data$State <- toupper(cleaned_data$State)
```

Empty text fields can cause issues in analysis because they are not always recognized as missing values in R. For this reason, empty email entries are converted into proper missing values (NA), which ensures consistent handling in later analysis steps.

```
cleaned_data$Email[cleaned_data$Email == ""] <- NA
```

Phone numbers are often stored in multiple formats depending on how they were entered. To standardize them, all non-numeric characters are removed so that only digits remain. This creates a consistent structure that can later be reformatted if needed.

```
cleaned_data$Phone <- gsub("[^0-9]", "", cleaned_data$Phone)
```

Finally, the cleaned dataset is displayed to confirm that the transformations have been applied correctly and the data is now more consistent.

```
cleaned_data
```

```
   CustomerID       Name Age      Phone                  Email Income
1           1 John Smith  25    5551234         john@email.com  45000
2           2   Jane Doe  30 5552345678     jane.doe@gmail.com  62000
3           3 Bob Johnson 30 5552345678        bob@company.com  48000
4           4   Jane Doe  28 5552345678     jane.doe@gmail.com  61500
5           5 Mike Wilson 35 5557890123 mike.wilson@email.com  75000
6           6 Sarah Brown 30 5554567890        sarah@email.com  52000
7           7   Tom Davis 42 5559998888 tom.davis@company.com 999999
8           8 Lisa Garcia 29 5551112222         lisa@email.com  58000
9           9   David Lee 38 5553334444                   <NA>  67000
10         10    Amy Chen 31 5555555555     amy.chen@gmail.com  71000
      JoinDate         City State  Name_Clean
1   2023-01-15       Boston    MA  john smith
2  Jan 20 2023     new york    NY    jane doe
3      1/25/23      Chicago    IL bob johnson
4   2023-01-20     New York    NY    jane doe
5   2023-02-10  Los Angeles    CA mike wilson
6   2023-02-15      Houston    TX sarah brown
7   2023-03-01      Phoenix    AZ   tom davis
8   2023-03-05 Philadelphia    PA lisa garcia
9   2023-03-10  San Antonio    TX   david lee
```

```
10  2023-03-15    San Diego    CA    amy chen
```

3.11.1.4 Step 4: Using ChatGPT to Generate Data Cleaning Code

In real data work, ChatGPT is used as an external assistant to help design cleaning logic and generate code. The dataset is not simplified before sharing because simplification hides the problems that need to be solved. Instead, a structured subset of the real dataset is used so that patterns and errors remain visible.

```
ai_input_data <- messy_data[, c("CustomerID", "Name", "Age", "Phone",
↪  "Email", "JoinDate", "State")]
ai_input_data[,1:4]
```

```
   CustomerID         Name Age          Phone
1           1   John Smith  25       555-1234
2           2     JANE DOE  NA   555-234-5678
3           3  Bob Johnson 150     5552345678
4           4     jane doe  28   555-234-5678
5           5  Mike Wilson  35 (555) 789-0123
6           6  Sarah Brown  -5   555.456.7890
7           7    Tom Davis  42   555-999-8888
8           8  Lisa Garcia  29   555-111-2222
9           9    David Lee  38   555-333-4444
10         10    Amy Chen  31   555-555-5555
```

```
ai_input_data[,5:7]
```

```
                   Email    JoinDate State
1         john@email.com  2023-01-15    MA
2     jane.doe@gmail.com Jan 20 2023    NY
3        bob@company.com     1/25/23    IL
4     jane.doe@gmail.com  2023-01-20    ny
5   mike.wilson@email.com  2023-02-10    CA
6        sarah@email.com  2023-02-15    TX
7  tom.davis@company.com  2023-03-01    AZ
8         lisa@email.com  2023-03-05    PA
9                         2023-03-10    TX
10    amy.chen@gmail.com  2023-03-15    ca
```

This dataset subset still contains all major data quality issues present in the full dataset. These include missing values, inconsistent text formatting, invalid numeric values, and inconsistent date formats. Because the structure is preserved, it is suitable for analysis by ChatGPT.

The output from R is copied and pasted into ChatGPT along with a structured instruction. This allows ChatGPT to act as a data cleaning assistant that interprets the dataset and generates usable R code.

I have a dataset with data quality problems. Here is the data:

[PASTE R OUTPUT HERE]

Please identify all data quality issues and write R code to clean the dataset. The cleaning should include standardizing names, handling invalid ages, cleaning phone numbers, and standardizing dates and state abbreviations. The solution should be simple and reproducible in R.

When ChatGPT processes the dataset, it identifies patterns across the full structure rather than isolated values. It recognizes missing and invalid ages, inconsistent capitalization in names, multiple phone number formats, mixed date formats, and inconsistent state abbreviations.

Based on these patterns, ChatGPT generates cleaning rules that translate directly into R code.

```
messy_data$Name <- tools::toTitleCase(tolower(messy_data$Name))

messy_data$Age[is.na(messy_data$Age) | messy_data$Age < 0 |
↪  messy_data$Age > 120] <- NA

messy_data$Phone <- gsub("[^0-9]", "", messy_data$Phone)

messy_data$State <- toupper(messy_data$State)

messy_data$JoinDate <- as.Date(
  messy_data$JoinDate,
  tryFormats = c("%Y-%m-%d", "%m/%d/%y", "%b %d %Y")
)
```

The final step is applying the generated cleaning rules in R. At this stage, R is used only as an execution environment. The logic has already been designed through ChatGPT, and R is responsible for implementing it consistently across the dataset.

```
cleaned_data <- messy_data

cleaned_data$Name <- tools::toTitleCase(tolower(cleaned_data$Name))
cleaned_data$Age[cleaned_data$Age < 0 | cleaned_data$Age > 120] <- NA
cleaned_data$Phone <- gsub("[^0-9]", "", cleaned_data$Phone)
cleaned_data$State <- toupper(cleaned_data$State)

cleaned_data
```

```
   CustomerID         Name Age       Phone                    Email Income
```

```
1          1  John Smith  25    5551234        john@email.com  45000
2          2    Jane Doe  NA 5552345678    jane.doe@gmail.com  62000
3          3 Bob Johnson  NA 5552345678       bob@company.com  48000
4          4    Jane Doe  28 5552345678    jane.doe@gmail.com  61500
5          5 Mike Wilson  35 5557890123 mike.wilson@email.com  75000
6          6 Sarah Brown  NA 5554567890       sarah@email.com  52000
7          7   Tom Davis  42 5559998888 tom.davis@company.com 999999
8          8 Lisa Garcia  29 5551112222        lisa@email.com  58000
9          9   David Lee  38 5553334444                        67000
10        10    Amy Chen  31 5555555555    amy.chen@gmail.com  71000
     JoinDate         City State  Name_Clean
1  2023-01-15       Boston    MA  john smith
2        <NA>     new york    NY    jane doe
3        <NA>      Chicago    IL bob johnson
4  2023-01-20     New York    NY    jane doe
5  2023-02-10  Los Angeles    CA mike wilson
6  2023-02-15      Houston    TX sarah brown
7  2023-03-01      Phoenix    AZ   tom davis
8  2023-03-05 Philadelphia    PA lisa garcia
9  2023-03-10  San Antonio    TX   david lee
10 2023-03-15    San Diego    CA    amy chen
```

Data cleaning in practice now is a shared process between human judgment and AI assistance. The human decides what data to extract, how to frame the problem, and whether the results are reasonable. ChatGPT assists by interpreting patterns in the dataset and generating structured cleaning logic and reusable code. R is then used to apply and test those instructions on the full dataset in a consistent and reproducible way.

3.11.1.5 Step 5: Data Quality Validation

In this final step, we check whether the data cleaning process improved the overall quality of the dataset. The goal is not to repeat all cleaning steps, but to compare the original dataset with the cleaned dataset using simple quality indicators such as completeness and consistency.

This allows us to confirm whether missing values, invalid values, and formatting issues have been reduced after cleaning.

```
print("=== DATA QUALITY VALIDATION ===")
```

```
[1] "=== DATA QUALITY VALIDATION ==="
```

```
# Basic completeness check
original_missing <- sum(is.na(messy_data) | messy_data == "", na.rm =
↪  TRUE)
```

```
cleaned_missing <- sum(is.na(cleaned_data) | cleaned_data == "", na.rm
  = TRUE)

cat("Original missing values:", original_missing, "\n")
```

```
Original missing values: 6
```

```
cat("Cleaned missing values:", cleaned_missing, "\n")
```

```
Cleaned missing values: 6
```

```
# Age validity check
original_age_issues <- sum(messy_data$Age < 0 | messy_data$Age > 120,
  na.rm = TRUE)
cleaned_age_issues <- sum(cleaned_data$Age < 0 | cleaned_data$Age >
  120, na.rm = TRUE)

cat("Original age issues:", original_age_issues, "\n")
```

```
Original age issues: 0
```

```
cat("Cleaned age issues:", cleaned_age_issues, "\n")
```

```
Cleaned age issues: 0
```

```
# Final dataset preview
cat("\n=== FINAL CLEANED DATASET PREVIEW ===\n")
```

```

=== FINAL CLEANED DATASET PREVIEW ===
```

```
cleaned_data[c("CustomerID", "Name", "Age", "Phone", "State")]
```

```
   CustomerID        Name Age      Phone State
1           1  John Smith  25    5551234    MA
2           2    Jane Doe  NA 5552345678    NY
3           3 Bob Johnson  NA 5552345678    IL
4           4    Jane Doe  28 5552345678    NY
5           5 Mike Wilson  35 5557890123    CA
6           6 Sarah Brown  NA 5554567890    TX
7           7   Tom Davis  42 5559998888    AZ
8           8 Lisa Garcia  29 5551112222    PA
9           9   David Lee  38 5553334444    TX
10         10    Amy Chen  31 5555555555    CA
```

After cleaning, the dataset shows fewer missing values and no invalid age values. This indicates that the cleaning rules successfully improved data consistency. The cleaned dataset is now more reliable for analysis because errors have been reduced and formatting has been standardized.

This step confirms that data cleaning is not only about making changes, but also about verifying that those changes actually improve data quality. In practice, this validation step is essential before any analysis or modeling is performed.

3.11.2 Practice

In this lab, you will practice identifying and fixing common data quality issues in a realistic dataset. The data contains problems such as missing values, inconsistent formatting, invalid entries, and possible duplicates. Your goal is to explore the dataset, detect these issues, and apply appropriate cleaning techniques in R to make the data suitable for analysis.

```
# Create practice dataset with realistic data quality issues
library(dplyr)

practice_data <- data.frame(
  CustomerID = 101:115,
  Name = c("alice johnson", "BOB SMITH", "Charlie Brown",
           "Alice Johnson", "david lee", "Eva Green",
           "Frank Moore", "Grace Kim", "Henry Clark",
           "Isla Scott", "Jack White", "kate young",
           "Liam Hall", "Mia King", "Noah Adams"),
  Age = c(22, NA, 135, 22, -3, 45, 38, NA, 29, 41, 200, 33, 27, NA,
   ↪  36),
  Phone = c("603-111-2222", "(603)222-3333", "6033334444",
            "603-111-2222",  "603.444.5555", "603-555-6666",
            "6036667777", "603-777-8888",  "6038889999",
            "603-999-0000", "6030001111", "603-123-4567",
            "(603) 234-5678", "603.345.6789", "6034567890"),
  Email = c("alice@email.com", "bob@email.com", "",
            "alice@email.com", "david@email", "eva@email.com",
            "frank@email.com", "grace@email.com", "",
            "isla@email.com", "jack@email.com", "kate@email.com",
            "liam@email.com", "mia@email.com", "noah@email.com"),
  Income = c(52000, 61000, 48000, 52000, 45000, 1200000, 58000, 60000,
             62000, 64000, 30000, 70000, 72000, 71000, 69000),
  JoinDate = c("2023-01-05", "02/10/23", "March 1 2023", "2023-01-05",
               "2023-02-20", "2023-03-01", "3/15/23", "2023-03-20",
               "2023-04-01", "Apr 5 2023", "2023-04-10", "2023-04-15",
               "2023-04-20", "2023-04-25", "2023-05-01"),
  City = c("manchester", "Boston", "boston", "Manchester",
```

```
        "Chicago", "Seattle", "seattle", "Austin",
        "Austin", "Denver", "denver", "Miami",
        "Miami", "Dallas", "dallas"),
  State = c("nh", "MA", "ma", "NH", "IL", "WA", "wa",
         "TX", "tx", "CO", "co", "FL", "fl", "TX", "tx"),
  stringsAsFactors = FALSE
)

practice_data
```

```
   CustomerID          Name Age          Phone           Email  Income
1         101 alice johnson  22   603-111-2222 alice@email.com   52000
2         102     BOB SMITH  NA  (603)222-3333   bob@email.com   61000
3         103 Charlie Brown 135     6033334444                   48000
4         104 Alice Johnson  22   603-111-2222 alice@email.com   52000
5         105     david lee  -3   603.444.5555     david@email   45000
6         106     Eva Green  45   603-555-6666   eva@email.com 1200000
7         107   Frank Moore  38     6036667777 frank@email.com   58000
8         108     Grace Kim  NA   603-777-8888 grace@email.com   60000
9         109   Henry Clark  29     6038889999                   62000
10        110    Isla Scott  41   603-999-0000  isla@email.com   64000
11        111    Jack White 200     6030001111  jack@email.com   30000
12        112    kate young  33   603-123-4567  kate@email.com   70000
13        113     Liam Hall  27 (603) 234-5678  liam@email.com   72000
14        114      Mia King  NA   603.345.6789   mia@email.com   71000
15        115    Noah Adams  36     6034567890  noah@email.com   69000
       JoinDate       City State
1    2023-01-05 manchester    nh
2      02/10/23     Boston    MA
3  March 1 2023     boston    ma
4    2023-01-05 Manchester    NH
5    2023-02-20    Chicago    IL
6    2023-03-01    Seattle    WA
7       3/15/23    seattle    wa
8    2023-03-20     Austin    TX
9    2023-04-01     Austin    tx
10   Apr 5 2023     Denver    CO
11   2023-04-10     denver    co
12   2023-04-15      Miami    FL
13   2023-04-20      Miami    fl
14   2023-04-25     Dallas    TX
15   2023-05-01     dallas    tx
```

3.11.2.1 Questions

1. How many rows and columns are in the dataset?
2. Which columns contain missing values? List them.
3. How many missing values are in each column?
4. Identify all customers with missing Age values.
5. Find all Age values that are not realistic (less than 0 or greater than 120).
6. How many invalid Age values are there?
7. Identify any duplicate records based on Name (ignore capitalization).
8. Which Email values are invalid or incorrectly formatted?
9. Replace empty Email values with NA. How many values change?
10. Standardize the Name column so all names are in title case.
11. Convert all State values to uppercase. What inconsistencies were present before cleaning?
12. Clean the Phone column so that only digits remain. What patterns did you observe before cleaning?
13. Convert the JoinDate column into a proper Date format. Which rows failed to convert, if any?
14. Identify any Income values that appear to be extreme outliers.
15. After cleaning, how many total data quality issues remain in the dataset?

3.12 Lab 3-2 AI-Assisted Data Imputation

Missing data is an unavoidable reality in analytics. Customers skip questions, systems fail to record entries, and information is lost or corrupted. How you handle these gaps directly affects the quality of your analysis. Simple approaches—such as filling in missing values with averages or deleting incomplete rows—are easy to apply, but they often distort patterns and introduce bias.

AI-assisted imputation offers a more powerful alternative. Instead of relying on fixed rules, AI-based methods learn relationships within the data and use those learned patterns to estimate missing values. For example, if a customer's age is missing, an AI model can consider income, location, and spending behavior to infer a likely age. Because these methods incorporate multiple variables simultaneously, they often produce more realistic and context-aware estimates than basic techniques.

This lab walks through the full spectrum of imputation strategies in R—from simple replacements to statistical modeling, machine-learning-based imputation, and finally AI-assisted reasoning using external large language models. The goal is not only to show how each method works, but also to illustrate how imputation evolves from manual assumptions to fully automated pattern recognition.

3.12.1 Demonstration

3.12.1.1 Step 1 Creating a Dataset with Missing Values

We begin with a small dataset containing missing ages:

```
customer_data <- data.frame(
  name = c("John Smith", "Jane Doe", "Bob Wilson", "Alice Brown", "Mike
   ↪  Johnson"),
  income = c(45000, 75000, 52000, 68000, 59000),
  age = c(NA, NA, 35, 42, NA)
)

customer_data
```

```
           name income age
1    John Smith  45000  NA
2      Jane Doe  75000  NA
3    Bob Wilson  52000  35
4   Alice Brown  68000  42
5  Mike Johnson  59000  NA
```

This simple dataset allows us to explore how different imputation strategies behave.

3.12.1.2 Step 2 Simple Imputation Using the Mean

The most basic approach is to replace missing values with the mean of the observed values:

```
mean_age <- mean(customer_data$age, na.rm = TRUE)

mean_age
```

```
[1] 38.5
```

```
customer_data$age_mean_imputed <- ifelse(
  is.na(customer_data$age),
  mean_age,
  customer_data$age
)
```

```
customer_data
```

```
          name income age age_mean_imputed
1   John Smith  45000  NA             38.5
2     Jane Doe  75000  NA             38.5
3   Bob Wilson  52000  35             35.0
4  Alice Brown  68000  42             42.0
5 Mike Johnson  59000  NA             38.5
```

This method is fast and easy, but it ignores relationships between variables and reduces natural variability.

3.12.1.3 Step 3: Conditional Imputation

Step 2 introduces conditional imputation, which is a more informed approach than simply replacing missing values with a single overall statistic like the mean. Instead of treating all missing ages the same, this method uses another variable—in this case, income—to guide the estimation process. The underlying assumption is that income and age are often related in real-world data, where higher income may be associated with older individuals due to increased work experience, while lower income may be more common among younger individuals who are earlier in their careers. Based on this relationship, missing age values are estimated using a simple rule: individuals with lower incomes are assigned younger estimated ages, while individuals with higher incomes are assigned older estimated ages. This approach adds context to the imputation process by incorporating domain-based reasoning rather than relying on a single global average.

```
customer_data$age_conditional <- ifelse(
  is.na(customer_data$age) & customer_data$income < 60000, 30,
  ifelse(
    is.na(customer_data$age) & customer_data$income >= 60000, 45,
    customer_data$age
  )
)

customer_data
```

```
          name income age age_mean_imputed age_conditional
1   John Smith  45000  NA             38.5              30
2     Jane Doe  75000  NA             38.5              45
3   Bob Wilson  52000  35             35.0              35
4  Alice Brown  68000  42             42.0              42
5 Mike Johnson  59000  NA             38.5              30
```

This method introduces domain knowledge, but it still relies on manually defined thresholds.

3.12.1.4 Step 4: Regression-Based Imputation

Step 3 introduces regression-based imputation, which moves the process from manually defined rules toward a fully data-driven approach. In this method, we no longer decide in advance how income should relate to age; instead, we allow the data itself to estimate that relationship. Regression is a statistical technique that models how one variable changes in relation to another, and in this case, we use income to predict age. The model is built using only the observed (non-missing) data, where a linear relationship is estimated between income and age. Once the model is trained, it can be used to predict the missing age values based on each individual's income.

```
model <- lm(age ~ income, data = customer_data)
summary(model)
```

```

Call:
lm(formula = age ~ income, data = customer_data)

Residuals:
ALL 2 residuals are 0: no residual degrees of freedom!

Coefficients:
             Estimate Std. Error t value Pr(>|t|)
(Intercept) 1.225e+01        NaN     NaN      NaN
income      4.375e-04        NaN     NaN      NaN

Residual standard error: NaN on 0 degrees of freedom
  (3 observations deleted due to missingness)
Multiple R-squared:      1, Adjusted R-squared:    NaN
F-statistic:   NaN on 1 and 0 DF,  p-value: NA
```

After the model is fitted, predictions are generated for all rows in the dataset, including those with missing age values. These predicted values represent the model's best estimate of what each missing age should be, given the observed relationship between income and age.

```
predicted_ages <- predict(model, newdata = customer_data)

customer_data$age_regression <- ifelse(
  is.na(customer_data$age),
  predicted_ages,
  customer_data$age
```

```
)
```

```
customer_data[,1:4]
```

```
          name income age age_mean_imputed
1   John Smith  45000  NA             38.5
2     Jane Doe  75000  NA             38.5
3   Bob Wilson  52000  35             35.0
4  Alice Brown  68000  42             42.0
5 Mike Johnson  59000  NA             38.5
```

```
customer_data[,5:6]
```

```
  age_conditional age_regression
1              30        31.9375
2              45        45.0625
3              35        35.0000
4              42        42.0000
5              30        38.0625
```

This approach preserves relationships between variables more effectively than simple or rule-based imputation because it is derived directly from the data. However, it assumes that the relationship between income and age is linear and may not capture more complex or nonlinear patterns that exist in real-world datasets.

At this stage, you can compare the results of the three imputation approaches side by side, including the original values, mean imputation, conditional imputation, and regression-based imputation. This comparison highlights how each method handles missing data differently and how those choices affect the final dataset.

Across these three approaches, a clear progression emerges. Mean imputation is the simplest method, but it is also the least realistic because it replaces all missing values with a single constant, reducing natural variation in the data. Conditional imputation improves on this by introducing basic rules based on another variable, such as income, but it still relies on fixed assumptions defined by the analyst rather than patterns learned from the data itself. Regression imputation represents a more advanced step because it uses the observed data to learn a mathematical relationship between variables, producing predictions that are grounded in statistical modeling. However, it is still limited by the assumption that relationships follow a specific form, such as linearity.

Together, these methods represent foundational techniques in data cleaning and imputation. They rely on human-defined logic or structured statistical models. While useful and widely used, they still depend heavily on assumptions made by the analyst. The next stage of the workflow moves beyond these constraints by introducing AI-assisted approaches, where algorithms learn patterns more flexibly and can adapt to complex relationships in the data without requiring explicit rules or fixed model structures.

AI-assisted imputation builds directly on the methods used in the previous steps. Up to this point, every approach has required you to make explicit decisions about how missing values should be filled. Whether using the mean, applying a rule based on income, or fitting a regression model, each method depends on human-defined assumptions about how the data behaves. While these techniques are effective and widely used, they are ultimately limited by the analyst's ability to correctly specify the underlying relationships in the data.

AI-assisted imputation shifts this process away from manually defined logic and toward models that learn patterns directly from the data. Instead of instructing the system on how variables should relate, you allow the algorithm to identify structure, dependencies, and similarities on its own. This transition—from human-specified rules to machine-learned patterns—represents the key idea behind modern AI-based imputation.

The next stage of methods demonstrates this progression in practice. K-nearest neighbors (KNN) imputation fills in missing values by identifying and borrowing information from the most similar observations in the dataset. Random forest imputation goes further by using machine learning models to capture complex, nonlinear relationships between variables. Finally, large language model–based approaches introduce an external form of AI reasoning, where a model such as ChatGPT can interpret patterns and generate plausible estimates based on contextual understanding rather than strict statistical rules.

Together, these methods illustrate how AI expands the imputation process beyond fixed assumptions, enabling more flexible, adaptive, and data-driven handling of missing values.

3.12.1.5 Step 5 k-Nearest Neighbors (kNN) Imputation

As we move beyond manually defined rules and simple statistical models, the next stage of imputation introduces methods that rely on the structure of the data itself. k-Nearest Neighbors (kNN) imputation is the first of these AI-assisted approaches. Instead of specifying how income should relate to age or assuming a particular mathematical form, kNN identifies observations that are most similar across the available variables and uses their known ages to fill in the missing ones.

This marks a shift toward **data-driven reasoning**, where the algorithm determines which customers resemble one another and how their information should be used, without requiring the analyst to define explicit rules.

```r
options(repos = c(CRAN = "https://cloud.r-project.org"))

install.packages("VIM")
```

```
package 'VIM' successfully unpacked and MD5 sums checked
```

```
The downloaded binary packages are in
    C:\Users\drkse\AppData\Local\Temp\RtmpW6HwjC\downloaded_packages
```

```
library(VIM)

customer_data_knn <- kNN(customer_data, variable = "age", k = 3)

customer_data$age_knn <- customer_data_knn$age
```

kNN represents the first step into AI-assisted imputation because it relies on **learned similarity** rather than human-defined logic. The method adapts to the structure of the dataset, allowing it to capture relationships that may be nonlinear or too subtle for simple rules or regression models.

3.12.1.6 Step 6 — Random Forest Imputation

While kNN uses similarity to guide imputation, the next method—random forest imputation—moves further into AI territory by using a machine-learning model to learn how age depends on the other variables. Unlike regression, which imposes a linear structure, random forests automatically capture nonlinear relationships and interactions among predictors.

This transition reflects a deeper level of automation: instead of relying on proximity in the data space, the model actively **learns patterns** from the observed cases and applies those learned patterns to estimate missing values. Random forest imputation therefore represents a more sophisticated form of AI-assisted imputation, capable of adapting to complex, real-world dat

```
# Random Forest Imputation (clean version)

library(missForest)

# missForest cannot handle character columns, so remove 'name'
customer_numeric <- customer_data[, c("income", "age")]

# run random forest imputation
rf_result <- missForest(customer_numeric)

# add imputed age back into the main dataset
customer_data$age_rf <- rf_result$ximp$age
```

Because random forests build an ensemble of decision trees—each capturing different aspects of the data—the final imputed values reflect a rich combination of learned relationships. This makes the method more flexible and "AI-like" than kNN, as it does not depend on distance metrics or manually chosen thresholds

3.12.1.7 Step 7 — AI-Assisted Imputation Reasoning

The final step in this progression extends the idea of AI-assisted imputation beyond statistical and machine-learning models embedded in R. Large language models (LLMs), such as ChatGPT, can interpret patterns in a more flexible, human-like way. Rather than relying on predefined equations, similarity metrics, or tree-based models, an LLM can reason about the relationship between income and age using contextual understanding and pattern recognition.

This approach represents the broadest form of AI assistance in imputation: the model is not constrained by a specific algorithmic structure and can incorporate domain intuition, proportional reasoning, and contextual cues that traditional models cannot access. It is particularly useful when patterns are subtle, when the dataset is small, or when human-like reasoning is desirable.

A structured prompt describing the known data and missing values guides the model:

Code

You are a data analyst helping to impute missing values.

We have customer income and age data:

Income 45000 → age missing

Income 75000 → age missing

Income 52000 → age 35

Income 68000 → age 42

Income 59000 → age missing

Income 82000 → age 50

Income 61000 → age missing

Based on the relationship between income and age, estimate reasonable values for the missing ages.

Return only the missing ages in order, as a comma-separated list.

A model such as ChatGPT might respond with:

32, 47, 36, 44

These values reflect the AI's interpretation of the pattern, combining statistical intuition with contextual reasoning. Once obtained, the values can be inserted back into R:

```
ai_values <- c(32, 47, 36, 44)

customer_data$age_ai <- customer_data$age
customer_data$age_ai[is.na(customer_data$age_ai)] <- ai_values
```

This final method demonstrates how modern AI systems can extend imputation beyond the limits of traditional statistical and machine-learning techniques, offering a flexible and adaptive form of reasoning that complements the earlier approaches.

Across all seven methods explored in this lab, a clear progression emerges—from simple, assumption-driven techniques to increasingly flexible, data-driven, and ultimately AI-assisted approaches. Mean imputation provides a quick but crude fix, replacing all missing values with a single constant and erasing natural variation. Conditional imputation improves on this by incorporating domain knowledge, but it still depends on manually defined rules. Regression-based imputation represents a more advanced step, allowing the data to determine the relationship between variables, yet it remains limited by its linear structure.

The transition into AI-assisted methods marks a fundamental shift. kNN imputation abandons explicit rules entirely, instead relying on similarity patterns learned directly from the data. Random forest imputation goes further by using machine-learning models to capture nonlinear relationships and interactions that would be difficult or impossible to specify manually. Finally, large language model–based imputation introduces an even broader form of reasoning, where an AI system can interpret patterns, infer context, and generate plausible estimates using flexible, human-like logic.

Together, these methods illustrate how imputation evolves from rigid, analyst-defined assumptions to adaptive, pattern-driven intelligence. AI-assisted imputation does not replace traditional techniques; rather, it expands the toolkit available to analysts, offering more nuanced, context-aware, and realistic ways to handle missing data. As datasets grow in complexity and scale, these AI-based approaches become increasingly valuable, enabling analysts to preserve structure, reduce bias, and produce more reliable insights from imperfect data.

3.12.2 Practice

The following exercises allow you to apply the imputation methods introduced in this lab. You will begin by generating a small dataset with missing values, then explore how different imputation strategies affect the results. These questions reinforce the progression from simple, assumption-driven methods to more flexible, AI-assisted approaches.

```
set.seed(42)

practice_data <- data.frame(
```

```
customer_id = 1:15,

monthly_spend = c(120, 200, 150, NA, 310, 180, NA, 260, 140, 195, 330,
NA, 175, 205, NA),

visits_per_month = c(3, 5, 4, 2, 6, 3, 4, NA, 2, 5, 7, 3, NA, 4, 2),

satisfaction_score = c(8, 9, NA, 6, 10, 7, 8, 9, 6, NA, 10, 7, 8, 9,
↪ NA)

)

practice_data
```

```
   customer_id monthly_spend visits_per_month satisfaction_score
1            1           120                3                  8
2            2           200                5                  9
3            3           150                4                 NA
4            4            NA                2                  6
5            5           310                6                 10
6            6           180                3                  7
7            7            NA                4                  8
8            8           260               NA                  9
9            9           140                2                  6
10          10           195                5                 NA
11          11           330                7                 10
12          12            NA                3                  7
13          13           175               NA                  8
14          14           205                4                  9
15          15            NA                2                 NA
```

3.12.2.1 Questions

1. Identify which variables contain missing values in the dataset and determine how many values are missing in each variable.
2. Calculate the mean monthly_spend using only complete cases. What value would be used to replace missing monthly_spend values under simple mean imputation?
3. Describe how replacing all missing monthly_spend values with the mean would affect the distribution of that variable.
4. Create a simple conditional rule for imputing monthly_spend based on visits_per_month. Explain the reasoning behind your rule.

5. Using your rule from Question 4, determine which rows would receive lower versus higher imputed spending values. How does this differ from mean imputation?
6. Fit a regression model predicting monthly_spend from visits_per_month using only complete cases. What relationship does the model estimate between these variables?
7. Using the regression model, generate predicted monthly_spend values for all rows. Which predicted values would replace the missing entries?
8. Compare the imputed monthly_spend values produced by mean imputation, conditional imputation, and regression imputation. Which method appears most realistic for this dataset, and why?
9. Explain how k Nearest Neighbors imputation determines similarity between customers in this dataset. Which variables would influence the similarity calculation?
10. After performing kNN imputation with k = 3, compare the imputed satisfaction_score values to those produced by regression. What differences do you observe?
11. Describe how a random forest model learns to predict missing values in satisfaction_score. What advantages does it have over regression in this dataset?
12. Compare the imputed values from random forest and kNN for visits_per_month. Which method seems to capture more nuanced patterns, and why?
13. Write a structured prompt that could be sent to a large language model to estimate missing satisfaction_score values in this dataset.
14. Explain how a large language model might infer satisfaction_score from monthly_spend and visits_per_month, even without explicit formulas. What kinds of reasoning might it apply?
15. Evaluate the differences between kNN, random forest, and large language model based imputation. In what situations might each method be most appropriate for this dataset.

3.13 Lab 3-3 Duplication and Record Consistency

Imagine you're working as a data analyst for a growing e-commerce company. Customer data has come in from multiple sources—online registrations, phone orders, and imported records from acquisitions. A quick count shows 15,000 customers, but a closer look reveals issues: "John Smith" appears multiple times with slight differences, "Jane Doe" and "J. Doe" may be the same person, and some records are exact duplicates.

This is a classic and costly data quality problem: duplicate records. Duplicates don't just clutter your data—they distort key metrics, waste marketing resources, and create confusion about which information is correct. They can also lead to poor customer experience and potential compliance issues when accurate records are required.

Duplicates typically fall into three categories: exact duplicates (identical records), near duplicates (small variations in names or formatting), and partial duplicates (shared identifiers but differing details).

In this lab, you will learn how to identify and resolve these duplicate records using R, working with realistic data that reflects common challenges in real-world analytics.

3.13.1 Demonstration

3.13.1.1 Step 1: Create Dataset

We begin by loading the required R packages and creating a sample customer database. This dataset reflects common real-world issues where customer records come from multiple systems (online forms, point-of-sale systems, imports, etc.), often leading to duplicate and inconsistent entries. We will use it throughout the lab to demonstrate how duplicates form and how they can be identified and cleaned.

```
options(repos = c(CRAN = "https://cloud.r-project.org"))

install.packages("RecordLinkage")
```

```
package 'RecordLinkage' successfully unpacked and MD5 sums checked

The downloaded binary packages are in
    C:\Users\drkse\AppData\Local\Temp\RtmpW6HwjC\downloaded_packages
```

```
# Load required packages
library(dplyr)        # For data manipulation
library(stringdist)   # For string similarity calculations
library(RecordLinkage) # For record linkage and deduplication

# Create sample customer data with realistic duplicates
customer_data <- data.frame(
  CustomerID = 1:20,
  FirstName = c(
    "John", "Jane", "Robert", "John", "Mary", "Jane",
    "Bob", "Mary", "Michael", "Sarah", "John", "Robert",
    "J", "Mike", "Sara", "Jane", "Rob", "Mary", "John", "Michael"
  ),
  LastName = c(
    "Smith", "Johnson", "Brown", "Smith", "Davis", "Doe",
    "Brown", "Davis", "Wilson", "Miller", "Smith", "Brown",
    "Doe", "Wilson", "Miller", "Johnson", "Brown", "Davis", "Smith",
     ↪  "Wilson"
```

```
  ),
  Email = c(
    "john.smith@email.com", "jane.johnson@email.com",
     ↪ "rbrown@email.com",
    "j.smith@email.com", "mary.davis@email.com", "jane.doe@email.com",
    "bob.brown@email.com", "m.davis@email.com", "mwilson@email.com",
    "sarah.miller@email.com", "johnsmith@email.com",
     ↪ "robert.brown@email.com",
    "j.doe@email.com", "mike.wilson@email.com", "s.miller@email.com",
    "jane.johnson@email.com", "r.brown@email.com",
     ↪ "mary.davis@email.com",
    "john.smith@email.com", "michael.wilson@email.com"
  ),
  Phone = c(
    "555-1234", "555-5678", "555-9012", "555-1234", "555-3456",
    "555-7890", "555-9012", "555-3456", "555-2468", "555-1357",
    "(555) 123-4", "5559012", "555-7890", "555-2468", "555-1357",
    "555-5678", "555-9012", "555-3456", "555-1234", "555-2468"
  ),
  City = c(
    "New York", "Boston", "Chicago", "New York", "Miami", "Seattle",
    "Chicago", "Miami", "Denver", "Portland", "NYC", "Chicago",
    "Seattle", "Denver", "Portland", "Boston", "Chicago", "Miami",
    "New York", "Denver"
  ),
  stringsAsFactors = FALSE
)

# Display the dataset
print("Customer Database with Duplicates:")
```

```
[1] "Customer Database with Duplicates:"
```

```
print(customer_data[,1:3])
```

```
  CustomerID FirstName LastName
1          1      John    Smith
2          2      Jane  Johnson
3          3    Robert    Brown
4          4      John    Smith
5          5      Mary    Davis
6          6      Jane      Doe
7          7       Bob    Brown
8          8      Mary    Davis
```

```
9           9  Michael   Wilson
10         10    Sarah   Miller
11         11     John    Smith
12         12   Robert    Brown
13         13        J      Doe
14         14     Mike   Wilson
15         15     Sara   Miller
16         16     Jane  Johnson
17         17      Rob    Brown
18         18     Mary    Davis
19         19     John    Smith
20         20  Michael   Wilson
```

```
print(customer_data[,4:6])
```

```
                       Email        Phone     City
1       john.smith@email.com     555-1234 New York
2     jane.johnson@email.com     555-5678   Boston
3           rbrown@email.com     555-9012  Chicago
4         j.smith@email.com      555-1234 New York
5       mary.davis@email.com     555-3456    Miami
6         jane.doe@email.com     555-7890  Seattle
7        bob.brown@email.com     555-9012  Chicago
8         m.davis@email.com      555-3456    Miami
9          mwilson@email.com     555-2468   Denver
10    sarah.miller@email.com     555-1357 Portland
11       johnsmith@email.com (555) 123-4      NYC
12    robert.brown@email.com      5559012  Chicago
13           j.doe@email.com     555-7890  Seattle
14      mike.wilson@email.com    555-2468   Denver
15        s.miller@email.com     555-1357 Portland
16    jane.johnson@email.com     555-5678   Boston
17         r.brown@email.com     555-9012  Chicago
18      mary.davis@email.com     555-3456    Miami
19      john.smith@email.com     555-1234 New York
20 michael.wilson@email.com     555-2468   Denver
```

```
# Get basic information about the dataset
cat("\nDataset Summary:\n")
```

```
Dataset Summary:
```

```
cat("Total records:", nrow(customer_data), "\n")
```

```
Total records: 20
```

```
cat("Unique first names:", length(unique(customer_data$FirstName)),
↪  "\n")
```

```
Unique first names: 11
```

```
cat("Unique last names:", length(unique(customer_data$LastName)), "\n")
```

```
Unique last names: 7
```

```
cat("Unique email addresses:", length(unique(customer_data$Email)),
↪  "\n")
```

```
Unique email addresses: 17
```

When reviewing the dataset, pay attention to several common data quality issues. You will notice that some customer names appear multiple times with slight variations, which can make it difficult to identify duplicates. Email addresses may also represent the same individual but appear in different formats or with small inconsistencies. In addition, phone numbers are not standardized and may be written in different formats across records. Finally, city names may be inconsistent, with some entries using abbreviations while others use full names, further complicating efforts to clean and match records accurately.

3.13.1.2 Step 2: Exact Duplicate Detection

In this step, we begin identifying duplicate records using multiple approaches. In real-world data cleaning, there is rarely a single definition of a "duplicate," so we examine the dataset from different perspectives. First, we look for exact duplicates where every column matches. Then, we apply a more realistic business rule by identifying duplicates based on key identifying fields such as first name, last name, and email. Finally, we summarize repeated name patterns to understand how frequently duplicate structures appear in the dataset.

```
# Method 1: Find exact duplicates across all columns
exact_duplicates <- customer_data[
  duplicated(customer_data) | duplicated(customer_data, fromLast =
  ↪  TRUE),
]

cat("Exact Duplicates Found:\n")
```

```
Exact Duplicates Found:
```

```
if (nrow(exact_duplicates) > 0) {
  print(exact_duplicates)
```

```
} else {
  cat("No exact duplicates found.\n")
}
```

```
No exact duplicates found.
```

```
# Method 2: Find duplicates based on specific key fields
# Often, we want to check for duplicates based on business logic
key_duplicates <- customer_data[
  duplicated(customer_data[c("FirstName", "LastName", "Email")]) |
    duplicated(customer_data[c("FirstName", "LastName", "Email")],
               fromLast = TRUE),
]

cat("\nDuplicates based on Name + Email:\n")
```

```
Duplicates based on Name + Email:
```

```
if (nrow(key_duplicates) > 0) {
  print(key_duplicates[order(key_duplicates$FirstName,
                             key_duplicates$LastName), 1:4])
} else {
  cat("No key-based duplicates found.\n")
}
```

```
   CustomerID FirstName LastName                  Email
2           2      Jane  Johnson jane.johnson@email.com
16         16      Jane  Johnson jane.johnson@email.com
1           1      John    Smith   john.smith@email.com
19         19      John    Smith   john.smith@email.com
5           5      Mary    Davis   mary.davis@email.com
18         18      Mary    Davis   mary.davis@email.com
```

```
# Method 3: Count duplicate patterns
duplicate_counts <- customer_data %>%
  group_by(FirstName, LastName) %>%
  summarise(count = n(), .groups = "drop") %>%
  filter(count > 1) %>%
  arrange(desc(count))

cat("\nName combinations appearing multiple times:\n")
```

```
Name combinations appearing multiple times:
```

```
print(duplicate_counts)
```

```
# A tibble: 5 x 3
  FirstName LastName count
  <chr>     <chr>    <int>
1 John      Smith        4
2 Mary      Davis        3
3 Jane      Johnson      2
4 Michael   Wilson       2
5 Robert    Brown        2
```

From the results, we can see that duplicates are not always obvious and depend heavily on the definition being used. Exact duplicate detection identifies fully identical rows, but this approach often misses records that refer to the same individual with slight variations. When we shift to a business-rule approach using name and email, additional duplicate cases become visible. The grouped summary further highlights repeated name patterns, helping us understand where duplication is concentrated in the dataset. Together, these methods demonstrate why duplicate detection must be flexible and guided by context rather than relying on a single rule.

3.13.1.3 Step 3: Near Duplicate Detection with String Similarity

In this step, we move beyond exact matching and begin identifying near duplicates—records that likely refer to the same individual but contain small differences in spelling or formatting. These variations often occur due to manual data entry errors, inconsistent formatting across systems, or incomplete standardization. To detect these cases, we use string similarity measures to compare first and last names across all record pairs and flag those that exceed a defined similarity threshold.

```
# Function to calculate string similarity between two records
calculate_similarity <- function(str1, str2) {
  # Jaro-Winkler distance (converted to similarity below)
  stringdist(str1, str2, method = "jw")
}

# Create a similarity matrix for names
name_combinations <- expand.grid(
  i = 1:nrow(customer_data),
  j = 1:nrow(customer_data)
)

name_combinations <-
  name_combinations[name_combinations$i < name_combinations$j, ]
```

```
# Calculate similarities
similarities <- data.frame(
  Record1 = name_combinations$i,
  Record2 = name_combinations$j,
  Name1 = paste(
    customer_data$FirstName[name_combinations$i],
    customer_data$LastName[name_combinations$i]
  ),
  Name2 = paste(
    customer_data$FirstName[name_combinations$j],
    customer_data$LastName[name_combinations$j]
  ),
  FirstName_Similarity = 1 - mapply(
    calculate_similarity,
    customer_data$FirstName[name_combinations$i],
    customer_data$FirstName[name_combinations$j]
  ),
  LastName_Similarity = 1 - mapply(
    calculate_similarity,
    customer_data$LastName[name_combinations$i],
    customer_data$LastName[name_combinations$j]
  ),
  stringsAsFactors = FALSE
)

# Find potential near duplicates (high similarity threshold)
threshold <- 0.85

near_duplicates <- similarities[
  (similarities$FirstName_Similarity > threshold &
     similarities$LastName_Similarity > threshold) |
    (similarities$FirstName_Similarity > 0.95 |
       similarities$LastName_Similarity > 0.95),
]

cat("Potential Near Duplicates (Similarity > 85%):\n")
```

```
Potential Near Duplicates (Similarity > 85%):
```

```
if (nrow(near_duplicates) > 0) {
  print(near_duplicates[order(-near_duplicates$FirstName_Similarity),
  ↪  ])
} else {
  cat("No near duplicates found with current threshold.\n")
```

```
}

    Record1 Record2          Name1          Name2 FirstName_Similarity
4         1       4     John Smith     John Smith            1.0000000
12        2       6   Jane Johnson       Jane Doe            1.0000000
26        5       8     Mary Davis     Mary Davis            1.0000000
46        1      11     John Smith     John Smith            1.0000000
49        4      11     John Smith     John Smith            1.0000000
58        3      12   Robert Brown   Robert Brown            1.0000000
107       2      16   Jane Johnson   Jane Johnson            1.0000000
111       6      16       Jane Doe   Jane Johnson            1.0000000
141       5      18     Mary Davis     Mary Davis            1.0000000
144       8      18     Mary Davis     Mary Davis            1.0000000
154       1      19     John Smith     John Smith            1.0000000
157       4      19     John Smith     John Smith            1.0000000
164      11      19     John Smith     John Smith            1.0000000
180       9      20 Michael Wilson Michael Wilson            1.0000000
101      10      15   Sarah Miller    Sara Miller            0.9333333
123       3      17   Robert Brown      Rob Brown            0.8333333
132      12      17   Robert Brown      Rob Brown            0.8333333
127       7      17      Bob Brown      Rob Brown            0.7777778
72        6      13       Jane Doe          J Doe            0.7500000
87        9      14 Michael Wilson    Mike Wilson            0.7261905
185      14      20    Mike Wilson Michael Wilson            0.7261905
18        3       7   Robert Brown      Bob Brown            0.6666667
62        7      12      Bob Brown   Robert Brown            0.6666667
    LastName_Similarity
4             1.0000000
12            0.4920635
26            1.0000000
46            1.0000000
49            1.0000000
58            1.0000000
107           1.0000000
111           0.4920635
141           1.0000000
144           1.0000000
154           1.0000000
157           1.0000000
164           1.0000000
180           1.0000000
101           1.0000000
123           1.0000000
```

```
132            1.0000000
127            1.0000000
72             1.0000000
87             1.0000000
185            1.0000000
18             1.0000000
62             1.0000000
```

```
# Show the actual records for manual review
if (nrow(near_duplicates) > 0) {
  cat("\nDetailed comparison of potential duplicates:\n")

  for (i in 1:min(3, nrow(near_duplicates))) {
    cat("\n--- Potential Match", i, "---\n")

    rec1 <- customer_data[near_duplicates$Record1[i], ]
    rec2 <- customer_data[near_duplicates$Record2[i], ]

    cat(
      "Record", near_duplicates$Record1[i], ":",
      rec1$FirstName, rec1$LastName, "|",
      rec1$Email, "|",
      rec1$Phone, "\n"
    )

    cat(
      "Record", near_duplicates$Record2[i], ":",
      rec2$FirstName, rec2$LastName, "|",
      rec2$Email, "|",
      rec2$Phone, "\n"
    )

    cat("First Name Similarity:",
        round(near_duplicates$FirstName_Similarity[i], 3), "\n")

    cat("Last Name Similarity:",
        round(near_duplicates$LastName_Similarity[i], 3), "\n")
  }
}
```

```
Detailed comparison of potential duplicates:

--- Potential Match 1 ---
```

```
Record 1 : John Smith | john.smith@email.com | 555-1234
Record 4 : John Smith | j.smith@email.com | 555-1234
First Name Similarity: 1
Last Name Similarity: 1

--- Potential Match 2 ---
Record 2 : Jane Johnson | jane.johnson@email.com | 555-5678
Record 6 : Jane Doe | jane.doe@email.com | 555-7890
First Name Similarity: 1
Last Name Similarity: 0.492

--- Potential Match 3 ---
Record 3 : Robert Brown | rbrown@email.com | 555-9012
Record 7 : Bob Brown | bob.brown@email.com | 555-9012
First Name Similarity: 0.667
Last Name Similarity: 1
```

The results show how powerful similarity-based matching can be for identifying duplicates that traditional exact-matching methods would miss. Even when names are not identical, high similarity scores reveal likely matches that warrant further review. This step also highlights an important limitation: similarity thresholds require careful tuning, as too strict a value may miss true matches while too loose a value may introduce false positives. By manually reviewing top candidate pairs, we can validate potential duplicates before making final decisions in the cleaning process.

3.13.1.4 Step 4: Advanced Pattern Detection

In this step, we improve duplicate detection by first standardizing the data before comparisons are made. Real-world datasets often contain inconsistencies such as different capitalizations, extra spaces, abbreviations, and varying formats for phone numbers or city names. These inconsistencies can hide duplicates if we compare records directly.

To address this, we create cleaned versions of key fields such as names, phone numbers, email addresses, and cities. Once standardized, we re-run duplicate detection using these normalized values and also check for shared phone numbers, which often indicate the same customer across multiple records.

```r
# Function to standardize phone numbers for comparison
standardize_phone <- function(phone) {
  # Remove all non-digits
  gsub("[^0-9]", "", phone)
}

# Function to standardize city names
```

```r
standardize_city <- function(city) {
  city_mapping <- c(
    "NYC" = "New York",
    "LA" = "Los Angeles",
    "SF" = "San Francisco"
  )

  standardized <- city_mapping[city]
  ifelse(is.na(standardized), city, standardized)
}

# Create standardized version of the data
customer_clean <- customer_data %>%
  mutate(
    FirstName_Clean = tolower(trimws(FirstName)),
    LastName_Clean  = tolower(trimws(LastName)),
    Phone_Clean     = standardize_phone(Phone),
    City_Clean      = standardize_city(City),
    Email_Clean     = tolower(trimws(Email))
  )

# Find duplicates using multiple criteria
multi_criteria_duplicates <- customer_clean %>%
  group_by(FirstName_Clean, LastName_Clean) %>%
  filter(n() > 1) %>%
  arrange(FirstName_Clean, LastName_Clean, CustomerID)

cat("Potential duplicates using standardized names:\n")
```

```
Potential duplicates using standardized names:
```

```r
print(
  multi_criteria_duplicates[, c(
    "CustomerID", "FirstName", "LastName"
  )]
)
```

```
# A tibble: 13 x 3
   CustomerID FirstName LastName
        <int> <chr>     <chr>
 1          2 Jane      Johnson
 2         16 Jane      Johnson
 3          1 John      Smith
 4          4 John      Smith
```

```
 5          11 John      Smith
 6          19 John      Smith
 7           5 Mary      Davis
 8           8 Mary      Davis
 9          18 Mary      Davis
10           9 Michael   Wilson
11          20 Michael   Wilson
12           3 Robert    Brown
13          12 Robert    Brown
```

```r
# Check for phone number matches across different names
phone_duplicates <- customer_clean %>%
  group_by(Phone_Clean) %>%
  filter(n() > 1, Phone_Clean != "") %>%
  arrange(Phone_Clean, CustomerID)

cat("\nRecords sharing the same phone number:\n")
```

```

Records sharing the same phone number:
```

```r
if (nrow(phone_duplicates) > 0) {
  print(
    phone_duplicates[, c(
      "CustomerID", "FirstName", "LastName",
      "Phone", "Phone_Clean"
    )]
  )
} else {
  cat("No phone number duplicates found.\n")
}
```

```
# A tibble: 20 x 5
# Groups:   Phone_Clean [7]
   CustomerID FirstName LastName Phone        Phone_Clean
        <int> <chr>     <chr>    <chr>        <chr>
 1          1 John      Smith    555-1234     5551234
 2          4 John      Smith    555-1234     5551234
 3         11 John      Smith    (555) 123-4 5551234
 4         19 John      Smith    555-1234     5551234
 5         10 Sarah     Miller   555-1357     5551357
 6         15 Sara      Miller   555-1357     5551357
 7          9 Michael   Wilson   555-2468     5552468
 8         14 Mike      Wilson   555-2468     5552468
 9         20 Michael   Wilson   555-2468     5552468
```

```
10          5 Mary      Davis     555-3456     5553456
11          8 Mary      Davis     555-3456     5553456
12         18 Mary      Davis     555-3456     5553456
13          2 Jane      Johnson   555-5678     5555678
14         16 Jane      Johnson   555-5678     5555678
15          6 Jane      Doe       555-7890     5557890
16         13 J         Doe       555-7890     5557890
17          3 Robert    Brown     555-9012     5559012
18          7 Bob       Brown     555-9012     5559012
19         12 Robert    Brown     5559012      5559012
20         17 Rob       Brown     555-9012     5559012
```

```
# Summary of duplicate patterns found
cat("\n=== DUPLICATE ANALYSIS SUMMARY ===\n")
```

```
=== DUPLICATE ANALYSIS SUMMARY ===
```

```
cat("Total records in database:", nrow(customer_data), "\n")
```

```
Total records in database: 20
```

```
cat("Records with duplicate names:", nrow(multi_criteria_duplicates),
  ↪  "\n")
```

```
Records with duplicate names: 13
```

```
cat("Records with duplicate phone numbers:", nrow(phone_duplicates),
  ↪  "\n")
```

```
Records with duplicate phone numbers: 20
```

```
cat(
  "Estimated unique customers:",
  nrow(customer_data) - nrow(multi_criteria_duplicates) +
    length(unique(
      paste(
        multi_criteria_duplicates$FirstName_Clean,
        multi_criteria_duplicates$LastName_Clean
      )
    )),
  "\n"
)
```

```
Estimated unique customers: 12
```

This step demonstrates how much duplicate detection improves when data is standardized before analysis. Many records that appear different at first are revealed to belong to the same individual once formatting differences are removed. Phone numbers, in particular, provide a strong linking signal even when names or emails vary slightly.

Overall, this shows that duplicate detection is not just about comparing values—it depends heavily on preparing the data into a consistent structure first. Without this step, many hidden duplicates would remain undetected, leading to inaccurate counts and misleading business insights.

3.13.1.4.1 Step 5: AI-Assisted Duplicate Validation

In the final step, we demonstrate how artificial intelligence can be used as a decision-support tool for duplicate detection. While rule-based methods (exact matching, similarity scoring, and standardized comparisons) are effective, they can still produce borderline cases that are difficult to classify confidently.

In practice, AI can help evaluate these ambiguous record pairs by considering multiple fields at once and providing a reasoned judgment. To illustrate this, we take a small set of potential duplicate records identified in previous steps and pass them to an AI model for evaluation.

Example AI Prompt Used

You are a data quality assistant. Review the two customer records below and determine whether they represent the same individual. Consider name similarity, email patterns, phone numbers, and any inconsistencies in formatting.

Respond with YES (same person), NO (different people), or UNSURE, and briefly explain your reasoning.

```
Example Input
Record 1: John Smith | john.smith@email.com | 555-1234 | New York
Record 2: J. Smith | johnsmith@email.com | (555) 123-4 | NYC

Example AI Output (Illustration)
YES – The records likely refer to the same individual. The names are
highly similar, the phone numbers match after formatting, and the
email addresses follow a closely related pattern. The differences
in city formatting (New York vs NYC) are consistent with known
standardization issues.
```

3.13.2 Practice

Run the R code provided to create the dataset. Then answer each question using the data and the methods from the lab. Show any R code you used and write short explanations when needed.

```r
library(dplyr)
library(stringdist)

set.seed(42)

practice_data <- data.frame(
  CustomerID = 1:25,

  FirstName = c(
    "Anna", "Anne", "A.", "John", "Jon", "J.",
    "Maria", "Marie", "M.", "Chris", "Kris", "Christopher",
    "Sara", "Sarah", "S.", "David", "Dave", "D.",
    "Lily", "Lilly", "Li", "Mark", "Marc", "M.", "John"
  ),

  LastName = c(
    "Lee", "Lee", "Li",
    "Smith", "Smith", "Smith",
    "Garcia", "Garcia", "Garcia",
    "Brown", "Brown", "Brown",
    "Miller", "Miller", "Miller",
    "Davis", "Davis", "Davis",
    "Wilson", "Wilson", "Wilson",
    "Taylor", "Taylor", "Taylor",
    "Smith"
  ),

  Email = c(
    "anna.lee@email.com", "anne.lee@email.com", "a.lee@email.com",
    "john.smith@email.com", "jon.smith@email.com", "j.smith@email.com",
    "maria.garcia@email.com", "marie.garcia@email.com",
     ↪ "m.garcia@email.com",
    "chris.brown@email.com", "kris.brown@email.com",
     ↪ "christopher.brown@email.com",
    "sara.miller@email.com", "sarah.miller@email.com",
     ↪ "s.miller@email.com",
    "david.davis@email.com", "dave.davis@email.com",
     ↪ "d.davis@email.com",
    "lily.wilson@email.com", "lilly.wilson@email.com",
     ↪ "li.wilson@email.com",
    "mark.taylor@email.com", "marc.taylor@email.com",
     ↪ "m.taylor@email.com",
    "johnsmith@email.com"
```

```
  ),

  Phone = c(
    "555-1111", "5551111", "(555) 1111",
    "555-2222", "5552222", "(555) 2222",
    "555-3333", "5553333", "(555) 3333",
    "555-4444", "5554444", "(555) 4444",
    "555-5555", "5555555", "(555) 5555",
    "555-6666", "5556666", "(555) 6666",
    "555-7777", "5557777", "(555) 7777",
    "555-8888", "5558888", "(555) 8888",
    "555-2222"
  ),

  City = c(
    "New York", "NYC", "New York",
    "Boston", "Boston", "BOS",
    "Miami", "Miami", "MIA",
    "Chicago", "Chicago", "CHI",
    "Seattle", "Seattle", "SEA",
    "Denver", "Denver", "DEN",
    "Portland", "Portland", "PDX",
    "New York", "NYC", "New York",
    "Boston"
  ),

  stringsAsFactors = FALSE
)

practice_data[,1:4]
```

```
   CustomerID FirstName LastName                  Email
1           1      Anna      Lee     anna.lee@email.com
2           2      Anne      Lee     anne.lee@email.com
3           3        A.       Li        a.lee@email.com
4           4      John    Smith   john.smith@email.com
5           5       Jon    Smith    jon.smith@email.com
6           6        J.    Smith      j.smith@email.com
7           7     Maria   Garcia maria.garcia@email.com
8           8     Marie   Garcia marie.garcia@email.com
9           9        M.   Garcia     m.garcia@email.com
10         10     Chris    Brown  chris.brown@email.com
11         11      Kris    Brown   kris.brown@email.com
```

```
12          12 Christopher    Brown christopher.brown@email.com
13          13        Sara   Miller       sara.miller@email.com
14          14       Sarah   Miller      sarah.miller@email.com
15          15          S.   Miller          s.miller@email.com
16          16       David    Davis       david.davis@email.com
17          17        Dave    Davis        dave.davis@email.com
18          18          D.    Davis           d.davis@email.com
19          19        Lily   Wilson       lily.wilson@email.com
20          20       Lilly   Wilson      lilly.wilson@email.com
21          21          Li   Wilson         li.wilson@email.com
22          22        Mark   Taylor       mark.taylor@email.com
23          23        Marc   Taylor       marc.taylor@email.com
24          24          M.   Taylor          m.taylor@email.com
25          25        John    Smith         johnsmith@email.com
```

```
practice_data[,5:6]
```

```
          Phone     City
1      555-1111 New York
2       5551111      NYC
3    (555) 1111 New York
4      555-2222   Boston
5       5552222   Boston
6    (555) 2222      BOS
7      555-3333    Miami
8       5553333    Miami
9    (555) 3333      MIA
10     555-4444  Chicago
11      5554444  Chicago
12   (555) 4444      CHI
13     555-5555  Seattle
14      5555555  Seattle
15   (555) 5555      SEA
16     555-6666   Denver
17      5556666   Denver
18   (555) 6666      DEN
19     555-7777 Portland
20      5557777 Portland
21   (555) 7777      PDX
22     555-8888 New York
23      5558888      NYC
24   (555) 8888 New York
25     555-2222   Boston
```

3.13.2.1 Questions

1. Find any exact duplicate rows in the dataset. How many are there?
2. Using FirstName + LastName + Email, find records that appear to be the same person. List them.
3. Group by FirstName and LastName. Which name combinations appear more than once?
4. Calculate Jaro-Winkler similarity for all FirstName pairs. List three pairs with similarity above 0.90.
5. Identify at least five near-duplicate pairs using both first and last name similarity.
6. Standardize phone numbers by removing all non-numeric characters. After cleaning, how many records share the same phone number?
7. Standardize city names so that NYC, BOS, MIA, CHI, SEA, DEN, and PDX map to their full names. After cleaning, how many unique cities remain?
8. Using standardized FirstName, LastName, and Phone, find all groups where more than one record appears. Which field seems to be the strongest duplicate signal?
9. Identify email addresses that differ only by formatting (for example, dots or missing characters). List the pairs you find.
10. Choose two borderline pairs and decide whether they are the same person, different people, or unsure. Explain your reasoning briefly.

Chapter 4

Merging and Joining Data Sources

4.1 Learning Outcomes

4-1: Understand primary and foreign key concepts and their role in establishing relationships between data tables

4-2: Apply inner, left, right, and full joins in SQL to combine data from multiple sources appropriately

4-3: Identify and prevent common merge errors and duplicate detection issues when combining datasets

4-4: Use AI-assisted validation and cross-table consistency checks to ensure data integrity after merging

4-5: Design effective data integration strategies that maintain data quality while combining multiple sources

4.2 Introduction

In the real world, information about any business process is naturally scattered across multiple sources. When you make an online purchase, your customer information might be stored in a customer management system, product details maintained in an inventory database, and transaction records kept in a financial system. Each system serves a specific purpose and maintains its own data structure, creating a complex web of interconnected but separate information sources.

To understand why this separation exists and how to work with it effectively, let's examine a concrete example. Imagine you're analyzing customer behavior for an e-commerce company, and you have three separate datasets that need to be combined:

Customers

customer_id	name	email
1	John Smith	john@email.com
2	Jane Doe	jane@email.com
3	Bob Wilson	bob@email.com

Orders

order_id	customer_id	order_date	total_amount
1001	1	2023-01-15	99.99
1002	2	2023-01-16	149.50
1003	1	2023-01-20	75.25

Products

product_id	product_name	price
101	Laptop	899.99
102	Mouse	25.99
103	Keyboard	79.99

Each table contains valuable information, but to answer questions like "Which customers buy the most expensive products?" you need to combine information from all three sources. This is where data merging and joining becomes essential for creating reliable datasets that support accurate analysis and effective AI applications.

4.2.1 Why Data Lives in Separate Tables

You might wonder why we don't simply store everything in one giant table. This question reveals a fundamental principle of data organization that every data analyst must understand. Consider what would happen if we tried to combine all customer and order information into a single table:

customer_id	name	address	order_id	order_date	product_name	price	quantity
1	John Smith	123 Main St	1001	2023-01-15	Laptop	899.99	1
1	John Smith	123 Main St	1001	2023-01-15	Mouse	25.99	2
1	John Smith	123 Main St	1003	2023-01-20	Keyboard	79.99	1

This approach quickly reveals serious problems. John's name, and address are repeated for every product he orders, creating data redundancy that wastes storage space and creates update anomalies. If John moves and needs to update his address, that change must be made in potentially hundreds of different rows. Miss even one row, and the data becomes inconsistent.

The solution is normalization, which involves separating information into logical groups and storing each piece of information in exactly one place. While this eliminates redundancy problems, it creates a new challenge: how do we reconnect related information when we need to analyze it? Understanding how to properly merge and join data sources is critical for creating reliable datasets that support accurate analysis and effective AI applications.

4.3 Primary and Foreign Keys - Data Relationships

4.3.1 Understanding Primary Keys

Every table in a relational database needs a way to uniquely identify each record, just as every person needs some form of identification in official contexts. While we might use names in casual conversation, official processes require more reliable identifiers like Social Security numbers because names alone can be ambiguous or duplicated. Database tables work according to the same principle.

A primary key serves as the "official ID" for each record in a table. Looking at our customers table above, customer_id is the primary key because each customer has a unique number that distinguishes them from all other customers. This unique identifier is essential because it makes relationships between tables possible and ensures data integrity over time.

4.3.1.1 Primary Keys Must Follow Specific Rules

Primary keys must be unique across all records, ensuring that no two customers can have the same customer_id. They must be non-null because every customer must have a customer_id (no empty values). The customer_id shouldn't change over time, providing stability for relationships. Finally, primary keys should be simple and efficient, making them easy to reference from other tables.

Let's examine some examples of good versus poor primary key choices:

Good Primary Key	Why It's Good	Poor Primary Key	Why It's Poor
customer_id (1, 2, 3...)	Unique, stable, simple	customer_name	Names can duplicate
order_id (1001, 1002...)	Auto-generated, unique	order_date	Multiple orders per day
product_id (101, 102...)	Business meaningful	product_price	Prices can change

Understanding these principles helps you recognize well-designed databases and avoid common pitfalls when working with data integration projects.

4.3.2 Foreign Keys

While primary keys provide unique identification within a table, foreign keys create the connections between tables that make relational databases powerful. A foreign key creates relationships between tables by referencing the primary key of another table. In our orders table, customer_id is a foreign key that points to the customer_id primary key in the customers table.

This connection represents a real-world relationship. When customer John Smith (customer_id = 1) places two orders, the relationship looks like this:

Customer: John Smith (ID: 1) His Orders: - Order 1001: $99.99 on 2023-01-15 - Order 1003: $75.25 on 2023-01-20

The foreign key customer_id in the orders table connects each order back to the correct customer, enabling us to answer questions about customer behavior, order patterns, and business performance.

4.3.3 Understanding Relationship Types

Most business relationships follow predictable patterns that determine how tables should be structured and connected. The most common pattern is one-to-many, where one record in a parent table relates to multiple records in a child table:

- One customer → Many orders
- One product → Many order items
- One department → Many employees

Many-to-many relationships are more complex but equally important. Students enroll in multiple courses while courses have multiple students. Products can belong to multiple categories while categories contain multiple products. These relationships require a special structure called a junction table.

Example Junction Table for Products and Categories:

product_id	category_id
101	1
101	3
102	2

This shows that product 101 (Laptop) belongs to both category 1 (Electronics) and category 3 (Computers), demonstrating how junction tables handle many-to-many relationships.

4.3.4 Maintaining Data Integrity Through Referential Integrity

Foreign key constraints enforce referential integrity, ensuring that relationships between tables remain valid and consistent. These constraints follow specific rules that prevent data corruption:

Insert Rule: You can't add an order for customer_id 999 if customer 999 doesn't exist Update Rule: If customer_id 1 changes to 100, all related orders must update too Delete Rule: If customer 1 is deleted, what happens to their orders?

The delete rule defines how the database handles related records when a record is deleted, with several possible options:

- Cascade: Deleting a customer automatically deletes all their associated orders.
- Restrict: Prevents deleting a customer if they have any existing orders.
- Set Null: Deleting a customer sets the customer_id in their orders to NULL, which can create orphaned orders.

Understanding these rules is important for designing robust databases and for troubleshooting issues that may arise when managing related data.

4.4 SQL Join Operations - Combining Data Systematically

4.4.1 Fundamental Logic of Joins

A join operation creates a new, temporary table by combining rows from two or more existing tables based on related columns. Think of it as creating a custom view that brings together information that was deliberately separated for storage efficiency. The process involves examining each row in one table, looking for corresponding rows in another table, and combining matching information according to the join type you specify.

The basic syntax for join operations follows this pattern:

```
SELECT columns
FROM table1
JOIN table2 ON table1.key = table2.key;
```

Understanding how this matching process works helps you predict what your results will look like and choose the appropriate join type for your analysis needs.

4.4.2 Inner Joins: Finding Complete Information

Inner joins return only rows that have matching values in both tables, representing the most restrictive approach to combining data. This approach is appropriate when you need complete information and incomplete records would compromise your analysis.

Example Scenario: Show customer names with their order information.

Before Join – Separate Tables

Customers Table:

customer_id	name
1	John
2	Jane
3	Bob

Orders Table:

order_id	customer_id
1001	1
1002	2
1003	1

This shows the two tables independently, with customer IDs linking orders to the corresponding customers.

SQL Query:

```
SELECT customers.name, orders.order_date, orders.total_amount
FROM customers
INNER JOIN orders ON customers.customer_id = orders.customer_id;
```

After Join – Combined Result

name	order_date	total_amount
John Smith	2023-01-15	99.99
Jane Doe	2023-01-16	149.50
John Smith	2023-01-20	75.25

This table shows the result of joining the Customers and Orders tables on customer_id, combining customer names with their respective orders. Notice that Bob Wilson doesn't appear because he has no orders. Inner joins only include customers with orders, making this approach ideal when you're analyzing active customers or when incomplete information would skew your results.

Inner joins are used when you want to include only the records that exist in both tables. For example, they are useful when analyzing active customers who have placed orders, finding products that have actually been sold, or identifying employees who have completed required training. Essentially, any scenario where you need complete information from all joined tables is appropriate for an inner join. Inner joins automatically exclude unmatched records, ensuring that your analysis is based only on data that exists in both tables.

4.4.3 Left Joins: Preserving Your Primary Dataset

Left joins take a different approach by preserving all rows from the left (first) table while adding matching information from the right (second) table where available. This prevents the "disappearing data" problem that can occur with inner joins.

Example Scenario: Show all customers and their order information (including customers with no orders).

SQL Query:

```
SELECT customers.name, orders.order_date, orders.total_amount
FROM customers
LEFT JOIN orders ON customers.customer_id = orders.customer_id;
```

Result

name	order_date	total_amount
John Smith	2023-01-15	99.99
John Smith	2023-01-20	75.25
Jane Doe	2023-01-16	149.50
Bob Wilson	NULL	NULL

Now Bob Wilson appears with NULL values because he exists in the customers table but has no orders. This complete view enables comprehensive analysis that includes inactive customers as a distinct segment.

Practical Application - Counting Orders per Customer:

```
SELECT customers.name, COUNT(orders.order_id) as order_count
FROM customers
LEFT JOIN orders ON customers.customer_id = orders.customer_id
GROUP BY customers.customer_id, customers.name;
```

Result

name	order_count
John Smith	2
Jane Doe	1
Bob Wilson	0

This analysis reveals customer activity levels, including inactive customers who represent potential marketing opportunities.

Left joins are useful when you want to keep all records from your primary table, even if there is no matching data in the related table. For example, they are ideal for customer analysis when you need to include inactive customers who have not placed any orders.

They are also helpful for product analysis to show products that have not been sold, or for employee reports to include staff members without recent activity. Essentially, use left joins whenever preserving the full dataset from your main table is important, regardless of whether related records exist.

4.4.4 Right Joins: Alternative Perspective for Data Quality

Right joins preserve all rows from the right (second) table and add matching information from the left (first) table where available. While less commonly used than left joins, right joins are valuable for data quality auditing and validation.

Example: Show all orders and customer information (including orders with invalid customer references).

Sample Data with Data Quality Issue:

order_id	customer_id	order_date	total_amount
1001	1	2023-01-15	99.99
1002	2	2023-01-16	149.50
1003	999	2023-01-20	75.25

The issue here is that customer_id 999 is an orphan record—there's no corresponding customer in the Customers table. This can cause problems in joins, reports, and data integrity.

SQL Query:

```
SELECT customers.name, orders.order_date, orders.total_amount
FROM customers
RIGHT JOIN orders ON customers.customer_id = orders.customer_id;
```

name	order_date	total_amount
John Smith	2023-01-15	99.99
Jane Doe	2023-01-16	149.50
NULL	2023-01-20	75.25

The NULL customer name in the last row reveals that order 1003 references customer_id 999, which doesn't exist in the customers table. This indicates a data quality problem that needs investigation.

4.4.5 Full Outer Joins: The Complete Picture

Full outer joins return all rows from both tables, with NULL values where matches don't exist. This provides the most comprehensive view of the relationship between two datasets.

Example: Show all customers and all orders, highlighting missing relationships.

SQL Query:

```
SELECT customers.name, orders.order_date, orders.total_amount
FROM customers
FULL OUTER JOIN orders ON
  customers.customer_id = orders.customer_id;
```

name	order_date	total_amount
John Smith	2023-01-15	99.99
John Smith	2023-01-20	75.25
Jane Doe	2023-01-16	149.50
Bob Wilson	NULL	NULL
NULL	2023-01-20	75.25

This comprehensive view shows both Bob Wilson (customer with no orders) and the last row (order with no valid customer), revealing both sides of any data quality issues.

4.4.6 Multiple Table Joins: Bringing Everything Together

Real-world analysis often requires combining information from more than two tables. Let's extend our example to include product information.

Order items

order_id	product_id	quantity
1001	101	1
1001	102	2
1002	103	1

SQL Query to Show Customer Names, Order Dates, and Product Names:

```
SELECT customers.name, orders.order_date, products.product_name,
  order_items.quantity
FROM customers
INNER JOIN orders ON customers.customer_id = orders.customer_id
INNER JOIN order_items ON orders.order_id = order_items.order_id
INNER JOIN products ON order_items.product_id = products.product_id;
```

Result

name	order_date	product_name	quantity
John Smith	2023-01-15	Laptop	1
John Smith	2023-01-15	Mouse	2
Jane Doe	2023-01-16	Keyboard	1

This multi-table join reveals the complete purchasing story, showing exactly which customers bought which products and when.

4.5 Common Merge Errors and Prevention Strategies

4.5.1 Understanding Why Merges Fail

Data integration in real-world environments is significantly more complex than textbook examples suggest. While academic exercises typically use clean, consistent data with perfect relationships, production systems contain data that has been entered by different people, imported from various sources, and modified over time by multiple applications. Understanding common failure patterns helps you anticipate and prevent problems before they affect your analysis.

4.5.2 Structural Issues: When Tables Don't Align Properly

4.5.2.1 Data Type Mismatches

A common issue in databases arises when the same logical information is stored using different data types in different tables. For example, one table might store a customer ID as a number, while another table stores it as text or includes leading zeros. Even though the values appear the same to us, the database treats them as different types. As a result, joins and other operations can fail or produce unexpected results, which can be confusing if you're not aware of the mismatch.

For instance, imagine three tables: one has customer_id as a number (1, 2, 3), another as text ("1", "2", "3"), and a third with leading zeros ("001", "002", "003"). If you try to join these tables directly, the database will not recognize these values as equal because it is comparing different data types. This is why it's crucial to ensure consistent data types across tables before performing joins.

To solve this, you can convert data types during the query. For example, if one table stores the ID as text, you can cast it to an integer so that it matches the numeric ID in the other table. This ensures that the join works as intended.

```
-- Example: joining tables with different data types
SELECT c.name, o.total_amount
FROM customers c
JOIN orders o
  ON c.customer_id = CAST(o.customer_id AS INTEGER);
```

You can also detect potential issues by checking the data types in each table using commands that describe the table structure. Additionally, examining patterns like the length of text-based IDs can reveal inconsistencies that could cause problems in joins.

```
-- Check data types of columns
DESCRIBE customers;  -- customer_id as INT
DESCRIBE orders;     -- customer_id as VARCHAR

-- Check lengths of text IDs for inconsistencies
SELECT customer_id, LENGTH(customer_id) AS id_length
FROM orders
GROUP BY customer_id, LENGTH(customer_id)
ORDER BY id_length;
```

By carefully checking and standardizing data types, you can prevent many common database errors and ensure accurate results.

4.5.3 Data Quality Issues: When Values Don't Match

4.5.3.1 Missing Key Values

Missing key values create orphaned records that can't participate in join operations. This can lead to incomplete analysis results without any warning, which may be confusing when your reports or queries return fewer rows than expected. For example, if an order references a customer_id that does not exist in the customers table, that order will be excluded in a standard inner join. Similarly, if the primary key in a table is missing or duplicated, it can cause incorrect aggregations or unexpected behavior in joins.

To detect missing key values, you can count how many NULL or missing entries exist in the foreign key column:

```
-- Count missing customer_id values in the orders table
SELECT COUNT(*) - COUNT(customer_id) AS missing_customer_ids
FROM orders;
```

This query subtracts the count of non-null customer_id values from the total number of rows, revealing how many orders are missing a valid customer reference.

4.5.3.2 Duplicate Key Values

It's important to check for duplicate primary keys because primary keys are meant to be unique. When duplicates exist, they can cause joins and aggregations to behave unpredictably, returning multiple matches or inflating results.

Example Problem:

Customers:

- ID 1: John Smith, john@email.com
- ID 1: John Smith, johnsmith@gmail.com (duplicate ID!)

Orders:

- Order 1001 → Customer ID 1 (Which John Smith does this belong to?)

Duplicates like this can lead to confusion and incorrect analysis because the database cannot determine which record to match.

To detect duplicate primary keys, you can use the following query:

```
-- Find duplicate customer_id values in the customers table
SELECT customer_id, COUNT(*) AS duplicate_count
FROM customers
GROUP BY customer_id
HAVING COUNT(*) > 1;
```

By running these checks, you can identify inconsistent records before performing joins. Once detected, duplicates can be corrected, merged, or handled appropriately in queries. For example, using LEFT JOIN can help preserve unmatched records, but resolving duplicates ensures data integrity and reliable analysis.

Multiple records with the same key violate uniqueness rules and can corrupt join results, so proactively detecting and addressing duplicate keys is essential for accurate database operations.

4.5.4 Business Logic Issues: When Relationships Don't Make Sense

4.5.4.1 Orphaned Records

Orphaned records occur in child tables when they reference parent records that no longer exist. This creates logical inconsistencies and can lead to inaccurate analysis. For example, an order might reference a customer that has been deleted, making it impossible to link the order to a valid customer.

To detect orphaned records, you can use a left join to find child table entries without matching parent records. For instance:

```
-- Find orphaned orders (orders without valid customers)
SELECT o.*
FROM orders o
LEFT JOIN customers c ON o.customer_id = c.customer_id
WHERE c.customer_id IS NULL;
```

You can also assess the business impact of these orphaned records, such as how many there are and the potential revenue they represent:

```
-- Calculate business impact of orphaned records
SELECT
    COUNT(*) AS orphaned_orders,
    SUM(total_amount) AS lost_revenue_tracking,
    AVG(total_amount) AS avg_orphaned_order_value
FROM orders o
LEFT JOIN customers c ON o.customer_id = c.customer_id
WHERE c.customer_id IS NULL;
```

By identifying orphaned records early, you can correct or handle them properly in your analysis, ensuring more accurate results and avoiding misleading business insights.

4.5.5 Duplicate Detection in Merged Data

When merging data from multiple sources, unexpected duplicates can appear. These duplicates can distort analysis results, such as inflating customer activity or total sales. Detecting and resolving these duplicates is crucial to maintain accurate reporting.

For example, if customer records appear multiple times after a merge, you can count the appearances to identify unexpected duplicates:

```
-- Count how many times each customer appears in merged data
SELECT customer_id, name, COUNT(*) AS appearance_count
FROM (
    SELECT c.customer_id, c.name, o.order_id
    FROM customers c
```

```
    LEFT JOIN orders o ON c.customer_id = o.customer_id
) merged_data
GROUP BY customer_id, name
HAVING COUNT(*) > 2;  -- More than expected for active customers
```

Once duplicates are detected, there are two common ways to resolve them. The first approach is aggregation, which summarizes all relevant information per customer:

```
-- Aggregate orders per customer
SELECT customer_id,
       name,
       COUNT(order_id) AS total_orders,
       SUM(total_amount) AS total_spending
FROM customers c
LEFT JOIN orders o ON c.customer_id = o.customer_id
GROUP BY customer_id, name;
```

Resulting table:

customer_id	name	total_orders	total_spending
1	John Smith	2	175.24
2	Jane Doe	1	149.50
3	Bob Wilson	0	0.00

The second approach is filtering, for example keeping only the most recent order per customer:

```
-- Keep only the most recent order per customer
SELECT c.name, o.order_date, o.total_amount
FROM customers c
JOIN (
    SELECT customer_id, MAX(order_date) AS latest_date
    FROM orders
    GROUP BY customer_id
) latest ON c.customer_id = latest.customer_id
JOIN orders o ON latest.customer_id = o.customer_id
             AND latest.latest_date = o.order_date;
```

By using aggregation or filtering strategies, you can remove duplicate effects and ensure your merged dataset accurately reflects each customer's activity.

4.5.6 Prevention Strategies: Building Robust Integration

The Pre-Merge Validation Checklist is designed to ensure your data is accurate and consistent before combining tables. The first step is to check key column quality. This means verifying that the columns you plan to join on, such as customer_id, have consistent data types across all tables. If one table stores customer IDs as numbers while another stores them as text, the database will not recognize them as matching values.

```
-- Validate data types before joining
SELECT
    'customers' as table_name,
    'customer_id' as column_name,
    DATA_TYPE as data_type
FROM INFORMATION_SCHEMA.COLUMNS
WHERE TABLE_NAME = 'customers' AND COLUMN_NAME = 'customer_id'

UNION ALL

SELECT
    'orders' as table_name,
    'customer_id' as column_name,
    DATA_TYPE as data_type
FROM INFORMATION_SCHEMA.COLUMNS
WHERE TABLE_NAME = 'orders' AND COLUMN_NAME = 'customer_id';
```

The second step is to verify referential integrity by checking that foreign keys reference valid primary keys:

```
-- Check for orphaned foreign keys
SELECT COUNT(*) as orphaned_orders
FROM orders o
LEFT JOIN customers c ON o.customer_id = c.customer_id
WHERE c.customer_id IS NULL;
```

The third step is to identify duplicate primary keys that could cause join problems:

```
-- Check for duplicate primary keys
SELECT customer_id, COUNT(*) as duplicate_count
FROM customers
GROUP BY customer_id
HAVING COUNT(*) > 1;
```

Finally, examine data distribution to understand the relationship patterns:

```
-- Analyze relationship patterns
SELECT
```

```
    'customers_without_orders' as metric,
    COUNT(*) as count
FROM customers c
LEFT JOIN orders o ON c.customer_id = o.customer_id
WHERE o.customer_id IS NULL

UNION ALL

SELECT
    'customers_with_orders' as metric,
    COUNT(DISTINCT c.customer_id) as count
FROM customers c
INNER JOIN orders o ON c.customer_id = o.customer_id;
```

By following this validation checklist, you can identify and resolve potential issues before they affect your analysis, ensuring more reliable and accurate results.

4.6 AI-Assisted Validation and Cross-Table Consistency

4.6.1 Using AI for Data Quality Assessment

AI tools can significantly enhance your ability to detect and resolve data quality issues in merged datasets. These tools can analyze patterns, suggest validation approaches, and help automate quality checks that would be time-consuming to perform manually.

What you might ask AI: "Help me validate the quality of my customer-order join"

AI might suggest:

```
-- Comprehensive data quality assessment
SELECT
    'Total Customers' as metric,
    COUNT(*) as value
FROM customers

UNION ALL

SELECT
    'Total Orders' as metric,
    COUNT(*) as value
FROM orders

UNION ALL

SELECT
```

```
    'Customers with Orders' as metric,
    COUNT(DISTINCT c.customer_id) as value
FROM customers c
INNER JOIN orders o ON c.customer_id = o.customer_id

UNION ALL

SELECT
    'Orders with Valid Customers' as metric,
    COUNT(*) as value
FROM orders o
INNER JOIN customers c ON o.customer_id = c.customer_id

UNION ALL

SELECT
    'Orphaned Orders' as metric,
    COUNT(*) as value
FROM orders o
LEFT JOIN customers c ON o.customer_id = c.customer_id
WHERE c.customer_id IS NULL;
```

This comprehensive assessment provides a complete picture of your data quality and relationship integrity.

4.6.2 AI-Powered Anomaly Detection

AI can help identify unusual patterns in your merged data that might indicate quality issues:

What you might ask AI: "Find unusual patterns in my customer order data"

AI might suggest:

```
-- Detect potential data anomalies
SELECT
    c.customer_id,
    c.name,
    COUNT(o.order_id) as order_count,
    SUM(o.total_amount) as total_spending,
    AVG(o.total_amount) as avg_order_value,
    CASE
        WHEN COUNT(o.order_id) > 10 THEN 'High Frequency'
        WHEN SUM(o.total_amount) > 1000 THEN 'High Value'
        WHEN AVG(o.total_amount) > 200 THEN 'High Average'
```

```
        ELSE 'Normal'
    END as anomaly_flag
FROM customers c
LEFT JOIN orders o ON c.customer_id = o.customer_id
GROUP BY c.customer_id, c.name
HAVING COUNT(o.order_id) > 5
    OR SUM(o.total_amount) > 500
    OR AVG(o.total_amount) > 150
ORDER BY total_spending DESC;
```

This analysis helps identify customers with unusual purchasing patterns that might warrant further investigation.

4.7 Conclusion

Merging and joining data sources is a fundamental skill for data analysis that requires understanding both technical implementation and business logic. Through proper use of primary and foreign keys, you can create reliable relationships between tables that support accurate analysis and reporting.

The various types of SQL joins—inner, left, right, and full outer—each serve specific purposes in data integration. Understanding when to use each type ensures that your analysis includes the appropriate data and excludes irrelevant or incomplete information.

Common merge errors can significantly impact analysis quality, but they can be prevented through systematic validation and quality checks. By understanding data type mismatches, missing values, duplicates, and orphaned records, you can build robust integration processes that maintain data integrity.

AI-assisted validation provides powerful tools for detecting and resolving data quality issues, enabling more efficient and accurate data integration. These tools can help automate quality checks and identify patterns that might be missed in manual validation processes.

As you continue developing your data analysis skills, remember that successful data integration requires both technical proficiency and business understanding. The goal is not just to combine data, but to create reliable, meaningful datasets that support accurate analysis and informed decision-making.

4.8 Key Terms

Primary Key – A unique identifier for each record in a database table that ensures no two records can have the same value.

Foreign Key – A field in one table that references the primary key of another table, creating relationships between tables.

Referential Integrity – Database rules that ensure relationships between tables remain valid and consistent.

Normalization – The process of organizing data into separate tables to eliminate redundancy and improve data integrity.

Inner Join – A join operation that returns only rows with matching values in both tables.

Left Join – A join operation that returns all rows from the left table and matching rows from the right table.

Right Join – A join operation that returns all rows from the right table and matching rows from the left table.

Full Outer Join – A join operation that returns all rows from both tables, with NULL values where matches don't exist.

Junction Table – A table used to implement many-to-many relationships between two other tables.

Orphaned Records – Records in a child table that reference parent records that no longer exist.

Data Type Mismatch – When the same logical information is stored using different data types in different tables.

Duplicate Detection – The process of identifying and resolving duplicate records in merged datasets.

Cross-Table Validation – Checking data consistency and integrity across multiple related tables.

One-to-Many Relationship – A relationship where one record in a parent table relates to multiple records in a child table.

Many-to-Many Relationship – A relationship where records in one table can relate to multiple records in another table and vice versa.

Cascade Delete – A referential integrity rule where deleting a parent record automatically deletes related child records.

Data Integration – The process of combining data from multiple sources into a unified dataset.

Join Condition – The criteria used to match records between tables in a join operation.

Null Values – Missing or unknown data values that require special handling in join operations.

Data Quality Assessment – The process of evaluating data accuracy, completeness, and consistency.

Anomaly Detection – Identifying unusual patterns or outliers in data that may indicate quality issues.

Validation Checklist – A systematic approach to verifying data quality before performing merge operations.

4.9 Review Questions

1. What is the difference between a primary key and a foreign key, and why are both necessary for relational databases?
2. Explain the four main types of SQL joins and provide a business scenario where each would be most appropriate.
3. How can data type mismatches cause join operations to fail, and what strategies can prevent these issues?
4. What are orphaned records, and how can they impact data analysis results?
5. Describe the difference between one-to-many and many-to-many relationships, providing examples of each.
6. How do duplicate primary keys affect join operations, and what methods can detect these duplicates?
7. What is referential integrity, and how do cascade, restrict, and set null rules work?
8. When would you choose a left join over an inner join for customer analysis?
9. How can AI tools assist in validating data quality after merge operations?
10. What steps should be included in a pre-merge validation checklist?
11. How do full outer joins help identify data quality issues in merged datasets?
12. What are the advantages and disadvantages of storing all information in a single table versus using normalized tables with joins?

4.10 References

[1] W3Schools. (2024). SQL Joins Tutorial. https://www.w3schools.com/sql/sql_join.asp

[2] SQLBolt. (2024). Interactive SQL Tutorial - Multi-table Queries with JOINs. https://sqlbolt.com/lesson/select_queries_with_joins

[3] Mode Analytics. (2024). SQL Tutorial - JOINs and UNIONs. https://mode.com/sql-tutorial/sql-joins/

[4] Codecademy. (2024). Learn SQL - Multiple Tables. https://www.codecademy.com

[5] PostgreSQL Documentation. (2024). Queries - Joins Between Tables. https://www.postgresql.org/docs/current/tutorial-join.html

4.11 Lab 4-1 Merging and Joining Data Sources

In this lab, you will learn how to combine data from multiple tables into one dataset for analysis. This is called joining or merging data. It is necessary because real-world data is usually stored in separate tables rather than one large file.

For example, an online bookstore stores customer information in one table, orders in another, and books in a third. Each table holds a different type of data. If you want to answer a question like “Which customers spend the most money?”, you must join these tables using shared IDs such as customer ID and book ID so that customers, orders, and prices can be linked together.

This structure exists to reduce duplication. If everything were stored in one table, customer details like name and email would be repeated for every order, making updates harder and increasing errors. Because of this structure, data analysis often requires joining tables to bring related information together for analysis.

4.11.1 Demonstration

4.11.1.1 Step 1: Create data

Our demonstration uses three related tables from an online bookstore: customers, orders, and books. This structure reflects how real businesses organize their data to maintain efficiency and consistency.

First, let's create our three related datasets and examine their structure.

```
# Load required packages
library(dplyr)  # For data manipulation and joins
library(DT)     # For displaying nice tables

# Create the Customers table
customers_text <- "customer_id,name,email,city
1,John Smith,john@email.com,Seattle
2,Jane Doe,jane@email.com,Portland
3,Bob Wilson,bob@email.com,Vancouver
4,Alice Brown,alice@email.com,Seattle"

customers <- read.csv(text = customers_text, stringsAsFactors =
↪ FALSE)
```

```
# Create the Orders table
orders_text <- "order_id,customer_id,order_date,total_amount
1001,1,2023-01-15,135.98
1002,2,2023-01-16,89.99
1003,1,2023-01-20,79.99
1004,3,2023-01-22,125.50"

orders <- read.csv(text = orders_text, stringsAsFactors = FALSE)

# Create the Books table
books_text <- "book_id,title,author,price,category
101,Data Science Handbook,Smith & Jones,89.99,Technical
102,Python Programming,Johnson,45.99,Programming
103,Machine Learning,Davis,79.99,Technical
104,Web Development,Miller,65.50,Programming
105,Statistics Guide,Wilson,59.99,Technical"

books <- read.csv(text = books_text, stringsAsFactors = FALSE)

# Display each table
print("=== CUSTOMERS TABLE ===")
```

```
[1] "=== CUSTOMERS TABLE ==="
```

```
print(customers)
```

```
  customer_id        name            email      city
1           1  John Smith  john@email.com   Seattle
2           2    Jane Doe  jane@email.com  Portland
3           3  Bob Wilson   bob@email.com Vancouver
4           4 Alice Brown alice@email.com   Seattle
```

```
print("=== ORDERS TABLE ===")
```

```
[1] "=== ORDERS TABLE ==="
```

```
print(orders)
```

```
  order_id customer_id order_date total_amount
1     1001           1 2023-01-15       135.98
2     1002           2 2023-01-16        89.99
3     1003           1 2023-01-20        79.99
4     1004           3 2023-01-22       125.50
```

```
print("=== BOOKS TABLE ===")
```

```
[1] "=== BOOKS TABLE ==="
```

```
print(books)
```

```
  book_id                  title         author price    category
1     101 Data Science Handbook Smith & Jones 89.99   Technical
2     102     Python Programming       Johnson 45.99 Programming
3     103       Machine Learning         Davis 79.99   Technical
4     104        Web Development        Miller 65.50 Programming
5     105        Statistics Guide       Wilson 59.99   Technical
```

4.11.1.2 Step 2: Understanding Keys

Before we can combine data from multiple tables, we need to understand how the tables are connected. In relational data, these connections are defined using keys. A primary key uniquely identifies each record in a table, while a foreign key creates a link between two tables. In this dataset, customers, orders, and books are stored separately, but they are related through shared identifiers. Understanding these relationships is essential because joins depend entirely on correctly matching keys across tables.

```
# Examine the key relationships
print("=== PRIMARY KEYS ===")
```

```
[1] "=== PRIMARY KEYS ==="
```

```
print("Customers table: customer_id (unique identifier for each
 ↪  customer)")
```

```
[1] "Customers table: customer_id (unique identifier for each customer)"
```

```
print("Orders table: order_id (unique identifier for each order)")
```

```
[1] "Orders table: order_id (unique identifier for each order)"
```

```
print("Books table: book_id (unique identifier for each book)")
```

```
[1] "Books table: book_id (unique identifier for each book)"
```

```
print("\n=== FOREIGN KEYS ===")
```

```
[1] "\n=== FOREIGN KEYS ==="
```

```
print("Orders table: customer_id (references
 ↪  customers.customer_id)")
```

```
[1] "Orders table: customer_id (references customers.customer_id)"
```

```r
print("This creates a relationship: one customer can have many
  ↪  orders")
```

```
[1] "This creates a relationship: one customer can have many orders"
```

```r
# Verify key uniqueness
print("\n=== KEY UNIQUENESS CHECK ===")
```

```
[1] "\n=== KEY UNIQUENESS CHECK ==="
```

```r
print(paste("Unique customers:",
  ↪  length(unique(customers$customer_id))))
```

```
[1] "Unique customers: 4"
```

```r
print(paste("Total customer records:", nrow(customers)))
```

```
[1] "Total customer records: 4"
```

```r
print(paste("Unique orders:", length(unique(orders$order_id))))
```

```
[1] "Unique orders: 4"
```

```r
print(paste("Total order records:", nrow(orders)))
```

```
[1] "Total order records: 4"
```

```r
# Show the relationship
print("\n=== CUSTOMER-ORDER RELATIONSHIPS ===")
```

```
[1] "\n=== CUSTOMER-ORDER RELATIONSHIPS ==="
```

```r
relationship_summary <- orders %>%
  group_by(customer_id) %>%
  summarise(order_count = n(), total_spent = sum(total_amount))
print(relationship_summary)
```

```
# A tibble: 3 x 3
  customer_id order_count total_spent
        <int>       <int>       <dbl>
1           1           2       216.
2           2           1        90.0
3           3           1       126.
```

This step establishes the structure that makes relational analysis possible. By identifying primary keys, we confirm that each table has a unique identifier for its records, and by identifying foreign keys, we see how the tables connect to one another. The relationship summary shows that a single customer can appear in multiple orders, reinforcing the idea of a one-to-many relationship. With these connections clearly defined, we are now ready to begin joining tables to build a complete, unified dataset for analysis.

4.11.1.3 Step 3: Inner Joins

Data tables rarely contain everything you need in one place, so we often combine them using joins. An inner join is the most selective type of join because it only keeps records that exist in both tables. If a customer does not have a matching order, that customer is removed from the result entirely. This makes inner joins useful when the focus is strictly on complete, matched records across datasets..

```r
# Inner join: Show customer names with their order information
customer_orders <- customers %>%
  inner_join(orders, by = "customer_id")

print("=== INNER JOIN: Customers with Orders ===")
```

```
[1] "=== INNER JOIN: Customers with Orders ==="
```

```r
print(customer_orders)
```

```
  customer_id       name           email      city order_id order_date
1           1 John Smith john@email.com   Seattle     1001 2023-01-15
2           1 John Smith john@email.com   Seattle     1003 2023-01-20
3           2   Jane Doe jane@email.com  Portland     1002 2023-01-16
4           3 Bob Wilson  bob@email.com Vancouver     1004 2023-01-22
  total_amount
1       135.98
2        79.99
3        89.99
4       125.50
```

```r
# Count results
print(paste("\nOriginal customers:", nrow(customers)))
```

```
[1] "\nOriginal customers: 4"
```

```r
print(paste("Customers with orders:", nrow(customer_orders)))
```

```
[1] "Customers with orders: 4"
```

```r
print(paste("Customers without orders:", nrow(customers) -
  ↪ length(unique(customer_orders$customer_id))))
```

```
[1] "Customers without orders: 1"
```

```
# Show which customers are missing
customers_with_orders <- unique(customer_orders$customer_id)
customers_without_orders <- customers[!customers$customer_id %in%
↪ customers_with_orders, ]
print("\n=== CUSTOMERS WITHOUT ORDERS (excluded by inner join)
 ↪  ===")
```

```
[1] "\n=== CUSTOMERS WITHOUT ORDERS (excluded by inner join) ==="
```

```
print(customers_without_orders)
```

```
  customer_id        name           email    city
4           4 Alice Brown alice@email.com Seattle
```

The inner join demonstrates how relational filtering works in practice. Only customers who have matching records in the orders table are included in the final output, while unmatched customers are automatically removed. This reduces the dataset to only meaningful linked records, which is useful when analyzing behavior such as purchasing activity. However, it also means that any customer without an order is excluded, which can be important to recognize when interpreting results or calculating totals.

4.11.1.4 Step 4: Left Joins

In real-world analysis, we often want to keep every record from a primary dataset, even when related data is missing. A left join accomplishes this by preserving all rows from the first (left) table and attaching matching records from the second table when they exist. If no match is found, the result is still included, but the missing values are filled with NA. This makes left joins especially useful for business questions where it is important to see both active and inactive entities in one view.

```
# Left join: Show all customers and their order information
all_customers_orders <- customers %>%
  left_join(orders, by = "customer_id")

print("=== LEFT JOIN: All Customers with Order Information ===")
```

```
[1] "=== LEFT JOIN: All Customers with Order Information ==="
```

```
print(all_customers_orders)
```

```
  customer_id        name           email     city order_id order_date
1           1  John Smith  john@email.com  Seattle     1001 2023-01-15
2           1  John Smith  john@email.com  Seattle     1003 2023-01-20
3           2    Jane Doe  jane@email.com Portland     1002 2023-01-16
```

```
4           3  Bob Wilson   bob@email.com Vancouver      1004 2023-01-22
5           4 Alice Brown alice@email.com   Seattle        NA       <NA>
  total_amount
1       135.98
2        79.99
3        89.99
4       125.50
5           NA
```

```
# Analyze customer activity
customer_activity <- all_customers_orders %>%
  group_by(customer_id, name, city) %>%
  summarise(
    order_count = sum(!is.na(order_id)),
    total_spent = sum(total_amount, na.rm = TRUE),
    .groups = 'drop'
  )

print("\n=== CUSTOMER ACTIVITY ANALYSIS ===")
```

```
[1] "\n=== CUSTOMER ACTIVITY ANALYSIS ==="
```

```
print(customer_activity)
```

```
# A tibble: 4 x 5
  customer_id name        city      order_count total_spent
        <int> <chr>       <chr>           <int>       <dbl>
1           1 John Smith  Seattle             2       216.
2           2 Jane Doe    Portland            1        90.0
3           3 Bob Wilson  Vancouver           1       126.
4           4 Alice Brown Seattle             0         0
```

```
# Identify inactive customers
inactive_customers <-
↪ customer_activity[customer_activity$order_count == 0, ]
print("\n=== INACTIVE CUSTOMERS (marketing opportunities) ===")
```

```
[1] "\n=== INACTIVE CUSTOMERS (marketing opportunities) ==="
```

```
print(inactive_customers)
```

```
# A tibble: 1 x 5
  customer_id name        city    order_count total_spent
        <int> <chr>       <chr>         <int>       <dbl>
1           4 Alice Brown Seattle           0           0
```

The left join expands the view of the dataset by retaining all customers, including those without any orders. This changes the analysis from a purely transactional perspective to a more complete customer perspective. Instead of losing records with no matches, we can now identify inactive customers, like Alice Brown, who appear with missing order values. This is particularly valuable in business contexts such as marketing and retention, where understanding who is not engaging is just as important as analyzing those who are.

4.11.1.5 Step 5: Right Joins and Full Joins

Different join types allow us to control how much of each dataset is preserved during merging. While left joins are the most commonly used in practice, right joins and full joins provide additional perspectives when we need to prioritize the second table or retain everything from both sources. A right join keeps all rows from the right table and matches data from the left when available, while a full join keeps every record from both tables regardless of whether matches exist. These joins are especially useful when comparing datasets or ensuring that no information is lost during integration.

```
# Right join: All orders with customer information (rarely used)
orders_customers <- customers %>%
  right_join(orders, by = "customer_id")

print("=== RIGHT JOIN: All Orders with Customer Information ===")
```

```
[1] "=== RIGHT JOIN: All Orders with Customer Information ==="
```

```
print(orders_customers)
```

```
  customer_id       name           email      city order_id order_date
1           1 John Smith john@email.com   Seattle     1001 2023-01-15
2           1 John Smith john@email.com   Seattle     1003 2023-01-20
3           2   Jane Doe jane@email.com  Portland     1002 2023-01-16
4           3 Bob Wilson  bob@email.com Vancouver     1004 2023-01-22
  total_amount
1       135.98
2        79.99
3        89.99
4       125.50
```

```
# Full join: All customers and all orders
full_customer_orders <- customers %>%
  full_join(orders, by = "customer_id")

print("\n=== FULL JOIN: Complete Dataset ===")
```

```
[1] "\n=== FULL JOIN: Complete Dataset ==="
```

```
print(full_customer_orders)
```

```
  customer_id        name             email      city order_id order_date
1           1  John Smith  john@email.com   Seattle     1001 2023-01-15
2           1  John Smith  john@email.com   Seattle     1003 2023-01-20
3           2    Jane Doe  jane@email.com  Portland     1002 2023-01-16
4           3  Bob Wilson   bob@email.com Vancouver     1004 2023-01-22
5           4 Alice Brown alice@email.com   Seattle       NA       <NA>
  total_amount
1       135.98
2        79.99
3        89.99
4       125.50
5           NA
```

```
# Compare join types
print("\n=== JOIN TYPE COMPARISON ===")
```

```
[1] "\n=== JOIN TYPE COMPARISON ==="
```

```
print(paste("Inner join rows:", nrow(customer_orders)))
```

```
[1] "Inner join rows: 4"
```

```
print(paste("Left join rows:", nrow(all_customers_orders)))
```

```
[1] "Left join rows: 5"
```

```
print(paste("Right join rows:", nrow(orders_customers)))
```

```
[1] "Right join rows: 4"
```

```
print(paste("Full join rows:", nrow(full_customer_orders)))
```

```
[1] "Full join rows: 5"
```

Right and full joins broaden the scope of our analysis by reducing restrictions on which records are included. A right join ensures that every order is retained even if customer details are missing, while a full join produces the most complete possible dataset by combining all records from both tables. Comparing the results across join types highlights an important principle in data integration: the more inclusive the join, the more potential there is for missing or unmatched values. Choosing between join types depends on whether the goal is precision (matching data only), coverage (keeping all records from one table), or completeness (retaining everything from both sources).

4.11.1.6 Step 6: Multiple Table Joins

In real business environments, data rarely lives in just two tables. Instead, information is distributed across multiple related tables to reduce redundancy and improve structure. To answer meaningful questions, analysts often need to combine three or more datasets in a single workflow. This requires chaining joins together, where each step adds another layer of detail. In this example, we move from customers to orders, then to order details, and finally to books, creating a complete view of what each customer purchased.

```
# Create order details table (many-to-many relationship through
 ↪  junction table)
order_details_text <- "order_id,book_id,quantity
1001,101,1
1001,102,2
1002,101,1
1003,103,1
1004,104,1
1004,105,1"

order_details <- read.csv(text = order_details_text,
↪  stringsAsFactors = FALSE)

print("=== ORDER DETAILS TABLE ===")
```

```
[1] "=== ORDER DETAILS TABLE ==="
```

```
print(order_details)
```

```
  order_id book_id quantity
1     1001     101        1
2     1001     102        2
3     1002     101        1
4     1003     103        1
5     1004     104        1
6     1004     105        1
```

```
# Complex join: Customer -> Orders -> Order Details -> Books
complete_analysis <- customers %>%
  inner_join(orders, by = "customer_id") %>%
  inner_join(order_details, by = "order_id") %>%
  inner_join(books, by = "book_id")

print("\n=== COMPLETE ANALYSIS: Customer Purchase Details ===")
```

```
[1] "\n=== COMPLETE ANALYSIS: Customer Purchase Details ==="
```

```r
print(complete_analysis[,1:6])
```

```
  customer_id       name           email      city order_id order_date
1           1 John Smith john@email.com   Seattle     1001 2023-01-15
2           1 John Smith john@email.com   Seattle     1001 2023-01-15
3           1 John Smith john@email.com   Seattle     1003 2023-01-20
4           2   Jane Doe jane@email.com  Portland     1002 2023-01-16
5           3 Bob Wilson  bob@email.com Vancouver     1004 2023-01-22
6           3 Bob Wilson  bob@email.com Vancouver     1004 2023-01-22
```

```r
print(complete_analysis[,7:10])
```

```
  total_amount book_id quantity                 title
1       135.98     101        1 Data Science Handbook
2       135.98     102        2    Python Programming
3        79.99     103        1      Machine Learning
4        89.99     101        1 Data Science Handbook
5       125.50     104        1       Web Development
6       125.50     105        1      Statistics Guide
```

```r
print(complete_analysis[,11:12])
```

```
         author price
1 Smith & Jones 89.99
2       Johnson 45.99
3         Davis 79.99
4 Smith & Jones 89.99
5        Miller 65.50
6        Wilson 59.99
```

```r
# Business insights from joined data
insights <- complete_analysis %>%
  group_by(name, category) %>%
  summarise(
    books_purchased = sum(quantity),
    total_spent = sum(price * quantity),
    .groups = 'drop'
  ) %>%
  arrange(desc(total_spent))

print("\n=== CUSTOMER PURCHASING PATTERNS BY CATEGORY ===")
```

```
[1] "\n=== CUSTOMER PURCHASING PATTERNS BY CATEGORY ==="
```

```
print(insights)
```

```
# A tibble: 5 x 4
  name       category    books_purchased total_spent
  <chr>      <chr>                 <int>       <dbl>
1 John Smith Technical                 2       170.
2 John Smith Programming               2        92.0
3 Jane Doe   Technical                 1        90.0
4 Bob Wilson Programming               1        65.5
5 Bob Wilson Technical                 1        60.0
```

This step demonstrates how relational data becomes powerful when multiple tables are combined into a single analytical view. By chaining joins together, we reconstruct the full business story—from who the customer is, to what they ordered, to the specific books and quantities purchased. This type of multi-table join is common in real databases where transactional systems are split into normalized structures.

The final output not only lists detailed transactions but also allows us to generate higher-level insights, such as total spending and purchasing patterns by category. This shows the key value of multi-table joins: they transform fragmented data into a coherent structure that supports both detailed reporting and strategic decision-making.

4.11.2 Practice

A company wants to analyze employee performance and project assignments. You have three related tables: employees, departments, and projects.

```
# Create the employee management dataset
employees_text <- "employee_id,name,department_id,hire_date,salary
1,Sarah Johnson,1,2022-01-15,75000
2,Mike Chen,2,2021-06-10,82000
3,Lisa Rodriguez,1,2023-03-20,68000
4,David Kim,3,2020-11-05,95000
5,Emma Wilson,2,2022-08-12,78000
6,James Brown,1,2021-12-01,71000"

employees <- read.csv(text = employees_text, stringsAsFactors =
↪ FALSE)

departments_text <-
↪ "department_id,department_name,manager_name,budget
1,Marketing,Jennifer Adams,250000
2,Engineering,Robert Taylor,400000
3,Sales,Michael Davis,300000
4,HR,Patricia Wilson,150000"
```

```
departments <- read.csv(text = departments_text, stringsAsFactors =
↪ FALSE)

projects_text <-
↪ "project_id,project_name,employee_id,start_date,end_date,budget
101,Website Redesign,2,2023-01-01,2023-06-30,50000
102,Mobile App,2,2023-07-01,2023-12-31,75000
103,Marketing Campaign,1,2023-02-15,2023-05-15,30000
104,Sales Training,4,2023-01-10,2023-03-10,20000
105,Data Analytics,5,2023-04-01,2023-09-30,60000
106,Brand Strategy,3,2023-03-01,2023-08-31,40000"

projects <- read.csv(text = projects_text, stringsAsFactors =
↪ FALSE)

print("=== EMPLOYEES TABLE ===")
```

```
[1] "=== EMPLOYEES TABLE ==="
```

```
print(employees)
```

```
  employee_id           name department_id  hire_date salary
1           1  Sarah Johnson             1 2022-01-15  75000
2           2      Mike Chen             2 2021-06-10  82000
3           3 Lisa Rodriguez             1 2023-03-20  68000
4           4      David Kim             3 2020-11-05  95000
5           5    Emma Wilson             2 2022-08-12  78000
6           6    James Brown             1 2021-12-01  71000
```

```
print("\n=== DEPARTMENTS TABLE ===")
```

```
[1] "\n=== DEPARTMENTS TABLE ==="
```

```
print(departments)
```

```
  department_id department_name    manager_name budget
1             1       Marketing  Jennifer Adams 250000
2             2     Engineering   Robert Taylor 400000
3             3           Sales   Michael Davis 300000
4             4              HR Patricia Wilson 150000
```

```
print("\n=== PROJECTS TABLE ===")
```

```
[1] "\n=== PROJECTS TABLE ==="
```

```
print(projects)
```

```
  project_id       project_name employee_id start_date   end_date budget
1        101   Website Redesign           2 2023-01-01 2023-06-30  50000
2        102         Mobile App           2 2023-07-01 2023-12-31  75000
3        103 Marketing Campaign           1 2023-02-15 2023-05-15  30000
4        104     Sales Training           4 2023-01-10 2023-03-10  20000
5        105     Data Analytics           5 2023-04-01 2023-09-30  60000
6        106     Brand Strategy           3 2023-03-01 2023-08-31  40000
```

4.11.2.1 Questions

1. Create an **inner join** between employees and departments using department_id. What does the resulting dataset include, and which employees (if any) are excluded?
2. Modify your join so that all employees are retained even if their department information is missing. What type of join should you use, and why?
3. Which employees belong to each department? Write a join that returns employee name, department name, and salary.
4. Perform a **left join** from departments to employees. What does this reveal about departments that have no employees?
5. Identify which department(s) have no assigned employees using a join-based approach.
6. Join employees and projects to show which employees are assigned to which projects. What happens to employees who are not assigned to any project?
7. Using a join, list all projects along with the employee name working on each project.
8. Perform a **multi-table join** combining employees, departments, and projects. What does the final dataset represent?
9. Which employee has worked on the highest number of projects? Use a join and summarization.
10. Which department has the highest total project budget (based on employees assigned to projects)?
11. Create a **full join** between employees and projects. What types of missing values appear, and what do they represent?
12. Compare an **inner join vs left join** between employees and projects. How do the row counts differ, and why?

Chapter 5

Filtering, Subsets, and Logical Selection

5.1 Learning Outcomes

5-1: Use WHERE clauses with conditional filters and Boolean logic to select specific data

5-2: Apply dynamic subsetting techniques to create flexible queries

5-3: Use AI tools to help generate and explain basic SQL filtering queries

5-4: Implement case filtering for simple exploratory data analysis

5.2 Introduction

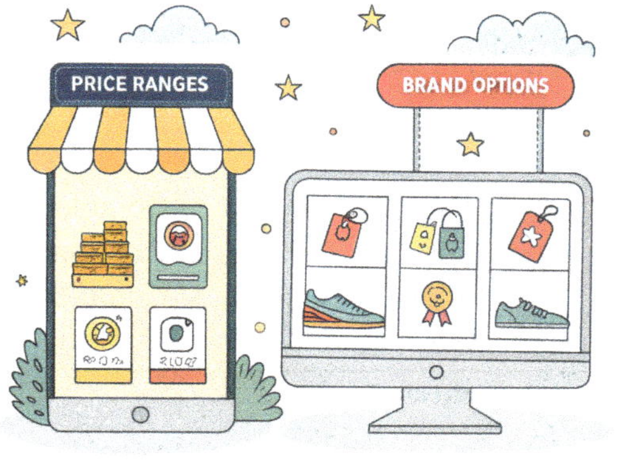

When working with databases, you rarely need all the data in a table. Most of the time, you want to find specific records that meet certain conditions. This is where filtering comes in - it's like using a search function to find exactly what you're looking for in a large dataset.

Filtering is essential because real-world databases often contain thousands or millions of records. Without the ability to filter data, you would be overwhelmed by information that isn't relevant to your current analysis. Learning to filter effectively is one of the most practical skills you can develop as a data analyst.

Think of filtering like shopping online. When you visit an e-commerce website, you don't want to see every single product. Instead, you use filters to narrow down your search - maybe you want shoes under $100, or electronics from a specific brand. SQL filtering works the same way, allowing you to specify exactly what criteria your data must meet.

The filtering techniques you'll learn in this module form the foundation for virtually all data analysis work. Whether you're creating reports, analyzing trends, or preparing data for visualization, you'll use these filtering concepts daily in your professional work.

Let's use a simple example throughout this module. Imagine you work for a small online bookstore and have these tables:

Customers Table

customer_id	name	age	city	membership
1	Alice	25	New York	Premium
2	Bob	35	Chicago	Standard
3	Carol	28	New York	Premium
4	David	42	Miami	Standard
5	Emma	31	Chicago	Premium

Orders Table

order_id	customer_id	book_title	price	order_date	status
101	1	Python Basics	29.99	2024-01-15	Completed
102	2	Data Science	45.00	2024-01-20	Completed
103	1	Web Design	35.50	2024-02-01	Pending
104	3	SQL Guide	32.00	2024-02-05	Completed
105	4	AI Handbook	55.99	2024-02-10	Cancelled

This bookstore example provides a realistic context for learning filtering concepts. The data includes different types of information - text, numbers, and dates - which will help you understand how filtering works with various data types. Now let's learn how to filter this data to answer specific questions.

5.3 Conditional Filters and Boolean Logic

5.3.1 Basic WHERE Clause

The WHERE clause is your main tool for filtering data. It tells the database which rows you want to see based on conditions you specify. Think of the WHERE clause as a gatekeeper that examines each row and decides whether it meets your criteria.

Understanding the WHERE clause is crucial because it's the foundation of all data filtering in SQL. Every time you want to narrow down your results, you'll use a WHERE clause to specify your conditions. The power of the WHERE clause lies in its flexibility - you can create simple conditions or combine multiple criteria to create sophisticated filters.

Basic Structure:

```
SELECT columns
FROM table
WHERE condition;
```

This structure is straightforward but powerful. The SELECT clause determines what information you want to see, the FROM clause specifies which table to look in, and the WHERE clause defines which rows to include. This logical flow makes SQL queries easy to read and understand.

Example 1: Find Premium customers

```
SELECT name, city, membership
FROM customers
WHERE membership = 'Premium';
```

Result Table showing Premium members:

name	city	membership
Alice	New York	Premium
Carol	New York	Premium
Emma	Chicago	Premium

This query demonstrates the most basic form of filtering - finding rows where a specific column equals a particular value. Notice how the result only includes customers whose membership status is exactly 'Premium'. This type of exact match filtering is very common in business analysis.

Example 2: Find expensive books (over $40)

```
SELECT order_id, book_title, price
FROM orders
WHERE price > 40;
```

Result Table for the selected orders:

order_id	book_title	price
102	Data Science	45.00
105	AI Handbook	55.99

This example shows how to filter using numeric comparisons. The greater-than operator (>) allows you to find all orders above a certain price threshold. This type of filtering is essential for business analysis, such as identifying high-value transactions or customers who spend above average amounts.

5.3.2 Comparison Operators

SQL provides several operators to compare values, each serving different analytical purposes. Understanding when to use each operator is key to creating effective filters that answer your business questions accurately.

The comparison operators are the building blocks of conditional logic in SQL. Each operator serves a specific purpose and helps you create precise filtering conditions. Learning to use these operators effectively will dramatically improve your ability to extract meaningful insights from data.

- **= (equals)** - finds exact matches
- **> (greater than)** - finds values above a threshold
- **< (less than)** - finds values below a threshold
- **>= (greater than or equal)** - includes the threshold value
- **<= (less than or equal)** - includes the threshold value
- **!= or <> (not equal)** - excludes specific values

The choice between >= and > (or <= and <) can be important depending on your business rules. For example, if you're looking for customers eligible for a senior discount at age 65, you would use >= to include 65-year-olds, not just those older than 65.

Example: Find customers under 30

```
SELECT name, age, city
FROM customers
WHERE age < 30;
```

Result Table with the selected customers:

name	age	city
Alice	25	New York
Carol	28	New York

This query helps identify younger customers, which might be useful for targeted marketing campaigns or demographic analysis. Age-based filtering is common in customer segmentation, where businesses want to understand different generational preferences and behaviors.

5.3.3 Text Filtering with LIKE

The LIKE operator is specifically designed for pattern matching in text data. This is incredibly useful because exact text matches are often too restrictive for real-world data analysis. Text data can vary in formatting, capitalization, or might contain additional words that prevent exact matches.

Pattern matching with LIKE gives you flexibility when working with text data that might not be perfectly standardized. This is particularly important when dealing with data entered by different people or imported from various sources, where consistency can't be guaranteed.

Use LIKE to search for patterns in text:

- **%** means "any characters" (including no characters)
- **_** means "any single character"

The percent sign (%) is the most commonly used wildcard because it allows you to find partial matches. This is essential when searching for product names, customer names, or any text field where you might not know the exact spelling or complete text.

Example: Find books with "Data" in the title

```
SELECT book_title, price
FROM orders
WHERE book_title LIKE '%Data%';
```

Result Table for the selected book:

book_title	price
Data Science	45.00

This pattern matching capability is extremely valuable for searching product catalogs, customer databases, or any situation where you need to find records containing specific words or phrases. The flexibility of LIKE makes it indispensable for exploratory data analysis.

5.3.4 Boolean Logic: AND, OR, NOT

Boolean logic allows you to combine multiple conditions to create sophisticated filtering criteria. This is where filtering becomes truly powerful, enabling you to answer complex business questions that require multiple criteria to be met simultaneously or alternatively.

Understanding Boolean logic is essential because real-world business questions rarely involve just one condition. You might want to find customers who are both Premium members AND live in specific cities, or orders that are either high-value OR from VIP customers. Boolean operators make these complex queries possible.

5.3.4.1 AND - Both conditions must be true

The AND operator creates more restrictive filters by requiring all conditions to be satisfied. This is useful when you need to narrow down your results to very specific criteria. AND logic is commonly used in business analysis to identify precise customer segments or transaction types.

```sql
SELECT name, age, city
FROM customers
WHERE age > 30 AND city = 'Chicago';
```

Result Table for the selected customer:

name	age	city
Emma	31	Chicago

This query finds customers who meet both criteria - they must be over 30 years old AND live in Chicago. Notice how this produces a more focused result than either condition alone would produce. This type of filtering is essential for targeted marketing or customer analysis.

5.3.4.2 OR - Either condition can be true

The OR operator creates more inclusive filters by accepting rows that meet any of the specified conditions. This is useful when you want to cast a wider net and include multiple categories or types of data in your analysis.

```sql
SELECT name, city, membership
FROM customers
WHERE city = 'New York' OR membership = 'Premium';
```

Result Table:

name	city	membership
Alice	New York	Premium
Carol	New York	Premium
Emma	Chicago	Premium

This query includes customers who either live in New York OR have Premium membership (or both). Notice that Alice and Carol appear because they meet both conditions, while Emma appears because she meets the Premium membership condition even though she doesn't live in New York.

5.3.4.3 NOT - Exclude certain conditions

The NOT operator allows you to exclude specific values or conditions from your results. This is particularly useful for removing unwanted data or focusing on everything except certain categories.

```
SELECT order_id, book_title, status
FROM orders
WHERE NOT status = 'Cancelled';
```

Result Table showing the selected orders with their status:

order_id	book_title	status
101	Python Basics	Completed
102	Data Science	Completed
103	Web Design	Pending
104	SQL Guide	Completed

This query shows all orders except those that were cancelled. Using NOT is often clearer than listing all the values you do want, especially when there are many possible values but only a few you want to exclude.

5.3.5 Combining Multiple Conditions

When you need to combine multiple Boolean operators, parentheses become essential for controlling the order of operations. Just like in mathematics, parentheses determine which conditions are evaluated together, ensuring your logic works as intended.

Proper use of parentheses is crucial for creating accurate filters. Without parentheses, SQL evaluates conditions in a specific order that might not match your intentions, potentially leading to incorrect results. Always use parentheses to make your logic explicit and clear.

Use parentheses to group conditions clearly:

```
SELECT name, age, city, membership
FROM customers
WHERE (age < 30 OR city = 'Miami') AND membership = 'Premium';
```

Result Table:

name	age	city	membership
Alice	25	New York	Premium
Carol	28	New York	Premium

This finds Premium customers who are either under 30 OR live in Miami. The parentheses ensure that the OR condition is evaluated first, then combined with the AND condition. Without parentheses, the logic would be interpreted differently and produce different results.

Understanding how to combine conditions effectively allows you to answer sophisticated business questions with a single query. This skill becomes increasingly valuable as you work with more complex datasets and business requirements.

5.4 Dynamic Subset and Query Prompts

5.4.1 Using IN for Multiple Values

The IN operator provides an efficient and readable way to check for multiple specific values in a single condition. This is much cleaner than writing multiple OR conditions and is easier to modify when your list of values changes.

The IN operator is particularly valuable when working with categorical data where you need to include several specific categories. Instead of writing long chains of OR conditions, IN allows you to specify all desired values in a simple, readable format.

Instead of writing multiple OR conditions, use IN to check for multiple values:

```
SELECT name, city
FROM customers
WHERE city IN ('New York', 'Chicago');
```

Result Table:

name	city
Alice	New York
Bob	Chicago

name	city
Carol	New York
Emma	Chicago

This query is equivalent to writing WHERE city = 'New York' OR city = 'Chicago', but it's much more concise and easier to read. The IN operator becomes even more valuable when you need to check for many values - imagine if you needed to include ten different cities!

The IN operator also makes your queries more maintainable. If you need to add or remove cities from your filter, you simply modify the list within the parentheses rather than restructuring the entire WHERE clause.

5.4.2 Date Range Filtering

Working with dates is a common requirement in business analysis, whether you're analyzing sales trends, customer behavior over time, or seasonal patterns. The BETWEEN operator provides an intuitive way to filter data within specific date ranges.

Date filtering is essential for time-based analysis, which is fundamental to understanding business trends and patterns. Most business questions involve some time component, making date filtering one of the most frequently used techniques in data analysis.

Use BETWEEN for ranges of values:

```
SELECT order_id, book_title, order_date
FROM orders
WHERE order_date BETWEEN '2024-01-01' AND '2024-01-31';
```

Result Table:

order_id	book_title	order_date
101	Python Basics	2024-01-15
102	Data Science	2024-01-20

The BETWEEN operator is inclusive, meaning it includes both the start and end dates in the results. This query finds all orders placed during January 2024, including orders on January 1st and January 31st. Understanding this inclusive behavior is important for accurate date range analysis.

BETWEEN works with any data type that can be ordered - numbers, dates, and even text. This makes it a versatile tool for range-based filtering across different types of data.

5.4.3 Creating Flexible Queries

Flexibility in query design means thinking about how your filtering criteria might change over time or for different analytical purposes. Building queries that can be easily modified saves time and reduces errors when your analysis requirements evolve.

Flexible query design is a hallmark of experienced data analysts. By anticipating how your filtering needs might change, you can create queries that are easy to modify and reuse for different scenarios.

You can make queries more flexible by thinking about different scenarios:

Example: Find recent high-value orders

```
SELECT order_id, customer_id, book_title, price, order_date
FROM orders
WHERE price >= 30
  AND order_date >= '2024-02-01'
  AND status = 'Completed';
```

Result Table:

order_id	customer_id	book_title	price	order_date
104	3	SQL Guide	32.00	2024-02-05

This query combines multiple filtering criteria to answer a specific business question: "What recent orders were both high-value and successfully completed?" Each condition serves a purpose - the price filter identifies high-value orders, the date filter focuses on recent activity, and the status filter ensures we only look at successful transactions.

The beauty of this approach is that you can easily modify any of these criteria. If you want to change the definition of "high-value" from $30 to $40, you simply change one number. If you want to look at a different time period, you modify the date. This flexibility makes your queries more valuable and reusable.

5.4.4 NULL Value Handling

NULL values represent missing or unknown data, and they require special handling in SQL because they don't behave like regular values. Understanding how to work with NULL values is crucial for accurate data analysis, especially when dealing with real-world data that often has missing information.

NULL values are a reality in most databases, occurring when information is not available, not applicable, or simply wasn't entered. Learning to handle NULL values properly ensures your analysis is accurate and complete.

Sometimes data is missing (NULL). Handle this with IS NULL or IS NOT NULL:

```
-- Find customers with missing age data (if any existed)
SELECT name, age, city
FROM customers
WHERE age IS NULL;

-- Find customers with complete age data
SELECT name, age, city
FROM customers
WHERE age IS NOT NULL;
```

It's important to note that you cannot use regular comparison operators (=, !=) with NULL values. The expression age = NULL will not work as expected because NULL represents "unknown," and you cannot compare something to an unknown value. This is why SQL provides the special IS NULL and IS NOT NULL operators.

Understanding NULL behavior is essential for data quality analysis. Before performing calculations or creating reports, you often need to understand how much of your data is complete and how missing values might affect your results.

5.5 Using AI to Generate or Explain SQL Queries

5.5.1 Getting Help from AI Tools

Modern AI tools have revolutionized how we approach SQL query writing by providing natural language interfaces that can translate business questions into working SQL code. This technology makes SQL more accessible to beginners while also helping experienced analysts work more efficiently.

AI query generation tools are particularly valuable for learning SQL because they can show you different ways to approach the same problem. By seeing how AI translates your natural language requests into SQL, you can learn new techniques and improve your own query-writing skills.

Modern AI tools can help you write SQL queries when you describe what you want in plain English. Here are some examples:

What you might ask AI: "Show me all premium customers from New York"

AI might generate:

```
SELECT name, city, membership
FROM customers
WHERE membership = 'Premium' AND city = 'New York';
```

This example demonstrates how AI can interpret natural language and convert it into proper SQL syntax. The AI correctly identified that you need to filter on two conditions (membership type and city) and combined them with an AND operator.

What you might ask AI: "Find orders over $40 that are completed"

AI might generate:

```
SELECT order_id, book_title, price, status
FROM orders
WHERE price > 40 AND status = 'Completed';
```

Notice how the AI translated "over $40" into the correct comparison operator (>) and understood that "completed" refers to the status field. This shows how AI can handle both numeric and text-based filtering requirements.

5.5.2 AI Query Explanations

One of the most valuable features of AI tools is their ability to explain existing SQL queries in plain English. This is particularly helpful when you encounter complex queries written by others or when you want to understand the logic behind a query you wrote some time ago.

AI explanations can help you learn SQL concepts by breaking down complex queries into understandable components. This educational aspect makes AI tools valuable not just for generating queries, but for improving your overall SQL knowledge.

AI can also explain existing queries in simple terms:

Query:

```
SELECT c.name, o.book_title, o.price
FROM customers c
JOIN orders o ON c.customer_id = o.customer_id
WHERE c.membership = 'Premium' AND o.price > 30;
```

AI Explanation: "This query finds the names of Premium customers along with the books they bought that cost more than $30. It connects the customers table with the orders table to show both customer information and their purchase details."

This explanation breaks down a complex query involving table joins and multiple conditions into understandable language. The AI identifies the key components: the data sources (customers and orders tables), the connection method (JOIN), and the filtering criteria (Premium membership and price threshold).

5.5.3 Simple AI Prompts for Filtering

When asking AI for help with filtering, being specific and clear in your requests will yield better results. The more precisely you describe what you want, the more accurate the generated SQL will be.

Effective communication with AI tools is a skill in itself. Learning to phrase your requests clearly and specifically will help you get better results and reduce the need for manual corrections to the generated code.

When asking AI for help with filtering, be specific:

- "Show customers older than 30"
- "Find orders from January 2024"
- "Get books that cost between $20 and $40"
- "List customers from Chicago or Miami"

Each of these prompts is clear and specific about what data you want and what conditions should be applied. The more specific your request, the more likely the AI will generate exactly the SQL you need.

5.5.4 Checking AI-Generated Queries

While AI tools are increasingly sophisticated, it's essential to review and validate any generated code before using it for important analysis. AI can make mistakes, especially with complex requirements or unusual data structures.

Developing the habit of reviewing AI-generated code will make you a better analyst and help you catch potential errors before they affect your results. This review process also helps you learn by seeing how different approaches can solve the same problem.

Always review AI-generated queries to make sure they:

1. Use the correct table and column names
2. Have the right filtering conditions
3. Make logical sense for your question

The first check ensures the query will actually run without errors. The second verifies that the logic matches your requirements. The third confirms that the overall approach makes sense for your analytical goals.

As you become more experienced with SQL, you'll develop an intuition for spotting potential issues in generated code. This skill is valuable not just for AI-generated queries, but for reviewing any SQL code, including your own.

5.6 Case Filtering for Exploratory Analysis

5.6.1 What is Exploratory Analysis?

Exploratory analysis is the process of investigating your data to discover patterns, relationships, and insights that might not be immediately obvious. Unlike confirmatory analysis where you test specific hypotheses, exploratory analysis involves asking open-ended questions and using various filtering techniques to examine your data from different angles.

This type of analysis is crucial in the early stages of any data project because it helps you understand what your data contains and what stories it might tell. Exploratory analysis often reveals unexpected patterns that lead to valuable business insights.

Exploratory analysis means looking at your data to discover patterns and answer questions you might not have thought of before. Filtering helps you examine different slices of your data.

The goal of exploratory analysis is to become familiar with your data and generate hypotheses for further investigation. This process often involves creating many different filters to examine various segments of your data, looking for interesting patterns or anomalies that warrant deeper analysis.

5.6.2 Basic Exploration Questions

Starting with simple, fundamental questions about your data helps establish a baseline understanding before moving to more complex analysis. These basic questions often reveal important characteristics of your dataset that influence how you approach more detailed analysis.

Every exploratory analysis should begin with basic questions that help you understand the overall structure and composition of your data. These foundational insights guide your subsequent analysis and help you identify areas that deserve deeper investigation.

Start with simple questions about your data:

Question 1: How many customers do we have by membership type?

```
SELECT membership, COUNT(*) as customer_count
FROM customers
GROUP BY membership;
```

Result Table:

membership	customer_count
Premium	3
Standard	2

This basic analysis reveals the distribution of customers across membership types. Understanding this distribution is important for business planning and helps you interpret other analyses in context. For example, if Premium customers behave differently, you need to know they represent 60% of your customer base.

Question 2: What's the average order value by status?

```sql
SELECT status, AVG(price) as average_price
FROM orders
GROUP BY status;
```

Result Table:

status	average_price
Completed	37.75
Pending	35.50
Cancelled	55.99

This analysis reveals an interesting pattern - cancelled orders have the highest average value. This might indicate that customers are more likely to cancel expensive orders, perhaps due to buyer's remorse or payment issues. This type of insight often emerges from basic exploratory analysis.

5.6.3 Exploring Customer Segments

Customer segmentation is a fundamental business analysis technique that involves dividing your customer base into groups with similar characteristics or behaviors. Filtering enables you to examine these different segments and understand how they differ from each other.

Segmentation analysis helps businesses understand their customer base better and develop targeted strategies for different groups. By using filtering to examine various customer segments, you can identify opportunities for personalized marketing, product development, and customer service improvements.

Example: Compare Premium vs Standard customers

```
-- Premium customer behavior
SELECT
    'Premium' as segment,
    COUNT(*) as customer_count,
    AVG(age) as avg_age
FROM customers
WHERE membership = 'Premium'

UNION ALL

-- Standard customer behavior
SELECT
    'Standard' as segment,
    COUNT(*) as customer_count,
    AVG(age) as avg_age
FROM customers
WHERE membership = 'Standard';
```

Result Table:

segment	customer_count	avg_age
Premium	3	28.0
Standard	2	38.5

This comparison reveals that Premium customers are younger on average than Standard customers. This insight could influence marketing strategies, product development, or customer acquisition efforts.

5.6.4 Geographic Analysis

Geographic filtering helps you understand regional patterns in your business, which can inform decisions about marketing, inventory, expansion, and customer service. Different regions often have distinct characteristics that affect business performance.

Understanding geographic patterns is essential for businesses that serve multiple markets. Regional differences in customer behavior, preferences, and economic conditions can significantly impact business strategy and operations.

Example: Analyze customers by city

```
SELECT
    city,
    COUNT(*) as customer_count,
    COUNT(CASE WHEN membership = 'Premium'
```

```
        THEN 1 END) as premium_count
FROM customers
GROUP BY city
ORDER BY customer_count DESC;
```

Result Table:

city	customer_count	premium_count
New York	2	2
Chicago	2	1
Miami	1	0

This analysis shows that New York has the highest concentration of Premium customers, while Miami has none. This geographic insight could influence decisions about premium service offerings or marketing investments in different cities.

5.6.5 Time-Based Patterns

Time-based analysis reveals trends, seasonality, and patterns that change over time. This type of analysis is crucial for understanding business cycles, planning inventory, and identifying growth opportunities.

Temporal patterns often reveal important business insights that aren't visible when looking at data in aggregate. Understanding how your business performs over time helps with forecasting, resource planning, and strategic decision-making.

Example: Orders by month

```
SELECT
    MONTH(order_date) as order_month,
    COUNT(*) as order_count,
    AVG(price) as avg_price
FROM orders
GROUP BY MONTH(order_date)
ORDER BY order_month;
```

Result Table:

order_month	order_count	avg_price
1	2	37.50
2	3	41.16

This temporal analysis shows that February had more orders and a higher average price than January. While this is a small sample, this type of analysis can reveal seasonal patterns, growth trends, and optimal timing for business activities.

5.7 Conclusion

Filtering is the foundation of effective data analysis, enabling you to focus on relevant information and extract meaningful insights from large datasets. Through WHERE clauses, Boolean logic, and various filtering techniques, you can answer specific business questions and explore your data systematically.

The skills you've learned in this chapter - from basic comparison operators to complex Boolean logic - form the building blocks for more advanced SQL techniques. Understanding how to filter data effectively will serve you well as you progress to more sophisticated analysis methods.

AI tools have made SQL more accessible by providing natural language interfaces for query generation and explanation. However, the fundamental understanding of filtering logic remains essential for creating accurate, meaningful analysis and for validating AI-generated code.

Exploratory analysis through filtering helps you discover patterns and insights that might not be immediately obvious. By systematically examining different segments of your data, you can generate hypotheses, identify opportunities, and make data-driven decisions that drive business value.

As you continue developing your SQL skills, remember that effective filtering is about more than just technical syntax - it's about asking the right questions and using logical thinking to extract insights that support business objectives.

5.8 Key Terms

WHERE Clause – The SQL clause used to specify conditions that filter which rows are returned in a query result.

Boolean Logic – A form of logic that uses operators like AND, OR, and NOT to combine multiple conditions.

Comparison Operators – Symbols used to compare values, including =, >, <, >=, <=, and != or <>.

LIKE Operator – A SQL operator used for pattern matching in text data, often used with wildcards.

Wildcards – Special characters used with LIKE for pattern matching: % (any characters) and _ (single character).

IN Operator – A SQL operator that allows checking for multiple specific values in a single condition.

BETWEEN Operator – A SQL operator used to filter data within a specific range of values.

NULL Values – Special values in databases that represent missing or unknown data.

IS NULL / IS NOT NULL – Special operators used to check for the presence or absence of NULL values.

Exploratory Analysis – The process of investigating data to discover patterns and generate insights without predetermined hypotheses.

Customer Segmentation – The practice of dividing customers into groups based on shared characteristics or behaviors.

Filtering – The process of selecting specific rows from a dataset based on defined criteria.

Conditional Logic – Programming logic that executes different actions based on whether conditions are true or false.

Pattern Matching – The technique of searching for specific patterns or sequences in text data.

Date Range Filtering – The process of selecting data within specific time periods or date ranges.

Geographic Analysis – Analysis that examines data patterns based on location or geographic regions.

Time-Based Analysis – Analysis that examines how data changes over time to identify trends and patterns.

AI Query Generation – The use of artificial intelligence tools to create SQL queries from natural language descriptions.

Query Validation – The process of reviewing and testing queries to ensure they produce accurate and expected results.

Dynamic Subsetting – Creating flexible filtering conditions that can be easily modified for different analytical purposes.

Logical Operators – Operators (AND, OR, NOT) used to combine or modify logical conditions in queries.

Data Quality Analysis – The process of examining data completeness, accuracy, and consistency, often involving NULL value analysis.

5.9 Review Questions

1. What is the purpose of the WHERE clause in SQL, and how does it function as a "gatekeeper" for data?
2. Explain the difference between the = and LIKE operators. When would you use each one?
3. How do AND, OR, and NOT operators differ in their effects on filtering results?
4. Why are parentheses important when combining multiple Boolean conditions in a WHERE clause?
5. What is the difference between the > and >= operators, and when might this distinction matter in business analysis?
6. How does the IN operator improve query readability compared to multiple OR conditions?
7. Explain why you cannot use regular comparison operators (= or !=) with NULL values.
8. What are the advantages and limitations of using AI tools for SQL query generation?
9. How does exploratory analysis differ from confirmatory analysis in terms of filtering approaches?
10. What types of business insights can be gained from geographic and time-based filtering?
11. How can the BETWEEN operator be used for both numeric and date range filtering?
12. What steps should you take to validate AI-generated SQL queries before using them for analysis?

5.10 References

[1] W3Schools. (2024). SQL WHERE Clause Tutorial.

[2] SQLBolt. (2024). Interactive SQL Tutorial - Filtering and Sorting Query Results. https://sqlbolt.com/lesson/filtering_sorting_query_results

[3] Mode Analytics. (2024). SQL Tutorial - Basic SQL. https://mode.com/sql-tutorial/introduction-to-sql/

[4] Codecademy. (2024). Learn SQL - Queries. https://www.codecademy.com/learn/learn-sql

[5] PostgreSQL Documentation. (2024). Pattern Matching. https://www.postgresql.org/docs/current/functions-matching.html

5.11 Lab 5-1 Introduction to SQL Using R

As datasets become larger and more complex, analysts often need tools that go beyond traditional R data manipulation functions. While R provides powerful functions for filtering, joining, and summarizing data, many real-world systems store and query data using SQL (Structured Query Language). SQL is the standard language used in databases across industries such as healthcare, finance, e-commerce, and government systems.

In this lab, we begin the transition from R-based data manipulation to SQL-style thinking using the sqldf package. This package allows us to write SQL queries directly inside R, using familiar data frames as if they were database tables. This creates an ideal bridge for learners: you can continue working in R while beginning to understand how database queries operate.

Rather than learning SQL in isolation, we will use existing R data frames and gradually introduce SQL concepts such as SELECT statements, filtering, ordering, aggregation, and joins. By the end of this lab, you will not only understand how SQL works but also how it connects directly to the data operations you have already learned in R.

5.11.1 Demonstration

5.11.1.1 Step 1: Setting Up SQL in R

Modern data analysis rarely involves working with a single table. Instead, data is typically stored across multiple related tables, similar to how databases are structured in real organizations. To prepare for working with these relational systems, we begin by introducing SQL-style querying directly inside R using the sqldf package.

The sqldf package creates a bridge between R and SQL by allowing data frames to be treated as database tables. This means we can write SQL queries—such as SELECT statements and JOIN operations—without leaving the R environment. This approach is especially useful for learners because it combines familiar R syntax with the structured logic of SQL, making the transition to database systems more intuitive.

In this step, we create two simple datasets that represent a typical relational structure found in business environments. One table contains individual-level information such as names and performance scores, while the second contains department-level and salary information. Both tables share a common identifier, ID, which will later be used to connect them through SQL joins.

```
options(repos = c(CRAN = "https://cloud.r-project.org"))
```

```r
# Load package
install.packages("sqldf")
```

```
package 'sqldf' successfully unpacked and MD5 sums checked

The downloaded binary packages are in
    C:\Users\drkse\AppData\Local\Temp\RtmpSKVmvR\downloaded_packages
```

```r
library(sqldf)

# Create dataset 1: individual performance data
df1 <- data.frame(
  ID = c(1, 2, 3, 4, 5, 6),
  Name = c("John", "Alice", "Bob", "Mary", "Tom", "Max"),
  Age = c(25, 30, 35, 40, 45, 27),
  Score = c(80, 85, 90, 95, 100, 99)
)

# Create dataset 2: department and salary data
df2 <- data.frame(
  ID = c(1, 2, 3, 5),
  Department = c("HR", "Finance", "IT", "Operations"),
  Salary = c(50000, 60000, 70000, 90000)
)

# Display datasets
print("=== DATASET 1: PERFORMANCE DATA ===")
```

```
[1] "=== DATASET 1: PERFORMANCE DATA ==="
```

```r
print(df1)
```

```
  ID  Name Age Score
1  1  John  25    80
2  2 Alice  30    85
3  3   Bob  35    90
4  4  Mary  40    95
5  5   Tom  45   100
6  6   Max  27    99
```

```r
print("=== DATASET 2: DEPARTMENT DATA ===")
```

```
[1] "=== DATASET 2: DEPARTMENT DATA ==="
```

```
print(df2)
```

```
  ID Department Salary
1  1         HR  50000
2  2    Finance  60000
3  3         IT  70000
4  5 Operations  90000
```

At this stage, we already have the foundation of a relational database structure. The ID column acts as a primary key in each table, allowing records to be matched across datasets. This shared structure is what makes SQL operations possible, since joins depend entirely on correctly aligned key fields. Even before writing any SQL queries, we can see that the data is already organized in a way that supports relational analysis.

5.11.1.2 Step 2: Understanding SQL Syntax Through Sorting Data

One of the best ways to begin learning SQL is by working with simple, readable operations that reveal how SQL structures its logic. Unlike R functions that often combine multiple steps implicitly, SQL requires each part of the operation to be written explicitly. This makes the process more transparent and easier to interpret, especially when working with large or complex datasets.

A fundamental SQL operation is sorting data using the ORDER BY clause. Sorting is commonly used in analysis and reporting to organize results in a meaningful sequence, such as ranking students by performance, ordering sales by revenue, or arranging records by date.

In SQL, we must explicitly state what we want to select, which table we are using, and how the results should be ordered.

```
score_asc <- sqldf("
  SELECT *
  FROM df1
  ORDER BY Score ASC
")

print("=== SORTED DATA (ASCENDING SCORE) ===")
```

```
[1] "=== SORTED DATA (ASCENDING SCORE) ==="
```

```
print(score_asc)
```

```
  ID  Name Age Score
1  1  John  25    80
2  2 Alice  30    85
3  3   Bob  35    90
```

```
4  4  Mary  40   95
5  6   Max  27   99
6  5   Tom  45  100
```

This query retrieves all columns from df1 and sorts the records based on the Score column in ascending order. The use of SELECT * indicates that all variables are included in the output, while ORDER BY Score ASC defines the sorting rule.

Unlike base R, where sorting can be performed with a single function call, SQL requires the analyst to explicitly describe both the data being selected and the logic used to arrange it. This structure may seem more verbose at first, but it reflects how database systems process queries internally and improves clarity when working with complex multi-step operations.

Sorting is widely used in real-world reporting systems. For example, analysts may rank employees by performance scores, order transactions by value, or identify the lowest and highest performing entities within a dataset. This foundational operation prepares you for more advanced SQL concepts such as filtering, grouping, and joining datasets.

5.11.1.3 Step 3: Aggregating Data with SQL Functions

One of the most important strengths of SQL is its ability to summarize data efficiently using aggregation functions. In traditional R workflows, summary statistics are often computed through a series of function calls or intermediate steps. SQL, however, allows these summaries to be expressed directly within a single query. This makes it especially powerful for reporting, dashboards, and database-level analysis where results must be computed quickly and consistently.

Common aggregation functions in SQL include SUM, COUNT, AVG, MIN, and MAX. These functions operate on entire columns and return a single summarized value, rather than returning row-level data.

5.11.1.3.1 Sum Function Calculation

The SUM function is used to calculate the total of all values in a numeric column. In this example, we compute the total of all scores in df1.

```
score_sum <- sqldf("
  SELECT SUM(Score)
  FROM df1
")

print("=== TOTAL SCORE (SUM) ===")
```

```
[1] "=== TOTAL SCORE (SUM) ==="
```

```
print(score_sum)
```

```
  SUM(Score)
1        549
```

5.11.1.3.2 Counting Distinct Values

Another commonly used aggregation function is COUNT, which can be combined with DISTINCT to identify the number of unique values in a column. This is particularly useful for understanding how many unique entities exist in a dataset.

```
n_ids <- sqldf("
  SELECT COUNT(DISTINCT ID)
  FROM df1
")

print("=== DISTINCT ID COUNT ===")
```

```
[1] "=== DISTINCT ID COUNT ==="
```

```
print(n_ids)
```

```
  COUNT(DISTINCT ID)
1                  6
```

This query counts the number of unique IDs in df1, helping confirm how many distinct individuals are represented in the dataset.

These aggregation operations highlight an important shift in analytical thinking. Instead of performing step-by-step transformations in R, SQL allows us to directly express the outcome we want. This declarative approach becomes especially valuable when working with large datasets stored in relational databases, where efficiency and clarity are essential.

5.11.1.4 Step 4: Introduction to SQL Joins

As datasets become more complex, it is no longer enough to analyze a single table in isolation. In real-world systems, related information is distributed across multiple tables to reduce redundancy and improve data organization. SQL joins are the mechanism that allows us to bring these separate tables together into a single, meaningful dataset by matching them on shared key values.

A join operation works by identifying a common column—often a primary key in one table and a foreign key in another—and using it to align related records. Among the different types of joins, the **inner join** is the most restrictive because it only returns records that have matching values in both tables. Any rows without a match are excluded from the result.

This makes inner joins particularly useful when the analysis requires complete, matched information from both datasets.

```
inner_join <- sqldf("
SELECT df1.ID, df1.Name, df1.Age, df1.Score,
df2.Department, df2.Salary
FROM df1
INNER JOIN df2 ON df1.ID = df2.ID
")

print("=== INNER JOIN RESULT ===")
```

```
[1] "=== INNER JOIN RESULT ==="
```

```
print(inner_join)
```

```
  ID  Name Age Score Department Salary
1  1  John  25    80         HR  50000
2  2 Alice  30    85    Finance  60000
3  3   Bob  35    90         IT  70000
4  5   Tom  45   100 Operations  90000
```

This query combines df1 and df2 by matching rows where the ID column exists in both tables. Only records with matching IDs are included in the final output, while non-matching rows are excluded automatically.

For example, IDs such as 4 and 6 from df1 are not present in df2, so those records do not appear in the result. This behavior illustrates an important concept in relational analysis: inner joins focus strictly on shared information across datasets.

Understanding inner joins is essential because they form the foundation for more advanced join types, including left joins, right joins, and full joins, which provide different levels of data inclusion depending on the analytical goal.

5.11.1.5 Step 5: Left Joins

While inner joins focus only on matching records between tables, real-world analysis often requires a more flexible approach. In many cases, analysts need to preserve all records from one dataset, even when matching information is missing from another. SQL provides additional join types—specifically left and right joins—that allow us to control which table is prioritized in the final result.

A **left join** keeps all records from the first (left) table and attempts to match records from the second table. When no match is found, the result still includes the original row from the left table, but missing values from the right table are filled with NULL. This is especially useful when the left table represents a complete list of entities, such as all customers or all employees.

```
left_join <- sqldf("
  SELECT df1.ID, df1.Name, df1.Age, df1.Score,
         df2.Department, df2.Salary
  FROM df1
  LEFT JOIN df2 ON df1.ID = df2.ID
")

print("=== LEFT JOIN RESULT ===")
```

```
[1] "=== LEFT JOIN RESULT ==="
```

```
print(left_join)
```

```
  ID  Name Age Score Department Salary
1  1  John  25    80         HR  50000
2  2 Alice  30    85    Finance  60000
3  3   Bob  35    90         IT  70000
4  4  Mary  40    95       <NA>     NA
5  5   Tom  45   100 Operations  90000
6  6   Max  27    99       <NA>     NA
```

This result shows that all records from df1 are preserved, even when no matching department information exists in df2. For example, IDs 4 and 6 appear in the output with missing values for Department and Salary. This is a key advantage of left joins: they allow analysts to maintain a complete view of the primary dataset while still integrating related information where available.

Additional Types

In addition to inner and left joins, SQL provides other join types that control how unmatched records are handled when combining tables.

A **right join** returns all rows from the second table, along with matching rows from the first table. If no match exists in the first table, the result still includes the row, but missing values are displayed as NULLs.

SELECT FROM TableA RIGHT JOIN TableB ON TableA.ID = TableB.ID;

A **full join** returns all rows from both tables, regardless of whether matches exist. When no match is found in either table, NULL values are shown in place of missing data.

SELECT *
FROM TableA FULL JOIN TableB ON TableA.ID = TableB.ID;

Overall, these join types expand flexibility in relational analysis by allowing analysts to decide whether to preserve one dataset, both datasets, or only matched records, depending on the needs of the analysis.

5.11.2 Practice

```
# Load package
library(sqldf)

# Create dataset
employees <- data.frame(
ID = c(1, 2, 3, 4, 5, 6, 7, 8),
Name = c("Anna", "Brian", "Cathy", "David", "Ella", "Frank", "Grace",
 ↪ "Henry"),
Department = c("HR", "Finance", "IT", "IT", "HR", "Marketing",
 ↪ "Finance", "IT"),
Age = c(25, 32, 29, 41, 38, 26, 45, 31),
Score = c(78, 88, 92, 85, 90, 76, 95, 89),
Salary = c(50000, 62000, 71000, 68000, 59000, 52000, 80000, 75000)
)

# View dataset
print(employees)
```

```
  ID  Name Department Age Score Salary
1  1  Anna         HR  25    78  50000
2  2 Brian    Finance  32    88  62000
3  3 Cathy         IT  29    92  71000
4  4 David         IT  41    85  68000
5  5  Ella         HR  38    90  59000
6  6 Frank  Marketing  26    76  52000
7  7 Grace    Finance  45    95  80000
8  8 Henry         IT  31    89  75000
```

5.11.2.1 Questions

1. Write a SQL query to display all columns from the employees table and show the output.
2. Write a SQL query to display only the Name and Score columns and show the output.
3. Write a SQL query to sort employees by Salary in descending order and show the output.

4. Write a SQL query to sort employees by Age in ascending order and show the output.
5. Write a SQL query to calculate the average Score of all employees and show the output.
6. Write a SQL query to calculate the total Salary paid to all employees and show the output.
7. Write a SQL query to count the total number of employees in the dataset and show the output.
8. Write a SQL query to count how many unique departments exist and show the output.
9. Write a SQL query to return all employees with a Score greater than 90 and show the output.
10. Write a SQL query to find the highest Salary in the dataset and show the output.
11. Write a SQL query to find the lowest Salary in the dataset and show the output.
12. Write a SQL query to calculate the average Salary for each Department and show the output

5.12 Lab 5-2 SQL Conditional Filters

In this lab, you will learn how to filter and extract meaningful subsets of data using SQL-style conditional logic within R. Real-world data is rarely useful in its raw form; analysts must continuously narrow, refine, and target specific records to answer business questions. This is where conditional filters such as WHERE clauses, comparison operators, pattern matching, and Boolean logic become essential tools.

We will work with a simulated e-commerce dataset from an online bookstore to represent a realistic business environment. The dataset includes customers and their purchasing behavior, along with order-level transaction data. Using the sqldf package, you will apply SQL queries directly to R data frames, allowing you to combine the clarity of SQL syntax with the analytical power of R.

Throughout this lab, you will progressively build more complex filters, starting with simple conditions and advancing to multi-condition logic using AND, OR, and NOT. By the end, you will be able to construct precise queries that isolate specific customer segments, identify high-value transactions, and support data-driven business decisions.

5.12.1 Demonstration

In this demonstration, we build a small e-commerce dataset representing customers and their book orders for an online bookstore. The goal is to use SQL-style conditional filters within R to explore how data can be selectively retrieved based on business rules such as membership level, spending behavior, product category, and order status.

We will use the sqldf package to apply SQL queries directly to R data frames, allowing us to combine structured query logic with R's data handling capabilities. This setup provides a practical foundation for learning how conditional filtering is used in real-world data analysis tasks such as customer segmentation and sales analysis.

5.12.1.1 Step 1: Setting Up

First, let's load the required packages and create our sample data frames.

```
# Load required packages
library(sqldf)      # For running SQL queries on data frames
library(dplyr)      # For additional data manipulation (optional)

# Create customers data frame
customers <- data.frame(
  customer_id = 1:8,
  name = c('Alice Johnson', 'Bob Smith', 'Carol Davis', 'David Wilson',
           'Emma Brown', 'Frank Miller', 'Grace Lee', 'Henry Taylor'),
  age = c(25, 34, 28, 45, 31, 52, 29, 38),
  city = c('New York', 'Chicago', 'New York', 'Miami',
           'Chicago', 'Boston', 'Seattle', 'Miami'),
  membership = c('Premium', 'Standard', 'Premium', 'VIP',
                 'Premium', 'Standard', 'VIP', 'Standard'),
  total_spent = c(450.75, 125.50, 680.25, 1250.00,
                  320.80, 89.99, 890.45, 156.30),
  join_date = as.Date(c('2023-01-15', '2023-02-20', '2023-01-10',
                        '2022-11-05', '2023-03-12', '2023-04-01',
                        '2022-12-18', '2023-02-28')),
  stringsAsFactors = FALSE
)

# Create orders data frame
orders <- data.frame(
  order_id = 101:110,
  customer_id = c(1, 2, 3, 1, 4, 5, 3, 6, 7, 4),
  book_title = c('Python Programming Basics',
                 'Data Science Fundamentals',
                 'Web Design Mastery',
                 'SQL for Beginners',
                 'Advanced Python Techniques',
                 'Machine Learning Guide',
                 'JavaScript Essentials',
```

```
                 'Digital Marketing 101',
                 'Data Visualization with Python',
                 'Cloud Computing Basics'),
  price = c(35.99, 45.00, 28.50, 32.75, 55.99, 48.25,
            39.99, 25.00, 42.50, 38.75),
  order_date = as.Date(c('2023-05-01', '2023-05-02', '2023-05-03',
                         '2023-05-04', '2023-05-05', '2023-05-06',
                         '2023-05-07', '2023-05-08',
                         '2023-05-09', '2023-05-10')),
  status = c('Shipped', 'Processing', 'Shipped', 'Delivered',
             'Shipped',  'Cancelled', 'Processing',
             'Delivered', 'Shipped', 'Processing'),
  category = c('Programming', 'Data Science', 'Design',
               'Database', 'Programming', 'Data Science',
               'Programming', 'Marketing', 'Data Science',
               'Technology'),
  stringsAsFactors = FALSE
)

# Display our sample data using R
cat("CUSTOMERS DATA FRAME:\n")
```

```
CUSTOMERS DATA FRAME:
```

```
print(customers[,1:4])
```

```
  customer_id          name age     city
1           1 Alice Johnson  25 New York
2           2     Bob Smith  34  Chicago
3           3   Carol Davis  28 New York
4           4  David Wilson  45    Miami
5           5    Emma Brown  31  Chicago
6           6  Frank Miller  52   Boston
7           7     Grace Lee  29  Seattle
8           8  Henry Taylor  38    Miami
```

```
print(customers[,5:7])
```

```
  membership total_spent  join_date
1    Premium      450.75 2023-01-15
2   Standard      125.50 2023-02-20
3    Premium      680.25 2023-01-10
4        VIP     1250.00 2022-11-05
5    Premium      320.80 2023-03-12
```

```
6   Standard      89.99 2023-04-01
7        VIP     890.45 2022-12-18
8   Standard     156.30 2023-02-28
```

```
cat("\nORDERS DATA FRAME:\n")
```

```
ORDERS DATA FRAME:
```

```
print(orders)
```

```
   order_id customer_id                          book_title price order_date
1       101           1      Python Programming Basics 35.99 2023-05-01
2       102           2      Data Science Fundamentals 45.00 2023-05-02
3       103           3             Web Design Mastery 28.50 2023-05-03
4       104           1             SQL for Beginners 32.75 2023-05-04
5       105           4     Advanced Python Techniques 55.99 2023-05-05
6       106           5        Machine Learning Guide 48.25 2023-05-06
7       107           3         JavaScript Essentials 39.99 2023-05-07
8       108           6          Digital Marketing 101 25.00 2023-05-08
9       109           7 Data Visualization with Python 42.50 2023-05-09
10      110           4         Cloud Computing Basics 38.75 2023-05-10
       status     category
1     Shipped  Programming
2  Processing Data Science
3     Shipped       Design
4   Delivered     Database
5     Shipped  Programming
6   Cancelled Data Science
7  Processing  Programming
8   Delivered    Marketing
9     Shipped Data Science
10 Processing   Technology
```

```
# Get basic information about our data
cat("\nData Summary:\n")
```

```
Data Summary:
```

```
cat("Number of customers:", nrow(customers), "\n")
```

```
Number of customers: 8
```

```
cat("Number of orders:", nrow(orders), "\n")
```

```
Number of orders: 10
```

```r
cat("Membership levels:", paste(unique(customers$membership), collapse
↪ = ", "), "\n")
```

```
Membership levels: Premium, Standard, VIP
```

```r
cat("Order statuses:", paste(unique(orders$status), collapse = ", "),
↪ "\n")
```

```
Order statuses: Shipped, Processing, Delivered, Cancelled
```

5.12.1.2 Step 2: Basic WHERE Clause Filtering

In this step, we introduce the SQL WHERE clause, which is used to filter rows in a dataset based on specific conditions. Instead of returning all records, WHERE allows us to select only the rows that meet a defined rule, such as a certain membership type, price range, or age group. This is the core mechanism for narrowing down data to the exact subset needed for analysis.

Using sqldf in R, we apply these SQL conditions directly to data frames to extract targeted groups of customers and orders. This demonstrates how WHERE acts as a filtering gate, controlling which records pass through for further analysis while leaving the original dataset unchanged.

```r
# Question 1: Who are our Premium customers?
premium_customers <- sqldf("
  SELECT name, city, membership, total_spent
  FROM customers
  WHERE membership = 'Premium'
")

cat("Premium Customers:\n")
```

```
Premium Customers:
```

```r
print(premium_customers)
```

```
           name     city membership total_spent
1 Alice Johnson New York    Premium      450.75
2   Carol Davis New York    Premium      680.25
3    Emma Brown  Chicago    Premium      320.80
```

```r
# Question 2: Which orders are worth more than $40?
expensive_orders <- sqldf("
  SELECT order_id, book_title, price, status
  FROM orders
```

```
  WHERE price > 40
")

cat("\nOrders over $40:\n")
```

```
Orders over $40:
```

```
print(expensive_orders)
```

```
  order_id                       book_title price     status
1      102      Data Science Fundamentals 45.00 Processing
2      105      Advanced Python Techniques 55.99    Shipped
3      106          Machine Learning Guide 48.25  Cancelled
4      109 Data Visualization with Python 42.50    Shipped
```

```
# Question 3: Find customers under 30 years old
young_customers <- sqldf("
  SELECT name, age, city, membership
  FROM customers
  WHERE age < 30
")

cat("\nCustomers under 30:\n")
```

```
Customers under 30:
```

```
print(young_customers)
```

```
           name age     city membership
1 Alice Johnson  25 New York    Premium
2   Carol Davis  28 New York    Premium
3     Grace Lee  29  Seattle        VIP
```

```
# Let's also create some business insights using R
cat("\n=== BUSINESS INSIGHTS ===\n")
```

```
=== BUSINESS INSIGHTS ===
```

```
cat("Premium customers:", nrow(premium_customers), "out of",
 ↪  nrow(customers),
    "(", round(nrow(premium_customers)/nrow(customers)*100, 1),
     ↪  "%)\n")
```

```
Premium customers: 3 out of 8 ( 37.5 %)
```

```r
cat("High-value orders:", nrow(expensive_orders), "out of",
 ↪ nrow(orders),
    "(", round(nrow(expensive_orders)/nrow(orders)*100, 1), "%)\n")
```

```
High-value orders: 4 out of 10 ( 40 %)
```

```r
cat("Young customers:", nrow(young_customers), "out of",
 ↪ nrow(customers),
    "(", round(nrow(young_customers)/nrow(customers)*100, 1),
     ↪ "%)\n")
```

```
Young customers: 3 out of 8 ( 37.5 %)
```

5.12.1.3 Step 3: Comparison Operators with SQL

In this step, we extend filtering beyond simple equality by using SQL comparison operators such as =, >=, <=, and !=. These operators allow us to define precise conditions for selecting data based on numeric thresholds and categorical differences. Instead of just asking whether a value matches something exactly, we can now identify ranges (such as high-value customers), boundaries (such as budget purchases), and exclusions (such as removing specific membership types). This makes queries more flexible and closer to real business decision-making.

Using sqldf in R, we apply these comparison rules directly to our customer and order data to isolate meaningful segments. The results are immediately returned as R data frames, allowing us to both inspect the filtered data and compute summary statistics for business insight.

```r
# Find customers who have spent exactly $450.75
exact_spender <- sqldf("
  SELECT name, total_spent, membership
  FROM customers
  WHERE total_spent = 450.75
")

cat("Customers who spent exactly $450.75:\n")
```

```
Customers who spent exactly $450.75:
```

```r
print(exact_spender)
```

```
           name total_spent membership
1 Alice Johnson      450.75    Premium
```

```
# Find customers who have spent $500 or more (high-value customers)
high_value_customers <- sqldf("
  SELECT name, total_spent, membership, city
  FROM customers
  WHERE total_spent >= 500
")

cat("\nHigh-value customers ($500+):\n")
```

```
High-value customers ($500+):
```

```
print(high_value_customers)
```

```
          name total_spent membership     city
1  Carol Davis      680.25    Premium New York
2 David Wilson     1250.00        VIP    Miami
3    Grace Lee      890.45        VIP  Seattle
```

```
# Find orders that are NOT expensive (under $35)
budget_orders <- sqldf("
  SELECT order_id, book_title, price, category
  FROM orders
  WHERE price <= 35
")

cat("\nBudget-friendly orders (under $35):\n")
```

```
Budget-friendly orders (under $35):
```

```
print(budget_orders)
```

```
  order_id             book_title price  category
1      103     Web Design Mastery 28.50    Design
2      104      SQL for Beginners 32.75  Database
3      108 Digital Marketing 101 25.00 Marketing
```

```
# Find customers who are NOT Standard members
non_standard <- sqldf("
  SELECT name, membership, total_spent
  FROM customers
  WHERE membership != 'Standard'
")
```

```r
cat("\nNon-Standard members:\n")
```

```
Non-Standard members:
```

```r
print(non_standard)
```

```
           name membership total_spent
1 Alice Johnson    Premium      450.75
2   Carol Davis    Premium      680.25
3  David Wilson        VIP     1250.00
4    Emma Brown    Premium      320.80
5     Grace Lee        VIP      890.45
```

```r
# Alternative syntax using <> (same result)
non_standard_alt <- sqldf("
  SELECT name, membership, total_spent
  FROM customers
  WHERE membership <> 'Standard'
")

cat("\nVerification - same query with <> operator:\n")
```

```
Verification - same query with <> operator:
```

```r
cat("Both queries return", nrow(non_standard), "rows\n")
```

```
Both queries return 5 rows
```

```r
# Create summary statistics using R
cat("\n=== BUSINESS ANALYSIS ===\n")
```

```
=== BUSINESS ANALYSIS ===
```

```r
cat("High-value customers represent",
↪  round(nrow(high_value_customers)/nrow(customers)*100, 1), "% of
↪  customer base\n")
```

```
High-value customers represent 37.5 % of customer base
```

```r
cat("Average spending by non-Standard members: $",
↪  round(mean(non_standard$total_spent), 2), "\n")
```

```
Average spending by non-Standard members: $ 718.45
```

```
cat("Budget orders represent",
↪  round(nrow(budget_orders)/nrow(orders)*100, 1), "% of all
↪  orders\n")
```

```
Budget orders represent 30 % of all orders
```

5.12.1.4 Step 4: Text Pattern Matching

In this step, we introduce the SQL LIKE operator, which is used to filter text data based on patterns rather than exact matches. This is especially useful when working with string fields such as names or book titles, where we may want to find partial matches, detect prefixes or suffixes, or search for keywords without knowing the full value. The LIKE operator makes it possible to search flexibly using wildcards such as %, which represents any sequence of characters.

Using sqldf in R, we apply these pattern-based filters to extract meaningful subsets of text data from our dataset. This allows us to move beyond exact comparisons and instead focus on how values are structured within strings, which is a common requirement in real-world text analysis and business reporting.

```
# Find all books with "Python" in the title
python_books <- sqldf("
  SELECT order_id, book_title, price, category
  FROM orders
  WHERE book_title LIKE '%Python%'
")

cat("Books with 'Python' in the title:\n")
```

```
Books with 'Python' in the title:
```

```
print(python_books)
```

```
  order_id                     book_title price     category
1      101       Python Programming Basics 35.99  Programming
2      105      Advanced Python Techniques 55.99  Programming
3      109 Data Visualization with Python 42.50 Data Science
```

```
# Find customers whose names start with 'A'
names_starting_a <- sqldf("
  SELECT name, city, membership
  FROM customers
  WHERE name LIKE 'A%'
")
```

```
cat("\nCustomers whose names start with 'A':\n")
```

```
Customers whose names start with 'A':
```

```
print(names_starting_a)
```

```
          name     city membership
1 Alice Johnson New York    Premium
```

```
# Find customers whose names end with 'son'
names_ending_son <- sqldf("
  SELECT name, age, city
  FROM customers
  WHERE name LIKE '%son'
")

cat("\nCustomers whose names end with 'son':\n")
```

```
Customers whose names end with 'son':
```

```
print(names_ending_son)
```

```
          name age     city
1 Alice Johnson  25 New York
2  David Wilson  45    Miami
```

```
# Find books with exactly 3 words in the title
three_word_titles <- sqldf("
  SELECT book_title, price, category
  FROM orders
  WHERE book_title LIKE '% % %' AND book_title NOT LIKE '% % % %'
")

cat("\nBooks with exactly 3 words in title:\n")
```

```
Books with exactly 3 words in title:
```

```
print(three_word_titles)
```

```
                 book_title price    category
1  Python Programming Basics 35.99 Programming
2  Data Science Fundamentals 45.00 Data Science
3        Web Design Mastery 28.50      Design
```

```
4          SQL for Beginners 32.75     Database
5 Advanced Python Techniques 55.99  Programming
6      Machine Learning Guide 48.25 Data Science
7       Digital Marketing 101 25.00    Marketing
8      Cloud Computing Basics 38.75   Technology
```

```
# Advanced pattern matching - find books with "Data" or "Science"
data_science_books <- sqldf("
  SELECT book_title, price, category
  FROM orders
  WHERE book_title LIKE '%Data%' OR book_title LIKE '%Science%'
")

cat("\nBooks related to Data or Science:\n")
```

```
Books related to Data or Science:
```

```
print(data_science_books)
```

```
                      book_title price     category
1      Data Science Fundamentals  45.0 Data Science
2 Data Visualization with Python  42.5 Data Science
```

5.12.1.5 Step 5: Boolean Logic - AND Operator in R

In this step, we introduce the Boolean AND operator, which is used to combine multiple conditions in a SQL query. Unlike single-condition filters, AND requires that **all conditions must be true at the same time** for a row to be included in the result. This makes it a powerful tool for narrowing data into very specific business segments, such as high-value customers in a specific location or products that meet multiple criteria.

Using sqldf in R, we apply AND logic to build more targeted queries across both customer and order data. This allows us to refine our analysis from broad filtering to precise segmentation, which is essential in real-world tasks like customer targeting, marketing analysis, and identifying high-value behavior patterns.

```
# Find Premium customers in New York
premium_ny <- sqldf("
  SELECT name, age, city, membership, total_spent
  FROM customers
  WHERE membership = 'Premium' AND city = 'New York'
")

cat("Premium customers in New York:\n")
```

```
Premium customers in New York:
```

```r
print(premium_ny)
```

```
          name age     city membership total_spent
1 Alice Johnson  25 New York    Premium      450.75
2   Carol Davis  28 New York    Premium      680.25
```

```r
# Find expensive Programming books (over $35)
expensive_programming <- sqldf("
  SELECT order_id, book_title, price, category, status
  FROM orders
  WHERE category = 'Programming' AND price > 35
")

cat("\nExpensive Programming books (>$35):\n")
```

```
Expensive Programming books (>$35):
```

```r
print(expensive_programming)
```

```
  order_id                  book_title price    category     status
1      101  Python Programming Basics 35.99 Programming    Shipped
2      105 Advanced Python Techniques 55.99 Programming    Shipped
3      107      JavaScript Essentials 39.99 Programming Processing
```

```r
# Find young, high-spending customers (under 35 AND spent over
↪ $400)
young_big_spenders <- sqldf("
  SELECT name, age, total_spent, membership
  FROM customers
  WHERE age < 35 AND total_spent > 400
")

cat("\nYoung, high-spending customers:\n")
```

```
Young, high-spending customers:
```

```r
print(young_big_spenders)
```

```
           name age total_spent membership
1 Alice Johnson  25      450.75    Premium
2   Carol Davis  28      680.25    Premium
3     Grace Lee  29      890.45        VIP
```

```
# Complex AND condition - Premium members who joined in 2023
recent_premium <- sqldf("
  SELECT name, membership, join_date, total_spent
  FROM customers
  WHERE membership = 'Premium' AND join_date >= '2023-01-01'
")

cat("\nPremium members who joined in 2023:\n")
```

```
Premium members who joined in 2023:
```

```
print(recent_premium)
```

```
[1] name        membership  join_date   total_spent
<0 rows> (or 0-length row.names)
```

5.12.1.6 Step 6: Boolean Logic - OR Operator in R

In this step, we introduce the Boolean OR operator, which is used to expand query results by including rows that satisfy **at least one of multiple conditions**. Unlike AND, which narrows results, OR broadens the selection and is useful when we want to capture multiple acceptable cases within a single query. This is commonly used in business analysis when defining flexible customer segments, product groups, or operational rules.

Using sqldf in R, we apply OR logic to identify broader patterns across customers and orders. This allows us to group related categories or behaviors together, such as combining multiple customer types or product categories into a single analysis.

```
# Find customers who are either VIP members OR have spent over $600
vip_or_big_spenders <- sqldf("
  SELECT name, membership, total_spent, city
  FROM customers
  WHERE membership = 'VIP' OR total_spent > 600
")

cat("VIP members OR big spenders (>$600):\n")
```

```
VIP members OR big spenders (>$600):
```

```
print(vip_or_big_spenders)
```

```
         name membership total_spent     city
1 Carol Davis    Premium      680.25 New York
```

```
2 David Wilson        VIP     1250.00    Miami
3    Grace Lee        VIP      890.45  Seattle
```

```
# Find books that are either Data Science OR Programming
tech_books <- sqldf("
  SELECT order_id, book_title, category, price
  FROM orders
  WHERE category = 'Data Science' OR category = 'Programming'
")

cat("\nData Science OR Programming books:\n")
```

```
Data Science OR Programming books:
```

```
print(tech_books)
```

```
  order_id                     book_title     category price
1      101      Python Programming Basics  Programming 35.99
2      102      Data Science Fundamentals Data Science 45.00
3      105     Advanced Python Techniques  Programming 55.99
4      106          Machine Learning Guide Data Science 48.25
5      107           JavaScript Essentials  Programming 39.99
6      109 Data Visualization with Python Data Science 42.50
```

```
# Find orders that are either high-value (>$45) OR already
↪ delivered
priority_orders <- sqldf("
  SELECT order_id, book_title, price, status
  FROM orders
  WHERE price > 45 OR status = 'Delivered'
")

cat("\nHigh-value OR delivered orders:\n")
```

```
High-value OR delivered orders:
```

```
print(priority_orders)
```

```
  order_id                 book_title price    status
1      104          SQL for Beginners 32.75 Delivered
2      105 Advanced Python Techniques 55.99   Shipped
3      106     Machine Learning Guide 48.25 Cancelled
4      108      Digital Marketing 101 25.00 Delivered
```

```
# Multiple OR conditions - customers in major cities
major_city_customers <- sqldf("
  SELECT name, city, membership, total_spent
  FROM customers
  WHERE city = 'New York' OR city = 'Chicago' OR city = 'Miami'
")

cat("\nCustomers in major cities (NY, Chicago, Miami):\n")
```

```
Customers in major cities (NY, Chicago, Miami):
```

```
print(major_city_customers)
```

```
          name     city membership total_spent
1 Alice Johnson New York    Premium      450.75
2     Bob Smith  Chicago   Standard      125.50
3   Carol Davis New York    Premium      680.25
4  David Wilson    Miami        VIP     1250.00
5    Emma Brown  Chicago    Premium      320.80
6  Henry Taylor    Miami   Standard      156.30
```

5.12.1.7 Step 7: Boolean Logic - NOT Operator in R

In this step, we introduce the Boolean NOT operator, which is used to **exclude specific conditions from a dataset**. Instead of selecting rows that match a condition, NOT filters them out, allowing us to focus on everything except a defined group. This is particularly useful in data analysis when removing unwanted categories, isolating non-target groups, or cleaning results to focus only on relevant records.

Using sqldf in R, we apply NOT logic across both customer and order data to demonstrate how exclusion-based filtering works in practice. This helps shift the focus from what meets a condition to what does not, which is a common requirement in business reporting, such as removing cancelled orders or excluding specific customer segments from analysis.

```
# Find all orders that are NOT cancelled
active_orders <- sqldf("
  SELECT order_id, book_title, status, price
  FROM orders
  WHERE NOT status = 'Cancelled'
")

cat("Active orders (NOT cancelled):\n")
```

```
Active orders (NOT cancelled):
```

```r
print(active_orders)
```

```
  order_id                     book_title     status price
1      101        Python Programming Basics    Shipped 35.99
2      102      Data Science Fundamentals Processing 45.00
3      103              Web Design Mastery    Shipped 28.50
4      104               SQL for Beginners  Delivered 32.75
5      105     Advanced Python Techniques    Shipped 55.99
6      107          JavaScript Essentials Processing 39.99
7      108            Digital Marketing 101  Delivered 25.00
8      109 Data Visualization with Python    Shipped 42.50
9      110           Cloud Computing Basics Processing 38.75
```

```r
# Alternative syntax using !=
active_orders_alt <- sqldf("
  SELECT order_id, book_title, status, price
  FROM orders
  WHERE status != 'Cancelled'
")

cat("\nVerification - same query with != operator:\n")
```

```
Verification - same query with != operator:
```

```r
cat("Both queries return", nrow(active_orders), "rows\n")
```

```
Both queries return 9 rows
```

```r
# Find customers who are NOT from New York or Chicago
non_metro_customers <- sqldf("
  SELECT name, city, membership, total_spent
  FROM customers
  WHERE NOT (city = 'New York' OR city = 'Chicago')
")

cat("\nCustomers NOT in NY or Chicago:\n")
```

```
Customers NOT in NY or Chicago:
```

```r
print(non_metro_customers)
```

```
         name    city membership total_spent
```

```
1 David Wilson   Miami        VIP    1250.00
2 Frank Miller  Boston   Standard      89.99
3    Grace Lee Seattle        VIP     890.45
4 Henry Taylor   Miami   Standard     156.30
```

```
# Find books that do NOT contain "Python" in the title
non_python_books <- sqldf("
  SELECT order_id, book_title, category, price
  FROM orders
  WHERE book_title NOT LIKE '%Python%'
")

cat("\nBooks NOT containing 'Python':\n")
```

```
Books NOT containing 'Python':
```

```
print(non_python_books)
```

```
  order_id                book_title     category price
1      102 Data Science Fundamentals Data Science 45.00
2      103         Web Design Mastery       Design 28.50
3      104          SQL for Beginners     Database 32.75
4      106    Machine Learning Guide Data Science 48.25
5      107     JavaScript Essentials  Programming 39.99
6      108      Digital Marketing 101    Marketing 25.00
7      110      Cloud Computing Basics   Technology 38.75
```

```
# Complex NOT condition - customers who are NOT Standard AND NOT
↪  under 30
mature_premium_customers <- sqldf("
  SELECT name, age, membership, total_spent
  FROM customers
  WHERE NOT membership = 'Standard' AND NOT age < 30
")

cat("\nMature premium customers (NOT Standard, NOT under 30):\n")
```

```
Mature premium customers (NOT Standard, NOT under 30):
```

```
print(mature_premium_customers)
```

```
          name age membership total_spent
1 David Wilson  45        VIP      1250.0
2   Emma Brown  31    Premium       320.8
```

5.12.1.8 Step 8: Combining Multiple Conditions in R

In this step, we combine multiple logical operators to build more advanced filters. Real business questions rarely rely on a single condition—instead, they often require combinations of AND, OR, and parentheses to control logic order. This allows us to define precise rules for selecting records that meet multiple criteria at once.

```
# Example: Young premium customers OR high spenders
young_valuable <- sqldf("
  SELECT name, age, membership, total_spent
  FROM customers
  WHERE age < 35 AND (membership = 'Premium' OR total_spent > 400)
")

cat("Young valuable customers:\n")
```

```
Young valuable customers:
```

```
print(young_valuable)
```

```
           name age membership total_spent
1 Alice Johnson  25    Premium      450.75
2    Carol Davis  28    Premium      680.25
3     Emma Brown  31    Premium      320.80
4      Grace Lee  29        VIP      890.45
```

This type of logic is commonly used for segmentation tasks where multiple business rules must be satisfied simultaneously, such as identifying high-value customer groups or prioritizing orders based on several conditions.

5.12.2 Practice

You're working as a data analyst for "TechBooks," an online retailer specializing in technology books. The company wants to better understand their customer base and optimize their marketing strategies using R and SQL.

```
# Create expanded dataset for exercises
tech_customers <- data.frame(
  customer_id = 201:210,
  first_name = c('Sarah', 'John', 'Maria', 'David', 'Lisa',
                 'Michael', 'Jennifer', 'Robert', 'Amanda',
                 'Kevin'),
  last_name = c('Connor', 'Smith', 'Garcia', 'Johnson', 'Wang',
                'Brown', 'Davis', 'Miller', 'Wilson', 'Taylor'),
  email = c('sarah.connor@email.com',
            'john.smith@email.com',
```

```
                 'maria.garcia@email.com',
                 'david.j@email.com',
                 'lisa.wang@email.com',
                 'mike.brown@email.com',
                 'jen.davis@email.com',
                 'rob.miller@email.com',
                 'amanda.w@email.com',
                 'kevin.taylor@email.com'),
  age = c(32, 28, 45, 35, 29, 52, 38, 41, 26, 33),
  city = c('Los Angeles', 'New York', 'Miami', 'Chicago',
           'Seattle', 'Boston', 'Austin', 'Denver',
           'Portland', 'Phoenix'),
  state = c('CA', 'NY', 'FL', 'IL', 'WA', 'MA', 'TX', 'CO',
            'OR', 'AZ'),
  membership_level = c('Gold', 'Silver', 'Platinum',
                       'Bronze', 'Gold', 'Silver', 'Platinum',
                       'Bronze', 'Gold', 'Silver'),
  account_balance = c(125.50, 89.25, 340.75, 45.00, 210.30,
                      156.80, 425.60, 67.90, 189.45, 98.75),
  last_purchase_date = as.Date(c('2023-04-15', '2023-05-02',
                                 '2023-04-28', '2023-03-20',
                                 '2023-05-10', '2023-04-05',
                                 '2023-05-08', '2023-03-15',
                                 '2023-05-12', '2023-04-22')),
  newsletter_subscriber = c(TRUE, FALSE, TRUE, TRUE, FALSE,
                            TRUE, TRUE, FALSE, TRUE, FALSE),
  stringsAsFactors = FALSE
)

# Display the exercise dataset
cat("TECHBOOKS CUSTOMER DATA:\n")
```

```
TECHBOOKS CUSTOMER DATA:
```

```
print(tech_customers[,1:5])
```

```
  customer_id first_name last_name                  email age
1         201      Sarah    Connor sarah.connor@email.com  32
2         202       John     Smith   john.smith@email.com  28
3         203      Maria    Garcia maria.garcia@email.com  45
4         204      David   Johnson      david.j@email.com  35
5         205       Lisa      Wang    lisa.wang@email.com  29
6         206    Michael     Brown   mike.brown@email.com  52
7         207   Jennifer     Davis    jen.davis@email.com  38
```

```
8           208     Robert     Miller   rob.miller@email.com  41
9           209     Amanda     Wilson      amanda.w@email.com  26
10          210      Kevin     Taylor kevin.taylor@email.com  33
```

```
print(tech_customers[,6:8])
```

```
          city state membership_level
1  Los Angeles    CA             Gold
2     New York    NY           Silver
3        Miami    FL         Platinum
4      Chicago    IL           Bronze
5      Seattle    WA             Gold
6       Boston    MA           Silver
7       Austin    TX         Platinum
8       Denver    CO           Bronze
9     Portland    OR             Gold
10     Phoenix    AZ           Silver
```

```
print(tech_customers[,9:10])
```

```
   account_balance last_purchase_date
1           125.50         2023-04-15
2            89.25         2023-05-02
3           340.75         2023-04-28
4            45.00         2023-03-20
5           210.30         2023-05-10
6           156.80         2023-04-05
7           425.60         2023-05-08
8            67.90         2023-03-15
9           189.45         2023-05-12
10           98.75         2023-04-22
```

```
# Quick data overview using R
cat("\n=== DATASET OVERVIEW ===\n")
```

```
=== DATASET OVERVIEW ===
```

```
cat("Total customers:", nrow(tech_customers), "\n")
```

```
Total customers: 10
```

```
cat("Membership levels:",
↪  paste(unique(tech_customers$membership_level), collapse = ",
↪  "), "\n")
```

```
Membership levels: Gold, Silver, Platinum, Bronze
```

```
cat("States represented:", paste(unique(tech_customers$state),
  ↪ collapse = ", "), "\n")
```

```
States represented: CA, NY, FL, IL, WA, MA, TX, CO, OR, AZ
```

```
cat("Newsletter subscribers:",
  ↪ sum(tech_customers$newsletter_subscriber), "out of",
  ↪ nrow(tech_customers), "\n")
```

```
Newsletter subscribers: 6 out of 10
```

```
cat("Average account balance: $",
  ↪ round(mean(tech_customers$account_balance), 2), "\n")
```

```
Average account balance: $ 174.93
```

5.12.2.1 Questions

1. Write an SQL query in R using sqldf to display all customers who are in the **Gold membership level**.
2. Find all customers who are **older than 35 years** and display their first name, last name, and age.
3. Retrieve all customers who live in **either New York, Chicago, or Seattle** using an OR condition.
4. Write a query to find customers whose **account balance is greater than $150**.
5. Identify all customers who are **NOT Silver members**.
6. Use a WHERE clause to list customers who **subscribed to the newsletter (TRUE)**.
7. Find customers who are **younger than 40 AND have an account balance greater than $100**.
8. Write a query to find customers whose **first name starts with the letter "J"**.
9. Retrieve customers whose **last name contains the letter "a" anywhere in the name**.
10. Find customers who are in **Platinum membership AND live in Texas (TX or Austin city)**.
11. Write a query to find customers who have a **last purchase date after May 1, 2023**.

12. Identify customers who are **either Gold members OR have account balance greater than $200**.
13. Find all customers who are **NOT newsletter subscribers AND have account balance under $100**.
14. Write a query that returns customers who are **between ages 30 and 45 inclusive**.
15. Create a query that finds customers who live in **California, Florida, or Arizona AND are Silver or Gold members**.

Chapter 6

Derived Fields and Transformations

6.1 Learning Outcomes

6-1: Create calculated fields and formulas to derive new information from existing data

6-2: Use conditional logic (CASE statements) to transform and categorize data

6-3: Apply text, date, and numeric transformations to clean and format data

6-4: Leverage AI tools for transformation suggestions and automation

6.2 Introduction

Sometimes the data you need for analysis doesn't exist directly in your database tables. Instead, you need to create new information by combining, calculating, or transforming the data you already have. This process of creating derived fields and transformations is

fundamental to data analysis and allows you to unlock insights that aren't immediately visible in raw data.

Derived fields are new columns that you create by performing calculations or transformations on existing data. These might be simple mathematical calculations like totals or percentages, or more complex transformations like categorizing customers based on their purchase behavior. The ability to create derived fields dramatically expands your analytical capabilities.

Think of derived fields like cooking - you start with basic ingredients (your raw data) and combine them in different ways to create something new and useful (insights). Just as a chef might combine flour, eggs, and milk to make pancakes, you might combine order quantities and prices to calculate total sales, or combine customer ages and purchase amounts to create customer segments.

Understanding how to create effective derived fields is crucial because it allows you to answer business questions that can't be answered with raw data alone. Questions like "What percentage of our revenue comes from premium customers?" or "Which customers should be classified as high-value?" require creating new calculated fields from existing data.

Let's continue with our bookstore example from Module 5, using the same tables but now focusing on how to create new, useful information from this existing data:

Customers Table

customer_id	name	age	city	membership
1	Alice	25	New York	Premium
2	Bob	35	Chicago	Standard
3	Carol	28	New York	Premium
4	David	42	Miami	Standard
5	Emma	31	Chicago	Premium

Orders Table

order_id	customer_id	book_title	price	order_date	status
101	1	Python Basics	29.99	2024-01-15	Completed
102	2	Data Science	45.00	2024-01-20	Completed
103	1	Web Design	35.50	2024-02-01	Pending
104	3	SQL Guide	32.00	2024-02-05	Completed
105	4	AI Handbook	55.99	2024-02-10	Cancelled

From this basic data, we can create many useful derived fields like customer lifetime value, age categories, seasonal sales patterns, and much more. Let's explore how to create these transformations effectively.

6.3 Calculated Fields and Formulas

6.3.1 Understanding Calculated Fields

Calculated fields are new columns that you create by performing mathematical operations on existing data. These calculations can be simple arithmetic (addition, subtraction, multiplication, division) or more complex formulas that combine multiple fields and functions. The power of calculated fields lies in their ability to create meaningful business metrics from raw data.

Creating calculated fields is essential because raw data rarely contains all the information you need for analysis. Business metrics like profit margins, growth rates, and performance indicators almost always require calculations based on multiple data points. Learning to create these calculations effectively is a core skill for any data analyst.

The beauty of calculated fields is that they're computed in real-time based on the current data, so they always reflect the most up-to-date information. This means you don't need to store calculated values separately - they're generated fresh each time you run your query.

6.3.2 Basic Mathematical Operations

SQL supports all standard mathematical operations, allowing you to create calculated fields using familiar arithmetic. These basic operations form the building blocks for more complex business calculations.

Understanding how to perform basic calculations in SQL is fundamental because most business analysis involves some form of mathematical computation. Whether you're calculating totals, averages, percentages, or growth rates, you'll use these basic operations constantly.

Example: Calculate tax amount (assuming 8% sales tax)

```
SELECT
    order_id,
    book_title,
    price,
    price * 0.08 as tax_amount,
    price + (price * 0.08) as total_with_tax
FROM orders
WHERE status = 'Completed';
```

Result:

order_id	book_title	price	tax_amount	total_with_tax
101	Python Basics	29.99	2.40	32.39

order_id	book_title	price	tax_amount	total_with_tax
102	Data Science	45.00	3.60	48.60
104	SQL Guide	32.00	2.56	34.56

This example demonstrates how you can create multiple calculated fields in a single query. The tax_amount field calculates 8% of the price, while total_with_tax adds the tax to the original price. These types of calculations are common in business analysis for financial reporting and pricing analysis.

Notice how the calculated fields appear as new columns in the result set. You can use these calculated values just like any other column - you can sort by them, filter on them, or use them in further calculations.

Example: Calculate simple discount

```
SELECT
    order_id,
    book_title,
    price,
    CASE
        WHEN price > 40 THEN 5.00
        ELSE 0.00
    END as discount_amount,
    price - CASE
        WHEN price > 40 THEN 5.00
        ELSE 0.00
    END as final_price
FROM orders;
```

Result:

order_id	book_title	price	discount_amount	final_price
101	Python Basics	29.99	0.00	29.99
102	Data Science	45.00	5.00	40.00
103	Web Design	35.50	0.00	35.50
104	SQL Guide	32.00	0.00	32.00
105	AI Handbook	55.99	5.00	50.99

This example shows a simple discount calculation where books over $40 get a $5 discount. This type of straightforward calculation is easy to understand and implement, making it perfect for business scenarios where you need clear, simple pricing rules.

6.3.3 Working with Aggregate Functions

Aggregate functions allow you to perform calculations across multiple rows of data, creating summary statistics that provide insights into overall patterns and trends. These functions are essential for business reporting and analysis because they help you understand the big picture of your data.

Aggregate functions are particularly powerful when combined with GROUP BY clauses, allowing you to create calculated fields that summarize data by different categories or time periods. This capability is fundamental to business intelligence and reporting.

Example: Calculate customer statistics

```
SELECT
    c.customer_id,
    c.name,
    c.membership,
    COUNT(o.order_id) as total_orders,
    SUM(o.price) as total_spent,
    AVG(o.price) as avg_order_value
FROM customers c
LEFT JOIN orders o ON c.customer_id = o.customer_id
    AND o.status = 'Completed'
GROUP BY c.customer_id, c.name, c.membership;
```

Customer statistics:

customer_id	name	membership	total_orders	total_spent	avg_order_value
1	Alice	Premium	1	29.99	29.99
2	Bob	Standard	1	45.00	45.00
3	Carol	Premium	1	32.00	32.00
4	David	Standard	0	NULL	NULL
5	Emma	Premium	0	NULL	NULL

This query creates a simple customer profile by calculating basic metrics for each customer. These calculated fields provide valuable insights into customer behavior and value. Notice how customers without completed orders show NULL values for the calculated fields - this is normal behavior when no data exists to calculate from.

6.3.4 Date Calculations

Date calculations are crucial for time-based analysis, allowing you to calculate periods between dates, extract specific time components, and create time-based metrics. Most business analysis involves some element of time, making date calculations an essential skill.

Working with dates effectively allows you to answer important business questions about trends, seasonality, customer lifecycle, and performance over time. These insights are fundamental to strategic business planning and operational decision-making.

Example: Calculate days since order

```
SELECT
    order_id,
    customer_id,
    book_title,
    order_date,
    DATEDIFF(CURRENT_DATE, order_date) as days_since_order,
    CASE
        WHEN DATEDIFF(CURRENT_DATE, order_date) <= 30
            THEN 'Recent'
        WHEN DATEDIFF(CURRENT_DATE, order_date) <= 90
            THEN 'Moderate'
        ELSE 'Old'
    END as order_age_category
FROM orders
ORDER BY order_date DESC;
```

This example calculates how many days have passed since each order was placed and categorizes orders by age. This type of analysis is useful for understanding order patterns and identifying recent versus historical activity.

Example: Extract simple date components

```
SELECT
    order_id,
    book_title,
    order_date,
    YEAR(order_date) as order_year,
    MONTH(order_date) as order_month,
    DAYNAME(order_date) as day_of_week
FROM orders
ORDER BY order_date;
```

Simple dates:

order_id	book_title	order_date	order_year	order_month	day_of_week
101	Python Basics	2024-01-15	2024	1	Monday

order_id	book_title	order_date	order_year	order_month	day_of_week
102	Data Science	2024-01-20	2024	1	Saturday
103	Web Design	2024-02-01	2024	2	Thursday
104	SQL Guide	2024-02-05	2024	2	Monday
105	AI Handbook	2024-02-10	2024	2	Saturday

Breaking down dates into components allows you to analyze patterns by year, month, or day of week. This is essential for identifying seasonal trends, understanding customer behavior patterns, and planning business operations.

6.4 Conditional Logic (CASE Statements)

6.4.1 Understanding CASE Statements

CASE statements are SQL's primary tool for implementing conditional logic, allowing you to create different outputs based on specific conditions. Think of CASE statements as the SQL equivalent of "if-then-else" logic that you might use in everyday decision-making.

CASE statements are incredibly powerful because they allow you to transform and categorize data based on business rules. This capability is essential for creating meaningful segments, applying business logic, and transforming raw data into actionable insights.

The flexibility of CASE statements makes them one of the most useful tools in SQL. You can use them to create simple categories, implement complex business rules, handle missing data, and transform values to make them more meaningful for analysis.

6.4.2 Simple CASE Statements

Simple CASE statements evaluate a single column against multiple possible values. This is useful when you want to transform or categorize data based on specific values in a field.

Simple CASE statements are perfect for creating readable labels from coded values, standardizing inconsistent data, or creating categories based on specific field values. They make your analysis results more understandable and business-friendly.

Example: Create readable membership labels

```
SELECT
    customer_id,
    name,
    membership,
    CASE membership
```

```
        WHEN 'Premium' THEN 'VIP Customer'
        WHEN 'Standard' THEN 'Regular Customer'
        ELSE 'Unknown Status'
    END as membership_label
FROM customers;
```

Membership Labels:

customer_id	name	membership	membership_label
1	Alice	Premium	VIP Customer
2	Bob	Standard	Regular Customer
3	Carol	Premium	VIP Customer
4	David	Standard	Regular Customer
5	Emma	Premium	VIP Customer

This example shows how CASE statements can create descriptive labels that make reports more readable and user-friendly. The membership_label field makes it immediately clear what each membership type means.

6.4.3 Searched CASE Statements

Searched CASE statements use conditions (like WHERE clauses) to evaluate multiple criteria. This is more flexible than simple CASE statements because you can use any logical condition, not just equality comparisons.

Searched CASE statements are essential for implementing business logic that involves ranges, multiple conditions, or calculations. They allow you to create sophisticated categorizations and transformations that reflect real-world business rules.

Example: Categorize customers by age

```
SELECT
    customer_id,
    name,
    age,
    CASE
        WHEN age < 30 THEN 'Young Customer'
        WHEN age < 40 THEN 'Middle-Age Customer'
        WHEN age >= 40 THEN 'Mature Customer'
        ELSE 'Unknown Age'
    END as age_category
FROM customers;
```

Customer Age Categories:

customer_id	name	age	age_category
1	Alice	25	Young Customer
2	Bob	35	Middle-Age Customer
3	Carol	28	Young Customer
4	David	42	Mature Customer
5	Emma	31	Middle-Age Customer

This example demonstrates how CASE statements can create age-based segments that are useful for marketing analysis and customer targeting. The age categories make it easy to group customers for different business strategies.

Example: Categorize orders by value

```
SELECT
    order_id,
    book_title,
    price,
    CASE
        WHEN price < 30 THEN 'Budget Order'
        WHEN price < 50 THEN 'Standard Order'
        WHEN price >= 50 THEN 'Premium Order'
        ELSE 'Unknown Value'
    END as order_category
FROM orders;
```

Order Category:

order_id	book_title	price	order_category
101	Python Basics	29.99	Budget Order
102	Data Science	45.00	Standard Order
103	Web Design	35.50	Standard Order
104	SQL Guide	32.00	Standard Order
105	AI Handbook	55.99	Premium Order

This value-based categorization helps identify different types of orders, which can be useful for inventory planning, pricing strategies, and understanding customer purchasing patterns.

6.4.4 Using CASE with Aggregate Functions

CASE statements become even more powerful when combined with aggregate functions, allowing you to create conditional counts, sums, and averages. This technique is essential for creating business metrics that depend on specific conditions.

Combining CASE statements with aggregate functions allows you to answer complex business questions like "How many high-value customers do we have?" or "What percentage of our revenue comes from premium members?" These insights are crucial for business strategy and planning.

Example: Calculate conditional metrics by membership type

```
SELECT
    c.membership,
    COUNT(c.customer_id) as total_customers,
    COUNT(o.order_id) as total_orders,
    SUM(CASE WHEN o.status = 'Completed'
        THEN o.price ELSE 0 END) as completed_revenue,
    COUNT(CASE WHEN o.price > 40 THEN 1 END)
        as high_value_orders
FROM customers c
LEFT JOIN orders o ON c.customer_id = o.customer_id
GROUP BY c.membership;
```

Membership Summary:

membership	total_customers	total_orders	completed_revenue	high_value_orders
Premium	3	2	61.99	0
Standard	2	3	45.00	2

This analysis provides insights into how different membership types perform across various metrics. The conditional aggregations allow you to calculate specific metrics like revenue from completed orders only, or count only high-value orders.

6.5 Text, Date, and Numeric Transformations

6.5.1 Text Transformations

Text transformations are essential for cleaning, standardizing, and extracting information from text data. Real-world data often contains inconsistent formatting, mixed cases, extra spaces, or embedded information that needs to be extracted or standardized.

Working with text data effectively is crucial because text fields often contain valuable information that needs to be cleaned or transformed before analysis. Learning these transformation techniques helps you handle messy real-world data and extract maximum value from text fields.

Example: Clean and standardize customer names

```
SELECT
    customer_id,
    name as original_name,
    UPPER(name) as name_uppercase,
    LOWER(name) as name_lowercase,
    LENGTH(name) as name_length
FROM customers;
```

Customer Name Transformations:

customer_id	original_name	name_uppercase	name_lowercase	name_length
1	Alice	ALICE	alice	5
2	Bob	BOB	bob	3
3	Carol	CAROL	carol	5
4	David	DAVID	david	5
5	Emma	EMMA	emma	4

This example demonstrates basic text transformation functions that are commonly used for data cleaning and standardization. These transformations are essential when working with data from multiple sources that might have different formatting conventions.

Example: Categorize books by title content

```
SELECT
    order_id,
    book_title,
    CASE
        WHEN book_title LIKE '%Python%' THEN 'Programming'
        WHEN book_title LIKE '%Data%' OR book_title LIKE '%SQL%'
          THEN 'Data Science'
        WHEN book_title LIKE '%Web%' THEN 'Web Development'
        WHEN book_title LIKE '%AI%' THEN 'Artificial Intelligence'
        ELSE 'General'
    END as book_category
FROM orders;
```

Book Categories:

order_id	book_title	book_category
101	Python Basics	Programming
102	Data Science	Data Science
103	Web Design	Web Development

order_id	book_title	book_category
104	SQL Guide	Data Science
105	AI Handbook	Artificial Intelligence

This example shows how you can extract meaningful categories from text data using pattern matching. This type of text analysis is valuable for content categorization and analysis.

6.5.2 Date Transformations

Date transformations allow you to extract specific components from dates, calculate time periods, and format dates for different purposes. These transformations are essential for time-based analysis and reporting.

Understanding date transformations is crucial because most business analysis involves time components. Whether you're analyzing trends, calculating ages, or creating time-based reports, you'll need to manipulate and format date data effectively.

Example: Extract date components

```
SELECT
    order_id,
    book_title,
    order_date,
    YEAR(order_date) as order_year,
    MONTH(order_date) as order_month,
    DAYNAME(order_date) as day_of_week,
    CASE
        WHEN DAYNAME(order_date) IN ('Saturday', 'Sunday')
```

```
            THEN 'Weekend'
        ELSE 'Weekday'
    END as day_type
FROM orders
ORDER BY order_date;
```

Order Date with Day Type:

order_id	book_title	order_date	order_year	order_month	day_of_week	day_type
101	Python Basics	2024-01-15	2024	1	Monday	Weekday
102	Data Science	2024-01-20	2024	1	Saturday	Weekend
103	Web Design	2024-02-01	2024	2	Thursday	Weekday
104	SQL Guide	2024-02-05	2024	2	Monday	Weekday
105	AI Handbook	2024-02-10	2024	2	Saturday	Weekend

This date analysis extracts useful components from the order date and creates additional insights like weekend versus weekday classification. These transformations enable detailed time-based analysis and reporting.

6.5.3 Numeric Transformations

Numeric transformations include rounding, mathematical functions, and formatting operations that make numeric data more useful for analysis and reporting. These transformations help you present numbers in meaningful ways and perform calculations that support business decision-making.

Numeric transformations are essential for creating clean, readable reports and performing calculations that match business requirements. Understanding these transformations helps you present data in ways that are meaningful to business stakeholders.

Example: Apply rounding and basic calculations to prices

```
SELECT
    order_id,
    book_title,
    price as original_price,
    ROUND(price, 0) as price_rounded,
    ROUND(price * 1.08, 2) as price_with_tax,
```

```
    CASE
        WHEN price < 35 THEN ROUND(price * 0.95, 2)
        ELSE ROUND(price * 0.90, 2)
    END as discounted_price
FROM orders;
```

Order Price Calculations:

order_id	book_title	price	price_rounded	price_with_tax	discounted_price
101	Python Basics	29.99	30	32.39	28.49
102	Data Science	45.00	45	48.60	40.50
103	Web Design	35.50	36	38.34	31.95
104	SQL Guide	32.00	32	34.56	30.40
105	AI Handbook	55.99	56	60.47	50.39

This example demonstrates basic numeric transformations including rounding, tax calculations, and conditional discounting. These transformations are commonly used in business analysis for pricing, financial calculations, and reporting.

6.5.4 Handling NULL Values

NULL values represent missing or unknown data, and they require special handling in transformations. Learning to work with NULL values effectively is crucial because real-world data often contains missing information that needs to be addressed appropriately.

Proper NULL handling ensures that your transformations produce accurate results even when some data is missing. This is essential for maintaining data quality and ensuring that missing values don't skew your analysis results.

Example: Handle NULL values in calculations

```
SELECT
    c.customer_id,
    c.name,
    c.age,
    COALESCE(SUM(o.price), 0) as total_spent,
    COALESCE(COUNT(o.order_id), 0) as order_count,
    CASE
        WHEN COALESCE(SUM(o.price), 0) = 0
            THEN 'No Purchases'
        WHEN COALESCE(SUM(o.price), 0) < 50
            THEN 'Low Spender'
```

```
        ELSE 'High Spender'
    END as spending_category
FROM customers c
LEFT JOIN orders o ON c.customer_id = o.customer_id
    AND o.status = 'Completed'
GROUP BY c.customer_id, c.name, c.age;
```

Customer Spending Categories:

customer_id	name	age	total_spent	order_count	spending_category
1	Alice	25	29.99	1	Low Spender
2	Bob	35	45.00	1	Low Spender
3	Carol	28	32.00	1	Low Spender
4	David	42	0.00	0	No Purchases
5	Emma	31	0.00	0	No Purchases

This example shows how to use COALESCE to handle NULL values in aggregations and how to create meaningful categories even when some customers have no purchase history. Proper NULL handling ensures accurate calculations and meaningful categorizations.

6.6 AI-Assisted Transformation Suggestions and Automation

6.6.1 Getting AI Help with Transformations

AI tools can significantly accelerate the process of creating data transformations by suggesting appropriate formulas, helping with complex calculations, and automating repetitive transformation tasks. These tools are particularly valuable when you're working with unfamiliar data or need to implement complex business logic.

AI assistance for transformations is especially helpful because it can suggest approaches you might not have considered and help you implement complex logic more efficiently. This capability allows you to focus on the analytical insights rather than getting bogged down in technical implementation details.

Modern AI tools can help you create transformations more efficiently and accurately. Here's how to leverage AI for common transformation tasks:

What you might ask AI: "Create a simple customer value score based on total spending"

AI might suggest:

```
SELECT
    c.customer_id,
    c.name,
```

```
    COALESCE(SUM(o.price), 0) as total_spent,
    CASE
        WHEN COALESCE(SUM(o.price), 0) >= 75
            THEN 'High Value'
        WHEN COALESCE(SUM(o.price), 0) >= 25
            THEN 'Medium Value'
        WHEN COALESCE(SUM(o.price), 0) > 0
            THEN 'Low Value'
        ELSE 'No Value'
    END as customer_value_score
FROM customers c
LEFT JOIN orders o ON c.customer_id = o.customer_id
    AND o.status = 'Completed'
GROUP BY c.customer_id, c.name;
```

This AI-generated transformation creates a simple customer value scoring system based on spending amount. The AI correctly handles NULL values and creates meaningful business categories.

What you might ask AI: "Calculate what percentage each customer contributes to total revenue"

AI might suggest:

```
SELECT
    c.customer_id,
    c.name,
    COALESCE(SUM(o.price), 0) as customer_revenue,
    ROUND(
        (COALESCE(SUM(o.price), 0) /
         (SELECT SUM(price) FROM orders
            WHERE status = 'Completed')) * 100,
        2
    ) as revenue_percentage
FROM customers c
LEFT JOIN orders o ON c.customer_id = o.customer_id
    AND o.status = 'Completed'
GROUP BY c.customer_id, c.name;
```

This AI solution calculates each customer's percentage contribution to total revenue, providing valuable insights into customer importance.

6.6.2 AI-Powered Data Cleaning Suggestions

AI tools can analyze your data and suggest appropriate cleaning and transformation strategies based on the patterns they detect. This capability is particularly valuable when working with messy or unfamiliar datasets.

AI-powered data cleaning suggestions can save significant time and help you identify transformation opportunities you might miss. These tools can spot patterns in your data and recommend standardization approaches that improve data quality and analytical value.

Example: AI suggestions for cleaning customer data

What you might ask AI: “Help me clean and standardize this customer data”

AI might analyze your data and suggest:

```
SELECT
    customer_id,
    -- Standardize name formatting
    UPPER(SUBSTRING(name, 1, 1)) ||
    LOWER(SUBSTRING(name, 2)) as standardized_name,
    -- Standardize city names
    UPPER(city) as city_standardized,
    -- Create age groups
    CASE
        WHEN age BETWEEN 18 AND 25 THEN '18-25'
        WHEN age BETWEEN 26 AND 35 THEN '26-35'
        WHEN age BETWEEN 36 AND 50 THEN '36-50'
        WHEN age > 50 THEN '50+'
        ELSE 'Unknown'
    END as age_group,
```

```
    -- Standardize membership
    CASE
        WHEN UPPER(membership) = 'PREMIUM' THEN 'Premium'
        WHEN UPPER(membership) = 'STANDARD' THEN 'Standard'
        ELSE 'Other'
    END as membership_clean
FROM customers;
```

This AI-suggested cleaning approach standardizes formatting, creates useful categories, and handles potential data inconsistencies.

6.6.3 Automating Complex Transformations

AI can help automate complex transformation workflows by suggesting efficient approaches and helping you implement multi-step transformations. This is particularly valuable for recurring analysis tasks or complex business logic implementation.

What you might ask AI: “Create a comprehensive customer analysis with multiple derived fields”

AI might suggest:

```
SELECT
    c.customer_id,
    c.name,
    c.age,
    c.city,
    c.membership,
    -- Order statistics
    COUNT(o.order_id) as total_orders,
    COALESCE(SUM(CASE WHEN o.status = 'Completed'
        THEN o.price END), 0) as total_revenue,
    COALESCE(AVG(CASE WHEN o.status = 'Completed'
        THEN o.price END), 0) as avg_order_value,
    -- Customer segmentation
    CASE
        WHEN COALESCE(SUM(CASE WHEN o.status = 'Completed'
            THEN o.price END), 0) >= 60 THEN 'High Value'
        WHEN COALESCE(SUM(CASE WHEN o.status = 'Completed'
            THEN o.price END), 0) >= 30 THEN 'Medium Value'
        WHEN COALESCE(SUM(CASE WHEN o.status = 'Completed'
            THEN o.price END), 0) > 0 THEN 'Low Value'
        ELSE 'No Value'
    END as customer_segment,
    -- Recency analysis
```

```
    CASE
        WHEN MAX(o.order_date) >= DATE_SUB(CURRENT_DATE,
            INTERVAL 30 DAY) THEN 'Recent'
        WHEN MAX(o.order_date) >= DATE_SUB(CURRENT_DATE,
            INTERVAL 90 DAY) THEN 'Moderate'
        WHEN MAX(o.order_date) IS NOT NULL THEN 'Inactive'
        ELSE 'Never Ordered'
    END as recency_status
FROM customers c
LEFT JOIN orders o ON c.customer_id = o.customer_id
GROUP BY c.customer_id, c.name, c.age, c.city, c.membership;
```

This comprehensive AI-generated analysis creates multiple derived fields that provide a complete customer profile including value segmentation and recency analysis.

6.7 Conclusion

Creating derived fields and transformations is fundamental to effective data analysis because it allows you to unlock insights that aren't immediately visible in raw data. Through calculated fields, conditional logic, and various transformation techniques, you can create meaningful business metrics and categories that drive decision-making.

The power of derived fields lies in their ability to transform raw data into actionable business intelligence. Whether you're calculating customer lifetime value, creating age-based segments, or implementing complex business rules through CASE statements, these techniques allow you to adapt your data to answer specific business questions.

Understanding how to work with text, dates, and numeric data through transformations ensures that you can handle the messy realities of real-world data. Combined with proper NULL handling and AI assistance, these skills enable you to create robust, reliable analysis that supports business objectives.

As you continue developing your SQL skills, remember that the goal of transformations isn't just to manipulate data, but to create meaningful insights that drive business value. The techniques you've learned in this chapter form the foundation for more advanced analytical work and will serve you well as you tackle increasingly complex business challenges.

6.8 Key Terms

Derived Fields – New columns created by performing calculations or transformations on existing data to generate additional insights.

Calculated Fields – Columns that result from mathematical operations performed on one or more existing fields in real-time.

CASE Statements – SQL conditional logic structures that allow different outputs based on specified conditions, similar to if-then-else logic.

Simple CASE – A CASE statement that evaluates a single column against multiple specific values.

Searched CASE – A CASE statement that uses conditional expressions (like WHERE clauses) to evaluate multiple criteria.

Aggregate Functions – SQL functions like SUM, COUNT, AVG, MIN, and MAX that perform calculations across multiple rows of data.

Text Transformations – Functions that modify text data, including UPPER, LOWER, LENGTH, and string manipulation operations.

Date Transformations – Functions that extract components from dates or calculate time periods, such as YEAR, MONTH, DATEDIFF.

Numeric Transformations – Operations that modify numeric data, including rounding, mathematical calculations, and formatting.

NULL Handling – Techniques for managing missing or unknown data values in calculations and transformations.

COALESCE – A SQL function that returns the first non-NULL value from a list of expressions, useful for handling missing data.

Conditional Aggregation – Using CASE statements within aggregate functions to create conditional counts, sums, or averages.

Business Logic – Rules and conditions that reflect real-world business requirements, often implemented through CASE statements.

Data Cleaning – The process of standardizing, correcting, and improving data quality through various transformation techniques.

Customer Segmentation – Dividing customers into groups based on shared characteristics, often created through derived fields.

Value Scoring – Creating metrics that quantify customer or transaction value, typically through calculated fields.

Recency Analysis – Evaluating how recently customers have engaged, often using date calculations and categorizations.

AI-Assisted Transformations – Using artificial intelligence tools to suggest, automate, or optimize data transformation processes.

Pattern Matching – Using LIKE operators and wildcards to identify and categorize data based on text patterns.

Time-Based Analysis – Analysis that focuses on temporal patterns and trends, enabled by date transformations.

Real-Time Calculations – Computed fields that are generated fresh each time a query runs, reflecting current data.

Data Standardization – Making data consistent in format, case, and structure across different sources or entries.

6.9 Review Questions

1. What are derived fields and why are they essential for data analysis?
2. How do calculated fields differ from stored data, and what are the advantages of real-time calculations?
3. Explain the difference between simple CASE and searched CASE statements, providing examples of when to use each.
4. How can CASE statements be combined with aggregate functions to create conditional metrics?
5. What are the key considerations when working with NULL values in transformations?
6. Describe common text transformation functions and their business applications.
7. How do date transformations support time-based analysis and business reporting?
8. What role do numeric transformations play in creating business-ready reports?
9. How can AI tools assist in creating and optimizing data transformations?
10. What are some best practices for handling missing data in calculated fields?
11. How do derived fields support customer segmentation and business intelligence?
12. What are the benefits and limitations of using AI for data cleaning suggestions?

6.10 References

[1] W3Schools. (2024). SQL CASE Statement Tutorial. https://www.w3schools.com/

[2] SQLBolt. (2024). Interactive SQL Tutorial - Expressions and Functions. https://sqlbolt.com/lesson/select_queries_with_expressions

[3] Mode Analytics. (2024). SQL Tutorial - CASE Statements and Conditional Logic. https://mode.com/sql-tutorial/sql-case/

[4] Codecademy. (2024). Learn SQL - Advanced Functions and Calculations. https://www.codecademy.com/learn/learn-sql

[5] PostgreSQL Documentation. (2024). Functions and Operators. https://www.postgresql.org/docs/current/functions.html

6.11 Lab 6-1 SQL Calculated Fields and Formulas

In this lab, you will take on the role of a business analyst at DataMart, a growing e-commerce company, tasked with answering key business questions such as identifying the most profitable products, calculating customer lifetime value, segmenting customers by age and spending behavior, and tracking sales performance over time. While the raw data contains essential details, it does not directly provide these insights—requiring you to create them using calculated fields.

Calculated fields are a core part of data analysis, allowing you to transform existing data into meaningful metrics through formulas, logic, and time-based calculations. Using SQL within R, you will build these calculations directly from the database and then use R to analyze and interpret the results. By the end of this lab, you will be able to turn raw data into actionable business insights that support real-world decision-making.

6.11.1 Demonstration

We'll work with DataMart's sales data to create various business metrics and insights. This scenario demonstrates typical e-commerce calculations that drive business decisions.

6.11.1.1 Step 1: Setting Up R Environment and Business Data

Let's create realistic business data with multiple tables for comprehensive analysis.

```
# Load required packages
library(sqldf)      # For SQL queries on data frames
library(dplyr)      # For additional data manipulation
library(lubridate)  # For advanced date handling

# Create products data frame
products <- data.frame(
  product_id = 1:8,
  product_name = c('Wireless Headphones', 'Smartphone Case',
                   'Bluetooth Speaker',
                   'Laptop Stand', 'USB Cable',
                   'Power Bank', 'Tablet Holder', 'Webcam'),
  category = c('Electronics', 'Accessories', 'Electronics',
               'Accessories', 'Accessories', 'Electronics',
               'Accessories', 'Electronics'),
  cost_price = c(45.00, 8.50, 25.00, 15.00, 3.00, 20.00, 12.00,
                 35.00),
```

```
  selling_price = c(79.99, 19.99, 49.99, 29.99, 9.99, 39.99,
                    24.99, 69.99),
  stringsAsFactors = FALSE
)

# Create customers data frame
customers <- data.frame(
  customer_id = 1:10,
  customer_name = c('Alice Johnson', 'Bob Smith', 'Carol Davis',
                    'David Wilson', 'Emma Brown', 'Frank Miller',
                    'Grace Lee', 'Henry Taylor',
                    'Iris Chen', 'Jack Robinson'),
  birth_date = as.Date(c('1990-03-15', '1985-07-22', '1992-11-08',
                         '1978-05-14', '1988-09-30', '1975-12-03',
                         '1995-02-18', '1982-08-25',
                         '1991-06-12', '1987-04-07')),
  registration_date = as.Date(c('2023-01-15', '2023-02-20',
                                '2023-01-10', '2022-11-05',
                                '2023-03-12', '2023-04-01',
                                '2022-12-18', '2023-02-28',
                                '2023-05-05', '2023-03-20')),
  city = c('New York', 'Chicago', 'New York', 'Miami', 'Chicago',
           'Boston', 'Seattle', 'Miami', 'Los Angeles', 'Boston'),
  stringsAsFactors = FALSE
)

# Create sales data frame
sales <- data.frame(
  sale_id = 1:15,
  customer_id = c(1, 2, 3, 1, 4, 5, 3, 6, 7, 2, 8, 9, 4, 10, 5),
  product_id = c(1, 2, 3, 4, 5, 1, 6, 7, 8, 3, 2, 4, 1, 5, 6),
  quantity = c(1, 2, 1, 1, 3, 1, 2, 1, 1, 1, 1, 1, 1, 2, 1),
  sale_date = as.Date(c('2023-06-01', '2023-06-02', '2023-06-03',
                        '2023-06-04', '2023-06-05', '2023-06-06',
                        '2023-06-07', '2023-06-08', '2023-06-09',
                        '2023-06-10', '2023-06-11', '2023-06-12',
                        '2023-06-13', '2023-06-14', '2023-06-15')),
  stringsAsFactors = FALSE
)

# Display our business data
cat("PRODUCTS DATA:\n")
```

```
PRODUCTS DATA:
```

```r
print(products)
```

```
  product_id        product_name    category cost_price selling_price
1          1 Wireless Headphones Electronics       45.0         79.99
2          2     Smartphone Case Accessories        8.5         19.99
3          3   Bluetooth Speaker Electronics       25.0         49.99
4          4        Laptop Stand Accessories       15.0         29.99
5          5           USB Cable Accessories        3.0          9.99
6          6          Power Bank Electronics       20.0         39.99
7          7       Tablet Holder Accessories       12.0         24.99
8          8              Webcam Electronics       35.0         69.99
```

```r
cat("\nCUSTOMERS DATA:\n")
```

```
CUSTOMERS DATA:
```

```r
print(customers)
```

```
   customer_id customer_name birth_date registration_date        city
1            1 Alice Johnson 1990-03-15        2023-01-15    New York
2            2     Bob Smith 1985-07-22        2023-02-20     Chicago
3            3   Carol Davis 1992-11-08        2023-01-10    New York
4            4  David Wilson 1978-05-14        2022-11-05       Miami
5            5    Emma Brown 1988-09-30        2023-03-12     Chicago
6            6  Frank Miller 1975-12-03        2023-04-01      Boston
7            7     Grace Lee 1995-02-18        2022-12-18     Seattle
8            8  Henry Taylor 1982-08-25        2023-02-28       Miami
9            9     Iris Chen 1991-06-12        2023-05-05 Los Angeles
10          10 Jack Robinson 1987-04-07        2023-03-20      Boston
```

```r
cat("\nSALES DATA:\n")
```

```
SALES DATA:
```

```r
print(sales)
```

```
   sale_id customer_id product_id quantity  sale_date
1        1           1          1        1 2023-06-01
2        2           2          2        2 2023-06-02
3        3           3          3        1 2023-06-03
4        4           1          4        1 2023-06-04
5        5           4          5        3 2023-06-05
6        6           5          1        1 2023-06-06
```

```
7          7          3          6          2 2023-06-07
8          8          6          7          1 2023-06-08
9          9          7          8          1 2023-06-09
10        10          2          3          1 2023-06-10
11        11          8          2          1 2023-06-11
12        12          9          4          1 2023-06-12
13        13          4          1          1 2023-06-13
14        14         10          5          2 2023-06-14
15        15          5          6          1 2023-06-15
```

6.11.1.2 Step 2: Basic Mathematical Operations

In this step, we begin transforming raw product and sales data into meaningful financial insights using basic mathematical operations. In real business environments, analysts regularly compute values such as profit, revenue, margins, and taxes to understand performance and support decision-making. Rather than calculating these values manually in spreadsheets, SQL allows us to generate them directly within queries, making the process faster, more consistent, and easier to reproduce.

Here, we focus on turning simple numbers like cost price, selling price, and quantity into more informative business metrics. This includes calculating profit per unit, profit margins, tax estimates, and total revenue generated from individual sales transactions. These derived values help reveal how profitable each product is and how each sale contributes to overall business performance.

We also extend these calculations to summarize performance across the dataset. By aggregating results, we can identify patterns such as total revenue, total profit, and the most profitable products. This combination of detailed and summary-level calculations provides a clearer picture of business health and sets the foundation for deeper financial analysis.

```
# Calculate profit margins and financial metrics
    product_metrics <- sqldf("
      SELECT
        product_id,
        product_name,
        category,
        cost_price,
        selling_price,
        selling_price - cost_price AS profit_per_unit,
        ROUND((selling_price - cost_price) / selling_price * 100, 2) AS
↪   profit_margin_percent,
        ROUND(selling_price * 0.08, 2) AS tax_amount,
        ROUND(selling_price + (selling_price * 0.08), 2) AS
↪   price_with_tax
```

```
  FROM products
  ORDER BY profit_margin_percent DESC
")

cat("Product Financial Metrics:\n")
```

```
Product Financial Metrics:
```

```
print(product_metrics)
```

```
  product_id         product_name    category cost_price selling_price
1          5            USB Cable Accessories        3.0          9.99
2          2     Smartphone Case Accessories        8.5         19.99
3          7        Tablet Holder Accessories       12.0         24.99
4          3    Bluetooth Speaker Electronics       25.0         49.99
5          6           Power Bank Electronics       20.0         39.99
6          8               Webcam Electronics       35.0         69.99
7          4         Laptop Stand Accessories       15.0         29.99
8          1  Wireless Headphones Electronics       45.0         79.99
  profit_per_unit profit_margin_percent tax_amount price_with_tax
1            6.99                 69.97        0.8          10.79
2           11.49                 57.48        1.6          21.59
3           12.99                 51.98        2.0          26.99
4           24.99                 49.99        4.0          53.99
5           19.99                 49.99        3.2          43.19
6           34.99                 49.99        5.6          75.59
7           14.99                 49.98        2.4          32.39
8           34.99                 43.74        6.4          86.39
```

```
# Calculate sales revenue and totals
sales_calculations <- sqldf("
  SELECT
    s.sale_id,
    s.customer_id,
    p.product_name,
    s.quantity,
    p.selling_price,
    s.quantity * p.selling_price AS total_revenue,
    s.quantity * p.cost_price AS total_cost,
    (s.quantity * p.selling_price) - (s.quantity * p.cost_price) AS
↪ total_profit,
    ROUND(s.quantity * p.selling_price * 0.08, 2) AS tax_collected
  FROM sales s
  JOIN products p ON s.product_id = p.product_id
```

```
  ORDER BY total_profit DESC
")

cat("\nSales Financial Calculations:\n")
```

```
Sales Financial Calculations:
```

```
print(head(sales_calculations[,1:5], 8))
```

```
  sale_id customer_id        product_name quantity selling_price
1       7           3          Power Bank        2         39.99
2       1           1 Wireless Headphones        1         79.99
3       6           5 Wireless Headphones        1         79.99
4       9           7              Webcam        1         69.99
5      13           4 Wireless Headphones        1         79.99
6       3           3    Bluetooth Speaker       1         49.99
7      10           2    Bluetooth Speaker       1         49.99
8       2           2      Smartphone Case       2         19.99
```

```
print(head(sales_calculations[,6:9], 8))
```

```
  total_revenue total_cost total_profit tax_collected
1         79.98         40        39.98           6.4
2         79.99         45        34.99           6.4
3         79.99         45        34.99           6.4
4         69.99         35        34.99           5.6
5         79.99         45        34.99           6.4
6         49.99         25        24.99           4.0
7         49.99         25        24.99           4.0
8         39.98         17        22.98           3.2
```

```
# Business insights using R
cat("\n=== FINANCIAL ANALYSIS ===\n")
```

```
=== FINANCIAL ANALYSIS ===
```

```
cat("Highest profit margin:",
↪  max(product_metrics$profit_margin_percent), "%\n")
```

```
Highest profit margin: 69.97 %
```

```
cat("Average profit margin:",
↪  round(mean(product_metrics$profit_margin_percent), 2), "%\n")
```

```
Average profit margin: 52.89 %
```

```r
cat("Total revenue from all sales: $",
 ↪  round(sum(sales_calculations$total_revenue), 2), "\n")
```

```
Total revenue from all sales: $ 724.8
```

```r
cat("Total profit from all sales: $",
 ↪  round(sum(sales_calculations$total_profit), 2), "\n")
```

```
Total profit from all sales: $ 362.3
```

```r
# Identify most profitable products
top_profit_products <-
↪ product_metrics[order(-product_metrics$profit_margin_percent),
↪ ][1:3, ]
cat("Top 3 most profitable products:\n")
```

```
Top 3 most profitable products:
```

```r
print(top_profit_products[, c("product_name",
 ↪  "profit_margin_percent")])
```

```
     product_name profit_margin_percent
1       USB Cable                 69.97
2 Smartphone Case                 57.48
3   Tablet Holder                 51.98
```

6.11.1.3 Step 3: Aggregate Functions for Business Summaries

In this step, we move beyond individual transactions and begin summarizing the data to understand overall business performance. While earlier steps focused on calculating values at the product or sale level, aggregate functions allow us to combine many rows of data into meaningful summaries such as totals, averages, and counts. These summaries are essential in real-world analytics because decision-makers are rarely interested in single transactions—they want patterns, trends, and key performance indicators.

Using aggregate functions, we can answer important business questions such as which customers are spending the most, which products generate the highest revenue, and which categories perform best overall. Instead of viewing sales as isolated events, we now group the data by customers, products, and categories to build a clearer picture of behavior and performance across the entire dataset.

This step introduces the idea of business-level reporting, where raw data is transformed into metrics like total spending per customer, total units sold per product, and total revenue per category. These summaries are the foundation of dashboards and executive reports, helping businesses identify high-value customers, best-selling products, and underperforming segments.

Now we will use SQL aggregate functions such as COUNT, SUM, and AVG to generate these business summaries and extract actionable insights from the data.

```
# Customer spending analysis
customer_summary <- sqldf("
  SELECT
    c.customer_id,
    c.customer_name,
    c.city,
    COUNT(s.sale_id) AS total_orders,
    SUM(s.quantity) AS total_items_purchased,
    SUM(s.quantity * p.selling_price) AS total_spent,
    AVG(s.quantity * p.selling_price) AS avg_order_value,
    MAX(s.sale_date) AS last_purchase_date
  FROM customers c
  LEFT JOIN sales s ON c.customer_id = s.customer_id
  LEFT JOIN products p ON s.product_id = p.product_id
  GROUP BY c.customer_id, c.customer_name, c.city
  ORDER BY total_spent DESC
")

cat("Customer Spending Summary:\n")
```

```
Customer Spending Summary:
```

```
print(customer_summary[,1:4])
```

```
   customer_id customer_name        city total_orders
1            3    Carol Davis    New York            2
2            5     Emma Brown     Chicago            2
3            1  Alice Johnson    New York            2
4            4   David Wilson       Miami            2
5            2      Bob Smith     Chicago            2
6            7      Grace Lee     Seattle            1
7            9      Iris Chen Los Angeles            1
8            6   Frank Miller      Boston            1
9            8   Henry Taylor       Miami            1
10          10 Jack Robinson      Boston            1
```

```
print(customer_summary[,5:6])
```

```
   total_items_purchased total_spent
1                      3      129.97
```

```
2                      2      119.98
3                      2      109.98
4                      4      109.96
5                      3       89.97
6                      1       69.99
7                      1       29.99
8                      1       24.99
9                      1       19.99
10                     2       19.98
```

```
print(customer_summary[,7:8])
```

```
   avg_order_value last_purchase_date
1           64.985              19515
2           59.990              19523
3           54.990              19512
4           54.980              19521
5           44.985              19518
6           69.990              19517
7           29.990              19520
8           24.990              19516
9           19.990              19519
10          19.980              19522
```

```
# Product performance analysis
product_performance <- sqldf("
  SELECT
    p.product_id,
    p.product_name,
    p.category,
    COUNT(s.sale_id) AS times_sold,
    SUM(s.quantity) AS total_units_sold,
    SUM(s.quantity * p.selling_price) AS total_revenue,
    SUM((s.quantity * p.selling_price) - (s.quantity *
↪ p.cost_price)) AS total_profit,
    AVG(s.quantity) AS avg_quantity_per_sale
  FROM products p
  LEFT JOIN sales s ON p.product_id = s.product_id
  GROUP BY p.product_id, p.product_name, p.category
  ORDER BY total_revenue DESC
")

cat("\nProduct Performance Analysis:\n")
```

```
Product Performance Analysis:
```

```r
print(product_performance)
```

```
  product_id         product_name    category times_sold total_units_sold
1          1 Wireless Headphones Electronics          3                3
2          6           Power Bank Electronics          2                3
3          3     Bluetooth Speaker Electronics          2                2
4          8               Webcam Electronics          1                1
5          4         Laptop Stand Accessories          2                2
6          2      Smartphone Case Accessories          2                3
7          5            USB Cable Accessories          2                5
8          7        Tablet Holder Accessories          1                1
  total_revenue total_profit avg_quantity_per_sale
1        239.97       104.97                   1.0
2        119.97        59.97                   1.5
3         99.98        49.98                   1.0
4         69.99        34.99                   1.0
5         59.98        29.98                   1.0
6         59.97        34.47                   1.5
7         49.95        34.95                   2.5
8         24.99        12.99                   1.0
```

```r
# Category analysis
category_summary <- sqldf("
  SELECT
    p.category,
    COUNT(DISTINCT p.product_id) AS products_in_category,
    COUNT(s.sale_id) AS total_sales,
    SUM(s.quantity * p.selling_price) AS category_revenue,
    AVG(s.quantity * p.selling_price) AS avg_sale_value
  FROM products p
  LEFT JOIN sales s ON p.product_id = s.product_id
  GROUP BY p.category
  ORDER BY category_revenue DESC
")

cat("\nCategory Performance Summary:\n")
```

```
Category Performance Summary:
```

```r
print(category_summary[,1:3])
```

```
     category products_in_category total_sales
```

```
1 Electronics                 4          8
2 Accessories                 4          7
```

```
print(category_summary[,4:5])
```

```
  category_revenue avg_sale_value
1           529.91       66.23875
2           194.89       27.84143
```

```
# Business insights using R
cat("\n=== AGGREGATE ANALYSIS ===\n")
```

```

=== AGGREGATE ANALYSIS ===
```

```
# Customer insights
active_customers <- sum(customer_summary$total_orders > 0, na.rm =
↪ TRUE)
cat("Active customers (made purchases):", active_customers, "out
  ↪ of", nrow(customers), "\n")
```

```
Active customers (made purchases): 10 out of 10
```

```
avg_customer_value <- round(mean(customer_summary$total_spent,
↪ na.rm = TRUE), 2)
cat("Average customer lifetime value: $", avg_customer_value, "\n")
```

```
Average customer lifetime value: $ 72.48
```

```
# Product insights
best_seller <- product_performance[which.max(product_performance$
↪ total_units_sold), ]
cat("Best selling product:", best_seller$product_name, "with",
  ↪ best_seller$total_units_sold, "units\n")
```

```
Best selling product: USB Cable with 5 units
```

```
# Category insights
if(nrow(category_summary) > 0) {
  top_category <- category_summary[1, ]
  cat("Top performing category:", top_category$category, "with $",
    ↪ round(top_category$category_revenue, 2), "revenue\n")
}
```

```
Top performing category: Electronics with $ 529.91 revenue
```

6.11.1.4 Step 4: CASE Statements for Business Logic

In this step, we introduce conditional logic using CASE statements, which allow us to apply business rules directly within SQL queries. While previous steps focused on calculating numeric values and summarizing data, this step is about transforming those numbers into meaningful categories that reflect real business decisions. In practice, businesses rarely interpret raw figures alone—they rely on labeled segments such as "VIP customer," "best seller," or "high-value sale" to guide marketing, inventory, and strategic planning.

CASE statements act like decision rules inside SQL, allowing us to evaluate conditions and assign labels based on thresholds or patterns in the data. This is especially useful for customer segmentation, product classification, and sales categorization. Instead of just knowing how much a customer spent or how many units were sold, we can now group customers into tiers, identify product performance levels, and classify transactions by value.

This step represents a shift from calculation to interpretation. We are no longer just computing numbers—we are embedding business intelligence directly into the dataset. These categorized outputs are what typically feed dashboards, reports, and decision-support systems, where clarity and interpretability matter more than raw values.

Now we will use CASE statements to apply business rules for customer segmentation, product categorization, and sales classification, turning numerical results into actionable business insights.

```
# Customer segmentation using CASE statements
customer_segments <- sqldf("
  SELECT
    c.customer_id,
    c.customer_name,
    COALESCE(SUM(s.quantity * p.selling_price), 0) AS total_spent,
    CASE
      WHEN COALESCE(SUM(s.quantity * p.selling_price), 0) >= 200
↪ THEN 'VIP Customer'
      WHEN COALESCE(SUM(s.quantity * p.selling_price), 0) >= 100
↪ THEN 'Premium Customer'
      WHEN COALESCE(SUM(s.quantity * p.selling_price), 0) > 0 THEN
↪ 'Regular Customer'
      ELSE 'New Customer'
    END AS customer_segment,
    CASE
      WHEN COUNT(s.sale_id) >= 3 THEN 'Frequent Buyer'
      WHEN COUNT(s.sale_id) >= 2 THEN 'Occasional Buyer'
      WHEN COUNT(s.sale_id) = 1 THEN 'One-time Buyer'
      ELSE 'No Purchases'
```

```
    END AS purchase_frequency
  FROM customers c
  LEFT JOIN sales s ON c.customer_id = s.customer_id
  LEFT JOIN products p ON s.product_id = p.product_id
  GROUP BY c.customer_id, c.customer_name
  ORDER BY total_spent DESC
")

cat("Customer Segmentation:\n")
```

```
Customer Segmentation:
```

```
print(customer_segments[,1:4])
```

```
   customer_id customer_name total_spent customer_segment
1            3    Carol Davis      129.97 Premium Customer
2            5     Emma Brown      119.98 Premium Customer
3            1  Alice Johnson      109.98 Premium Customer
4            4   David Wilson      109.96 Premium Customer
5            2      Bob Smith       89.97 Regular Customer
6            7      Grace Lee       69.99 Regular Customer
7            9      Iris Chen       29.99 Regular Customer
8            6   Frank Miller       24.99 Regular Customer
9            8   Henry Taylor       19.99 Regular Customer
10          10  Jack Robinson       19.98 Regular Customer
```

```
print(customer_segments[,4:5])
```

```
   customer_segment purchase_frequency
1  Premium Customer   Occasional Buyer
2  Premium Customer   Occasional Buyer
3  Premium Customer   Occasional Buyer
4  Premium Customer   Occasional Buyer
5  Regular Customer   Occasional Buyer
6  Regular Customer     One-time Buyer
7  Regular Customer     One-time Buyer
8  Regular Customer     One-time Buyer
9  Regular Customer     One-time Buyer
10 Regular Customer     One-time Buyer
```

```
# Product categorization by performance
product_categories <- sqldf("
  SELECT
    p.product_id,
```

```
      p.product_name,
      p.selling_price,
      COALESCE(SUM(s.quantity), 0) AS units_sold,
      CASE
        WHEN p.selling_price >= 50 THEN 'Premium Product'
        WHEN p.selling_price >= 25 THEN 'Mid-Range Product'
        ELSE 'Budget Product'
      END AS price_category,
      CASE
        WHEN COALESCE(SUM(s.quantity), 0) >= 3 THEN 'Best Seller'
        WHEN COALESCE(SUM(s.quantity), 0) >= 2 THEN 'Good Seller'
        WHEN COALESCE(SUM(s.quantity), 0) >= 1 THEN 'Slow Mover'
        ELSE 'No Sales'
      END AS sales_performance
    FROM products p
    LEFT JOIN sales s ON p.product_id = s.product_id
    GROUP BY p.product_id, p.product_name, p.selling_price
    ORDER BY units_sold DESC
  ")

  cat("\nProduct Categorization:\n")
```

```
Product Categorization:
```

```
  print(product_categories[,1:4])
```

```
  product_id       product_name selling_price units_sold
1          5          USB Cable          9.99          5
2          1 Wireless Headphones        79.99          3
3          2    Smartphone Case         19.99          3
4          6         Power Bank         39.99          3
5          3   Bluetooth Speaker        49.99          2
6          4       Laptop Stand         29.99          2
7          7      Tablet Holder         24.99          1
8          8             Webcam         69.99          1
```

```
  print(product_categories[,5:6])
```

```
     price_category sales_performance
1    Budget Product       Best Seller
2   Premium Product       Best Seller
3    Budget Product       Best Seller
4 Mid-Range Product       Best Seller
```

```
5 Mid-Range Product       Good Seller
6 Mid-Range Product       Good Seller
7    Budget Product        Slow Mover
8   Premium Product        Slow Mover
```

```r
# Sales analysis with conditional logic
sales_analysis <- sqldf("
  SELECT
    s.sale_id,
    s.sale_date,
    c.customer_name,
    p.product_name,
    s.quantity * p.selling_price AS sale_amount,
    CASE
      WHEN s.quantity * p.selling_price >= 100 THEN 'High Value
↪ Sale'
      WHEN s.quantity * p.selling_price >= 50 THEN 'Medium Value
↪ Sale'
      ELSE 'Low Value Sale'
    END AS sale_category,
    CASE
      WHEN s.quantity >= 3 THEN 'Bulk Purchase'
      WHEN s.quantity = 2 THEN 'Double Purchase'
      ELSE 'Single Item'
    END AS quantity_type
  FROM sales s
  JOIN customers c ON s.customer_id = c.customer_id
  JOIN products p ON s.product_id = p.product_id
  ORDER BY sale_amount DESC
")

cat("\nSales Analysis with Categories:\n")
```

```
Sales Analysis with Categories:
```

```r
print(head(sales_analysis, 8))
```

```
  sale_id  sale_date customer_name       product_name sale_amount
1       1 2023-06-01 Alice Johnson Wireless Headphones       79.99
2       6 2023-06-06    Emma Brown Wireless Headphones       79.99
3      13 2023-06-13  David Wilson Wireless Headphones       79.99
4       7 2023-06-07   Carol Davis          Power Bank       79.98
5       9 2023-06-09     Grace Lee              Webcam       69.99
6       3 2023-06-03   Carol Davis    Bluetooth Speaker       49.99
```

```
7      10 2023-06-10     Bob Smith   Bluetooth Speaker        49.99
8      15 2023-06-15   Emma Brown          Power Bank        39.99
      sale_category   quantity_type
1 Medium Value Sale     Single Item
2 Medium Value Sale     Single Item
3 Medium Value Sale     Single Item
4 Medium Value Sale Double Purchase
5 Medium Value Sale     Single Item
6    Low Value Sale     Single Item
7    Low Value Sale     Single Item
8    Low Value Sale     Single Item
```

```r
# Business insights using R
cat("\n=== SEGMENTATION ANALYSIS ===\n")
```

```
=== SEGMENTATION ANALYSIS ===
```

```r
# Customer segment distribution
segment_counts <- table(customer_segments$customer_segment)
cat("Customer segment distribution:\n")
```

```
Customer segment distribution:
```

```r
print(segment_counts)
```

```
Premium Customer Regular Customer
               4                6
```

```r
# Calculate segment percentages
segment_pct <- round(prop.table(segment_counts) * 100, 1)
cat("Customer segment percentages:\n")
```

```
Customer segment percentages:
```

```r
print(segment_pct)
```

```
Premium Customer Regular Customer
              40               60
```

```r
# Sales category analysis
sale_category_counts <- table(sales_analysis$sale_category)
cat("Sales category distribution:\n")
```

```
Sales category distribution:
```

```
print(sale_category_counts)
```

```
Low Value Sale Medium Value Sale
            10                 5
```

6.11.1.5 Step 5: Date Calculations for Time-Based Analysis

In this step, we shift our focus from static values to time-based patterns by working with date calculations. Time is one of the most important dimensions in business data because it reveals how customer behavior changes over days, months, and years. Understanding when events happen—such as when a customer registers, makes their first purchase, or returns to buy again—helps businesses evaluate engagement, retention, and long-term value.

Unlike basic numeric calculations, date operations allow us to measure duration, identify trends over time, and segment customers based on lifecycle stages. By calculating differences between dates, we can determine customer age, tenure, time to first purchase, and recency of activity. These measures are essential for answering questions like how quickly new customers convert, how long customers remain active, and which customers may be at risk of leaving.

This step also introduces the idea of customer lifecycle analysis, where we track behavior from registration through purchasing activity to identify stages such as new, active, at-risk, or inactive. These time-based insights are especially valuable in marketing and customer retention strategies, where timing often matters as much as behavior itself.

Now we will use date calculations in SQL to analyze customer demographics, purchase timing, and lifecycle patterns, helping us understand how customer relationships evolve over time.

```
# Customer age and tenure analysis
customer_demographics <- sqldf("
  SELECT
    customer_id,
    customer_name,
    birth_date,
    registration_date,
    ROUND((JULIANDAY('2023-06-15') - JULIANDAY(birth_date)) /
↪ 365.25) AS age_years,
    ROUND(JULIANDAY('2023-06-15') - JULIANDAY(registration_date))
↪ AS days_since_registration,
    CASE
      WHEN ROUND((JULIANDAY('2023-06-15') - JULIANDAY(birth_date))
↪ / 365.25) < 30 THEN 'Young (Under 30)'
```

```
        WHEN ROUND((JULIANDAY('2023-06-15') - JULIANDAY(birth_date))
↪   / 365.25) < 40 THEN 'Middle-aged (30-39)'
        WHEN ROUND((JULIANDAY('2023-06-15') - JULIANDAY(birth_date))
↪   / 365.25) < 50 THEN 'Mature (40-49)'
        ELSE 'Senior (50+)'
      END AS age_group,
      CASE
        WHEN JULIANDAY('2023-06-15') - JULIANDAY(registration_date)
↪   <= 90 THEN 'New Customer (0-3 months)'
        WHEN JULIANDAY('2023-06-15') - JULIANDAY(registration_date)
↪   <= 180 THEN 'Recent Customer (3-6 months)'
        ELSE 'Established Customer (6+ months)'
      END AS tenure_category
    FROM customers
    ORDER BY age_years
  ")

  cat("Customer Demographics and Tenure:\n")
```

```
Customer Demographics and Tenure:
```

```
  print(customer_demographics)
```

```
   customer_id customer_name birth_date registration_date age_years
1            7     Grace Lee 1995-02-18        2022-12-18      6710
2            3    Carol Davis 1992-11-08       2023-01-10      6713
3            9     Iris Chen 1991-06-12        2023-05-05      6714
4            1 Alice Johnson 1990-03-15        2023-01-15      6715
5            5    Emma Brown 1988-09-30        2023-03-12      6717
6           10 Jack Robinson 1987-04-07        2023-03-20      6718
7            2     Bob Smith 1985-07-22        2023-02-20      6720
8            8  Henry Taylor 1982-08-25        2023-02-28      6723
9            4  David Wilson 1978-05-14        2022-11-05      6727
10           6  Frank Miller 1975-12-03        2023-04-01      6729
   days_since_registration    age_group                  tenure_category
1                  2440767 Senior (50+) Established Customer (6+ months)
2                  2440744 Senior (50+) Established Customer (6+ months)
3                  2440629 Senior (50+) Established Customer (6+ months)
4                  2440739 Senior (50+) Established Customer (6+ months)
5                  2440683 Senior (50+) Established Customer (6+ months)
6                  2440675 Senior (50+) Established Customer (6+ months)
7                  2440703 Senior (50+) Established Customer (6+ months)
8                  2440695 Senior (50+) Established Customer (6+ months)
9                  2440810 Senior (50+) Established Customer (6+ months)
```

```
10                   2440663 Senior (50+) Established Customer (6+ months)
```

```
# Sales timing analysis
sales_timing <- sqldf("
  SELECT
    s.sale_id,
    s.sale_date,
    c.customer_name,
    c.registration_date,
    ROUND(JULIANDAY(s.sale_date) - JULIANDAY(c.registration_date))
↪ AS days_from_registration_to_purchase,
    ROUND(JULIANDAY('2023-06-15') - JULIANDAY(s.sale_date)) AS
↪ days_since_purchase,
    CASE
      WHEN JULIANDAY(s.sale_date) - JULIANDAY(c.registration_date)
↪ <= 7 THEN 'Immediate Purchase'
      WHEN JULIANDAY(s.sale_date) - JULIANDAY(c.registration_date)
↪ <= 30 THEN 'Quick Purchase'
      WHEN JULIANDAY(s.sale_date) - JULIANDAY(c.registration_date)
↪ <= 90 THEN 'Delayed Purchase'
      ELSE 'Long Delayed Purchase'
    END AS purchase_timing,
    CASE
      WHEN JULIANDAY('2023-06-15') - JULIANDAY(s.sale_date) <= 7
↪ THEN 'Very Recent'
      WHEN JULIANDAY('2023-06-15') - JULIANDAY(s.sale_date) <= 14
↪ THEN 'Recent'
      WHEN JULIANDAY('2023-06-15') - JULIANDAY(s.sale_date) <= 30
↪ THEN 'Moderate'
      ELSE 'Old'
    END AS recency_category
  FROM sales s
  JOIN customers c ON s.customer_id = c.customer_id
  ORDER BY days_since_purchase
")

cat("\nSales Timing Analysis:\n")
```

```
Sales Timing Analysis:
```

```
print(head(sales_timing[,1:4], 8))
```

```
  sale_id  sale_date customer_name registration_date
1      15 2023-06-15    Emma Brown        2023-03-12
```

```
2      14 2023-06-14 Jack Robinson        2023-03-20
3      13 2023-06-13  David Wilson        2022-11-05
4      12 2023-06-12     Iris Chen        2023-05-05
5      11 2023-06-11  Henry Taylor        2023-02-28
6      10 2023-06-10     Bob Smith        2023-02-20
7       9 2023-06-09     Grace Lee        2022-12-18
8       8 2023-06-08  Frank Miller        2023-04-01
```

```
print(head(sales_timing[,5:6], 8))
```

```
  days_from_registration_to_purchase days_since_purchase
1                                 95             2440588
2                                 86             2440589
3                                220             2440590
4                                 38             2440591
5                                103             2440592
6                                110             2440593
7                                173             2440594
8                                 68             2440595
```

```
print(head(sales_timing[,7:8], 8))
```

```
        purchase_timing recency_category
1 Long Delayed Purchase              Old
2      Delayed Purchase              Old
3 Long Delayed Purchase              Old
4      Delayed Purchase              Old
5 Long Delayed Purchase              Old
6 Long Delayed Purchase              Old
7 Long Delayed Purchase              Old
8      Delayed Purchase              Old
```

```
# Customer lifecycle analysis
customer_lifecycle <- sqldf("
  SELECT
    c.customer_id,
    c.customer_name,
    c.registration_date,
    MIN(s.sale_date) AS first_purchase_date,
    MAX(s.sale_date) AS last_purchase_date,
    COUNT(s.sale_id) AS total_purchases,
    ROUND(JULIANDAY(MIN(s.sale_date)) -
↪ JULIANDAY(c.registration_date)) AS days_to_first_purchase,
    ROUND(JULIANDAY('2023-06-15') - JULIANDAY(MAX(s.sale_date))) AS
↪ days_since_last_purchase,
```

```
    CASE
      WHEN JULIANDAY('2023-06-15') - JULIANDAY(MAX(s.sale_date)) <=
↪ 14 THEN 'Active'
      WHEN JULIANDAY('2023-06-15') - JULIANDAY(MAX(s.sale_date)) <=
↪ 30 THEN 'At Risk'
      ELSE 'Inactive'
    END AS customer_status
  FROM customers c
  LEFT JOIN sales s ON c.customer_id = s.customer_id
  GROUP BY c.customer_id, c.customer_name, c.registration_date
  ORDER BY days_since_last_purchase
")

cat("\nCustomer Lifecycle Analysis:\n")
```

```
Customer Lifecycle Analysis:
```

```
print(customer_lifecycle)
```

```
   customer_id customer_name registration_date first_purchase_date
1            5    Emma Brown        2023-03-12               19514
2           10 Jack Robinson        2023-03-20               19522
3            4  David Wilson        2022-11-05               19513
4            9     Iris Chen        2023-05-05               19520
5            8  Henry Taylor        2023-02-28               19519
6            2     Bob Smith        2023-02-20               19510
7            7     Grace Lee        2022-12-18               19517
8            6  Frank Miller        2023-04-01               19516
9            3   Carol Davis        2023-01-10               19511
10           1 Alice Johnson        2023-01-15               19509
   last_purchase_date total_purchases days_to_first_purchase
1               19523               2                     86
2               19522               1                     86
3               19521               2                    212
4               19520               1                     38
5               19519               1                    103
6               19518               2                    102
7               19517               1                    173
8               19516               1                     68
9               19515               2                    144
10              19512               2                    137
   days_since_last_purchase customer_status
```

```
1                    2440588        Inactive
2                    2440589        Inactive
3                    2440590        Inactive
4                    2440591        Inactive
5                    2440592        Inactive
6                    2440593        Inactive
7                    2440594        Inactive
8                    2440595        Inactive
9                    2440596        Inactive
10                   2440599        Inactive
```

```
# Business insights using R
cat("\n=== DATE-BASED ANALYSIS ===\n")
```

```
=== DATE-BASED ANALYSIS ===
```

```
# Age group analysis
age_distribution <- table(customer_demographics$age_group)
cat("Customer age distribution:\n")
```

```
Customer age distribution:
```

```
print(age_distribution)
```

```
Senior (50+)
          10
```

```
# Customer status analysis
status_counts <- table(customer_lifecycle$customer_status)
cat("Customer status distribution:\n")
```

```
Customer status distribution:
```

```
print(status_counts)
```

```
Inactive
      10
```

```
# Calculate average days to first purchase
avg_days_to_purchase <-
↪ round(mean(customer_lifecycle$days_to_first_purchase, na.rm =
↪ TRUE), 1)
cat("Average days from registration to first purchase:",
  ↪ avg_days_to_purchase, "\n")
```

```
Average days from registration to first purchase: 114.9
```

```
# Identify at-risk customers
at_risk_customers <- sum(customer_lifecycle$customer_status == 'At
↪ Risk', na.rm = TRUE)
cat("Customers at risk of churning:", at_risk_customers, "\n")
```

```
Customers at risk of churning: 0
```

6.11.2 Practice

You're working as a data analyst for "TechStore," an electronics retailer. The company wants comprehensive business metrics to improve operations and customer relationships.

```
# Create expanded dataset for exercises
tech_products <- data.frame(
  product_id = 1:12,
  product_name = c('Gaming Laptop', 'Wireless Mouse',
                   'Mechanical Keyboard', 'Monitor 24"',
                   'Graphics Card', 'SSD Drive', 'RAM Module',
                   'Cooling Fan',  'Power Supply', 'Motherboard',
                   'CPU Processor', 'Gaming Chair'),
  category = c('Computers', 'Accessories', 'Accessories',
               'Displays','Components', 'Storage', 'Components',
               'Components', 'Components', 'Components',
               'Components', 'Furniture'),
  cost_price = c(800, 25, 75, 180, 450, 85, 120, 35, 90, 200,
                 350, 250),
  selling_price = c(1299, 49, 129, 299, 699, 149, 199, 59,
                    149, 329, 549, 399),
  warranty_months = c(24, 12, 24, 36, 24, 60, 36, 12, 24,
                      24, 36, 12),
  stringsAsFactors = FALSE
)

tech_customers <- data.frame(
  customer_id = 1:15,
  customer_name = c('Alex Johnson', 'Beth Smith', 'Carlos Garcia',
                    'Diana Lee', 'Ethan Brown',
                    'Fiona Davis', 'George Wilson', 'Hannah
                    ↪ Miller',
                    'Ivan Chen', 'Julia Taylor',
                    'Kevin Martinez', 'Laura Anderson',
```

```
                   'Mike Thompson', 'Nina Rodriguez', 'Oscar
                   ↪  Kim'),
  birth_date = as.Date(c('1995-03-15', '1988-07-22', '1992-11-08',
                         '1985-05-14', '1990-09-30',
                         '1987-12-03', '1993-02-18', '1991-08-25',
                         '1989-06-12', '1994-04-07',
                         '1986-10-20', '1996-01-15', '1984-09-08',
                         '1997-03-25', '1983-11-12')),
  registration_date = as.Date(c('2023-01-15', '2023-02-20',
                                '2023-01-10', '2022-11-05',
                                '2023-03-12', '2023-04-01',
                                '2022-12-18', '2023-02-28',
                                '2023-05-05',
                                '2023-03-20',
                                '2022-10-15', '2023-04-10',
                                '2022-09-22', '2023-05-15',
                                '2022-08-30')),
  city = c('New York', 'Chicago', 'Los Angeles', 'Houston',
           'Phoenix', 'Philadelphia', 'San Antonio',
           'San Diego', 'Dallas', 'San Jose',
           'Austin', 'Jacksonville', 'Fort Worth', 'Columbus',
           'Charlotte'),
  stringsAsFactors = FALSE
)

tech_sales <- data.frame(
  sale_id = 1:20,
  customer_id = c(1, 2, 3, 1, 4, 5, 3, 6, 7, 2, 8, 9, 4, 10, 5, 11,
   ↪
                 12, 13, 14, 15),
  product_id = c(1, 2, 3, 4, 5, 6, 7, 8, 9, 10, 11, 12, 2, 3,
                4, 5, 6, 7, 8, 9),
  quantity = c(1, 2, 1, 1, 1, 2, 1, 3, 1, 1, 1, 1, 1, 1, 1, 1,
              1, 2, 1, 1),
  sale_date = as.Date(c('2023-06-01', '2023-06-02',
                        '2023-06-03', '2023-06-05',
                        '2023-06-06',
                        '2023-06-07', '2023-06-08',
                        '2023-06-10', '2023-06-11',
                        '2023-06-12',
                        '2023-06-13', '2023-06-14',
                        '2023-06-15', '2023-06-16',
                        '2023-06-17',
```

```
                            '2023-06-18', '2023-06-19',
                            '2023-06-20', '2023-06-21',
                            '2023-06-22')),
  stringsAsFactors = FALSE
)

# Display exercise data
cat("TECHSTORE EXERCISE DATA:\n")
```

```
TECHSTORE EXERCISE DATA:
```

```
cat("Products:", nrow(tech_products), "\n")
```

```
Products: 12
```

```
cat("Customers:", nrow(tech_customers), "\n")
```

```
Customers: 15
```

```
cat("Sales:", nrow(tech_sales), "\n")
```

```
Sales: 20
```

6.11.2.1 Questions

1. What is the profit per unit for each product in the tech_products dataset?
2. Which product has the highest profit margin percentage?
3. Calculate the total revenue generated from all sales in the tech_sales dataset.
4. Which customer has made the highest total spending across all purchases?
5. How many total units of each product have been sold?
6. Which product category generates the highest total revenue?
7. Create a new column that classifies products as "High Price" if selling_price is above 500, "Medium Price" if between 200–500, and "Low Price" if below 200.
8. What is the average order value per customer?
9. How many days passed between each customer's registration_date and their first purchase date?
10. Classify customers into age groups (Under 30, 30–39, 40–49, 50+) using birth_date.
11. Which customers have not made more than one purchase?

12. What is the total profit generated from each product category?
13. Identify the top 3 best-selling products based on quantity sold.
14. Create a column that labels sales as "High Value" if total sale amount is above 500, otherwise "Standard Value."
15. Which customers are most recently registered (within the last 60 days from 2023-06-22)?

Chapter 7

Reshaping and Reducing Data

7.1 Learning Outcomes

7-1: Reshape relational data using SQL techniques, including pivoting and unpivoting with CASE statements and UNION operations.

7-2: Create pivot-style summaries to compare counts, revenue, and performance across categories such as time periods, customer segments, and statuses.

7-3: Reduce dataset complexity through feature selection, derived variables, and simplified analytical views tailored to specific business questions.

7-4: Group and summarize transactional data using SQL aggregate functions to produce business-relevant metrics and performance indicators.

7-5: Validate reshaped and summarized data to ensure totals, relationships, and record counts are preserved throughout transformations.

7.2 Introduction

Data rarely comes in the exact format you need for analysis. Sometimes you need to reorganize rows into columns, combine multiple data points into summaries, or reduce complex datasets to their most essential elements. This process of reshaping and reducing data is fundamental to effective data analysis and helps you transform raw data into formats that reveal insights more clearly.

Data reshaping involves changing the structure of your data - converting rows to columns (pivoting), columns to rows (unpivoting), or reorganizing information to better suit your analytical needs. Data reduction involves simplifying datasets by focusing on the most important information, removing unnecessary complexity, and creating meaningful summaries.

Think of data reshaping like rearranging furniture in a room - the same pieces are there but organizing them differently can make the space more functional and reveal new possibilities. Similarly, reshaping data can make patterns and relationships more visible and analysis more straightforward.

Data reduction is like editing a long document down to its key points - you preserve the essential information while removing details that might obscure the main message. In data analysis, reduction helps you focus on what matters most and makes large datasets more manageable and understandable.

These skills are essential because real-world data analysis often requires you to work with data in formats that don't match your analytical needs. Learning to reshape and reduce data effectively allows you to adapt any dataset to your specific requirements and extract maximum value from your information.

Let's continue with our bookstore example, but now we'll explore how to reshape and reduce this data for different analytical purposes:

Customers Table

customer_id	name	age	city	membership
1	Alice	25	New York	Premium
2	Bob	35	Chicago	Standard
3	Carol	28	New York	Premium
4	David	42	Miami	Standard
5	Emma	31	Chicago	Premium

Orders Table

order_id	customer_id	book_title	price	order_date	status
101	1	Python Basics	29.99	2024-01-15	Completed
102	2	Data Science	45.00	2024-01-20	Completed
103	1	Web Design	35.50	2024-02-01	Pending
104	3	SQL Guide	32.00	2024-02-05	Completed
105	4	AI Handbook	55.99	2024-02-10	Cancelled
106	5	Python Basics	29.99	2024-02-15	Completed
107	2	Web Design	35.50	2024-02-20	Completed

From this data, we can create various reshaped views like customer purchase summaries by month, city-based sales pivots, or reduced datasets focusing only on the most important customer characteristics. Let's explore these techniques systematically.

7.3 Pivoting and Unpivoting Tables

7.3.1 Understanding Pivoting

Pivoting transforms data from a long format (many rows) to a wide format (many columns), making it easier to compare values across different categories. This transformation is particularly useful for creating summary reports, cross-tabulations, and comparative analyses.

Pivoting is essential because it allows you to reorganize data to answer specific business questions more effectively. Instead of scanning through many rows to compare categories, pivoting presents the information in a format that makes comparisons immediate and obvious.

The concept of pivoting comes from spreadsheet applications where you might create pivot tables to summarize data. In SQL, we achieve similar results using conditional aggregation with CASE statements, which gives us precise control over how the data is reorganized.

Understanding when and how to pivot data is crucial for creating effective business reports and dashboards. Pivoted data often provides clearer insights and is more suitable for visualization and presentation to business stakeholders.

7.3.2 Basic Pivoting with CASE Statements

Since many SQL databases don't have built-in PIVOT functions, we use CASE statements with aggregate functions to achieve pivoting. This approach is widely compatible and gives you complete control over the pivoting process.

Using CASE statements for pivoting is a fundamental skill because it works across different database systems and allows you to customize the pivoting logic to match your specific business requirements. This flexibility makes it more powerful than automated pivot functions.

Example: Pivot orders by status to see counts

```
SELECT
    customer_id,
    SUM(CASE WHEN status = 'Completed'
        THEN 1 ELSE 0 END) as completed_orders,
    SUM(CASE WHEN status = 'Pending'
        THEN 1 ELSE 0 END) as pending_orders,
    SUM(CASE WHEN status = 'Cancelled'
        THEN 1 ELSE 0 END) as cancelled_orders,
    COUNT(*) as total_orders
FROM orders
GROUP BY customer_id
ORDER BY customer_id;
```

Result:

customer_id	completed_orders	pending_orders	cancelled_orders	total_orders
1	1	1	0	2
2	2	0	0	2
3	1	0	0	1
4	0	0	1	1
5	1	0	0	1

This pivot transformation makes it easy to see each customer's order status distribution at a glance. Instead of scanning through multiple rows, you can immediately see how many orders each customer has in each status category.

Example: Pivot sales by month

```
SELECT
    YEAR(order_date) as order_year,
    SUM(CASE WHEN MONTH(order_date) = 1
        THEN price ELSE 0 END) as january_sales,
    SUM(CASE WHEN MONTH(order_date) = 2
        THEN price ELSE 0 END) as february_sales,
    SUM(price) as total_sales
FROM orders
WHERE status = 'Completed'
GROUP BY YEAR(order_date)
ORDER BY order_year;
```

Result:

order_year	january_sales	february_sales	total_sales
2024	74.99	97.49	172.48

This monthly sales pivot provides a clear view of seasonal patterns and makes it easy to compare performance across different time periods. This type of analysis is essential for business planning and trend identification.

7.3.3 Creating Customer Summary Pivots

Customer summary pivots help you understand customer behavior patterns by reorganizing customer data into comparative formats. These summaries are valuable for customer segmentation, marketing analysis, and business strategy development.

Customer pivots transform detailed transaction data into strategic insights about customer value, preferences, and behavior patterns. This transformation is essential for making data-driven decisions about customer relationships and business development.

Example: Pivot customer data by membership and city

```
SELECT
    city,
    SUM(CASE WHEN membership = 'Premium'
        THEN 1 ELSE 0 END) as premium_customers,
    SUM(CASE WHEN membership = 'Standard'
        THEN 1 ELSE 0 END) as standard_customers,
    COUNT(*) as total_customers
FROM customers
GROUP BY city
ORDER BY city;
```

Result:

city	premium_customers	standard_customers	total_customers
Chicago	1	1	2
Miami	0	1	1
New York	2	0	2

This geographic and membership pivot reveals important patterns about customer distribution and membership preferences by location. This information is valuable for targeted marketing and business expansion planning.

Example: Create customer purchase summary pivot

```
SELECT
    c.name,
    c.membership,
    SUM(CASE WHEN o.status = 'Completed'
        THEN o.price ELSE 0 END) as completed_revenue,
    SUM(CASE WHEN o.status = 'Pending'
        THEN o.price ELSE 0 END) as pending_revenue,
    COUNT(CASE WHEN o.status = 'Completed'
        THEN 1 END) as completed_count,
    COUNT(CASE WHEN o.status = 'Pending'
        THEN 1 END) as pending_count
FROM customers c
LEFT JOIN orders o ON c.customer_id = o.customer_id
GROUP BY c.customer_id, c.name, c.membership
ORDER BY completed_revenue DESC;
```

Result:

name	membership	completed_revenue	pending_revenue	completed_count	pending_count
Bob	Standard	80.50	0.00	2	0
Carol	Premium	32.00	0.00	1	0
Alice	Premium	29.99	35.50	1	1
Emma	Premium	29.99	0.00	1	0
David	Standard	0.00	0.00	0	0

This comprehensive customer pivot provides a complete view of each customer's purchase behavior, making it easy to identify top customers, pending revenue opportunities, and customers who might need attention.

7.3.4 Understanding Unpivoting

Unpivoting is the reverse of pivoting - it transforms data from a wide format (many columns) to a long format (many rows). This transformation is useful when you need to normalize data for analysis or when working with data that was previously pivoted.

Unpivoting is important because it allows you to work with data that might have been structured for reporting rather than analysis. Sometimes you receive data in a pivoted format that needs to be normalized before you can perform certain types of analysis or combine it with other datasets.

Example: Unpivot monthly sales data

Suppose we have this pivoted sales data:

```
-- Create a temporary pivoted table for demonstration
WITH pivoted_sales AS (
    SELECT
        'Books' as category,
        74.99 as january_sales,
        97.49 as february_sales
)
-- Unpivot it back to long format
SELECT
    category,
    'January' as month,
    january_sales as sales_amount
FROM pivoted_sales
UNION ALL
SELECT
    category,
    'February' as month,
    february_sales as sales_amount
FROM pivoted_sales;
```

Result:

category	month	sales_amount
Books	January	74.99
Books	February	97.49

This unpivoting transformation converts the wide monthly format back to a long format that's easier to analyze and combine with other time-series data.

7.4 Dimensionality Reduction Concepts (Feature Selection)

7.4.1 Understanding Dimensionality Reduction

Dimensionality reduction involves simplifying datasets by focusing on the most important variables and removing unnecessary complexity. In the context of SQL and business analysis, this typically means selecting the most relevant columns and creating simplified views of complex data.

Dimensionality reduction is crucial because real-world datasets often contain more information than you need for specific analyses. By focusing on the most relevant features, you can create cleaner, more focused analyses that are easier to understand and more likely to reveal meaningful insights.

The goal of dimensionality reduction is not just to make datasets smaller, but to make them more useful by eliminating noise and focusing attention on the variables that matter most for your specific analytical objectives.

Understanding which features to keep and which to eliminate requires both technical knowledge and business understanding. The most effective dimensionality reduction combines statistical techniques with domain expertise to preserve the most valuable information.

7.4.2 Identifying Key Features

Feature selection involves determining which columns and variables are most important for your analysis. This process requires understanding your business objectives and the relationships between different data elements.

Effective feature selection improves analysis quality by reducing complexity, eliminating redundant information, and focusing attention on the variables that drive the outcomes you care about. This skill is essential for creating meaningful and actionable insights.

Example: Select key customer features for analysis

```
-- Full customer dataset with all features
SELECT
    customer_id,
    name,
    age,
    city,
    membership,
    -- Calculate derived features
    CASE
        WHEN age < 30 THEN 'Young'
        WHEN age < 40 THEN 'Middle'
        ELSE 'Mature'
    END as age_group,
    COALESCE(SUM(o.price), 0) as total_spent,
    COUNT(o.order_id) as order_count
FROM customers c
LEFT JOIN orders o ON c.customer_id = o.customer_id
    AND o.status = 'Completed'
GROUP BY c.customer_id, c.name, c.age,
         c.city, c.membership;
```

Now, let's reduce this to key features for customer segmentation:

```
-- Reduced feature set focusing on segmentation
SELECT
    customer_id,
    name,
    CASE
        WHEN age < 30 THEN 'Young'
        WHEN age < 40 THEN 'Middle'
        ELSE 'Mature'
    END as age_group,
    membership,
    COALESCE(SUM(o.price), 0) as total_spent,
    CASE
        WHEN COALESCE(SUM(o.price), 0) >= 50
            THEN 'High Value'
        WHEN COALESCE(SUM(o.price), 0) > 0
            THEN 'Some Value'
        ELSE 'No Value'
    END as value_segment
```

```
FROM customers c
LEFT JOIN orders o ON c.customer_id = o.customer_id
    AND o.status = 'Completed'
GROUP BY c.customer_id, c.name, c.age, c.membership;
```

Result:

customer_id	name	age_group	membership	total_spent	value_segment
1	Alice	Young	Premium	29.99	Some Value
2	Bob	Middle	Standard	80.50	High Value
3	Carol	Young	Premium	32.00	Some Value
4	David	Mature	Standard	0.00	No Value
5	Emma	Middle	Premium	29.99	Some Value

This reduced dataset focuses on the most important features for customer analysis: age group, membership type, and value segment. By eliminating unnecessary details and creating meaningful categories, the data becomes more useful for strategic decision-making.

7.4.3 Creating Simplified Data Views

Simplified data views focus on essential information and eliminate complexity that might obscure important patterns. These views are particularly valuable for executive reporting and strategic analysis where clarity is more important than comprehensive detail.

Creating effective simplified views requires understanding what information is most critical for decision-making and how to present that information in the clearest possible format. This skill is essential for communicating insights to business stakeholders.

Example: Create simplified order summary view

```
-- Simplified order analysis focusing on key metrics
SELECT
    MONTH(order_date) as order_month,
    COUNT(*) as total_orders,
    SUM(CASE WHEN status = 'Completed'
        THEN 1 ELSE 0 END) as successful_orders,
    SUM(CASE WHEN status = 'Completed'
        THEN price ELSE 0 END) as revenue,
    ROUND(AVG(CASE WHEN status = 'Completed'
        THEN price END), 2) as avg_order_value
FROM orders
WHERE order_date >= '2024-01-01'
```

```
GROUP BY MONTH(order_date)
ORDER BY order_month;
```

Result:

order_month	total_orders	successful_orders	revenue	avg_order_value
1	2	2	74.99	37.50
2	5	3	97.49	32.50

This simplified view provides essential business metrics without overwhelming detail, making it perfect for executive dashboards and strategic planning discussions.

7.4.4 Focusing on Business-Critical Variables

Business-critical variables are the data elements that most directly impact your key business outcomes and decisions. Identifying and focusing on these variables is essential for creating analysis that drives real business value.

Understanding which variables are truly business-critical requires deep knowledge of your organization's goals, challenges, and success factors. This understanding allows you to create focused analyses that address the most important business questions.

Example: Focus on revenue-driving factors

```
-- Identify key factors that drive revenue
SELECT
    c.membership,
    c.city,
    COUNT(DISTINCT c.customer_id) as customer_count,
    SUM(CASE WHEN o.status = 'Completed'
        THEN o.price ELSE 0 END) as total_revenue,
    ROUND(
        SUM(CASE WHEN o.status = 'Completed'
           THEN o.price ELSE 0 END) /
        COUNT(DISTINCT c.customer_id),
        2
    ) as revenue_per_customer
FROM customers c
LEFT JOIN orders o ON c.customer_id = o.customer_ic
GROUP BY c.membership, c.city
HAVING COUNT(DISTINCT c.customer_id) > 0
ORDER BY total_revenue DESC;
```

Result:

membership	city	customer_count	total_revenue	revenue_per_customer
Standard	Chicago	1	80.50	80.50
Premium	New York	2	61.99	31.00
Premium	Chicago	1	29.99	29.99
Standard	Miami	1	0.00	0.00

This analysis focuses on the business-critical variables of membership type and geographic location, revealing which combinations drive the most revenue per customer.

7.5 Grouping and Summarizing Large Datasets

7.5.1 Understanding Data Summarization

Data summarization involves creating meaningful aggregates and summaries from detailed data, allowing you to understand patterns and trends that might not be visible in individual records. This process is fundamental to business intelligence and strategic analysis.

Effective summarization transforms overwhelming amounts of detail into actionable insights. By grouping related data and calculating meaningful aggregates, you can identify trends, compare performance, and make data-driven decisions based on clear patterns rather than individual data points.

The key to effective summarization is choosing the right level of aggregation for your analytical objectives. Too much detail can obscure patterns, while too much aggregation can hide important nuances. Finding the right balance is essential for creating useful business insights.

Summarization is particularly important when working with large datasets where individual records are too numerous to analyze effectively. By creating appropriate summaries, you can make large datasets manageable and meaningful.

7.5.2 Basic Grouping and Aggregation

Basic grouping and aggregation form the foundation of data summarization. These techniques allow you to organize data into meaningful categories and calculate summary statistics that reveal important patterns and trends.

Understanding how to group data effectively and choose appropriate aggregate functions is essential for creating business reports and analysis. These skills allow you to transform detailed transactional data into strategic insights.

Example: Summarize orders by customer and month

```
SELECT
    c.name,
    c.membership,
    MONTH(o.order_date) as order_month,
    COUNT(o.order_id) as order_count,
    SUM(CASE WHEN o.status = 'Completed'
        THEN o.price ELSE 0 END) as completed_revenue,
    SUM(o.price) as total_order_value
FROM customers c
JOIN orders o ON c.customer_id = o.customer_id
GROUP BY c.customer_id, c.name, c.membership,
         MONTH(o.order_date)
ORDER BY c.name, order_month;
```

Result:

name	membership	order_month	order_count	completed_revenue	total_order_value
Alice	Premium	1	1	29.99	29.99
Alice	Premium	2	1	0.00	35.50
Bob	Standard	1	1	45.00	45.00
Bob	Standard	2	1	35.50	35.50
Carol	Premium	2	1	32.00	32.00
David	Standard	2	1	0.00	55.99
Emma	Premium	2	1	29.99	29.99

This summary provides a clear view of customer activity patterns by month, making it easy to identify trends in customer behavior and revenue generation.

7.5.3 Creating Business Summaries

Business summaries focus on metrics that directly support business decision-making. These summaries should align with key performance indicators and strategic objectives, providing insights that can guide operational and strategic decisions.

Effective business summaries translate raw data into the language of business strategy, focusing on metrics like growth rates, customer value, market performance, and operational efficiency. These summaries are essential for executive reporting and strategic planning.

Example: Create monthly business performance summary

```
SELECT
    MONTH(order_date) as month,
```

```
    MONTHNAME(order_date) as month_name,
    COUNT(*) as total_orders,
    COUNT(DISTINCT customer_id) as active_customers,
    SUM(CASE WHEN status = 'Completed'
        THEN price ELSE 0 END) as revenue,
    SUM(CASE WHEN status = 'Completed'
        THEN 1 ELSE 0 END) as successful_orders,
    ROUND(
        SUM(CASE WHEN status = 'Completed'
          THEN 1 ELSE 0 END) * 100.0 / COUNT(*), 1
    ) as success_rate_percent
FROM orders
WHERE order_date >= '2024-01-01'
GROUP BY MONTH(order_date), MONTHNAME(order_date)
ORDER BY MONTH(order_date);
```

Result:

month	month_name	total_orders	active_customers	revenue	successful_orders	success_rate_percent
1	January	2	2	74.99	2	100.0
2	February	5	4	97.49	3	60.0

This business summary provides key performance indicators that help management understand monthly performance trends, customer engagement, and operational efficiency.

7.5.4 Using AI for Summarization Assistance

AI tools can help you create more effective summaries by suggesting appropriate grouping strategies, identifying important patterns, and recommending relevant metrics for your specific business context.

AI assistance for summarization is valuable because it can help you identify summarization approaches you might not consider and suggest metrics that could provide additional insights into your data. This capability can enhance your analytical effectiveness and efficiency.

What you might ask AI: "Help me create a customer performance summary for our bookstore"

AI might suggest:

```
-- AI-suggested customer performance summary
SELECT
    c.name,
    c.membership,
    c.city,
    COUNT(o.order_id) as total_orders,
    SUM(CASE WHEN o.status = 'Completed'
        THEN o.price ELSE 0 END) as revenue,
    CASE
        WHEN SUM(CASE WHEN o.status = 'Completed'
            THEN o.price ELSE 0 END) >= 60
            THEN 'High Value'
        WHEN SUM(CASE WHEN o.status = 'Completed'
            THEN o.price ELSE 0 END) >= 30
            THEN 'Medium Value'
        WHEN SUM(CASE WHEN o.status = 'Completed'
            THEN o.price ELSE 0 END) > 0
            THEN 'Low Value'
        ELSE 'No Value'
    END as customer_segment,
    ROUND(
        SUM(CASE WHEN o.status = 'Completed'
            THEN 1 ELSE 0 END) * 100.0 /
        NULLIF(COUNT(o.order_id), 0),
        1
    ) as success_rate
FROM customers c
LEFT JOIN orders o ON c.customer_id = o.customer_id
GROUP BY c.customer_id, c.name, c.membership, c.city
ORDER BY revenue DESC;
```

This AI-suggested summary provides a comprehensive view of customer performance with automatic segmentation and success rate calculations.

What you might ask AI: "Create a simple sales trend summary"

AI might suggest:

```
-- AI-suggested sales trend summary
SELECT
    DATE_FORMAT(order_date, '%Y-%m') as month,
    COUNT(*) as orders,
    SUM(CASE WHEN status = 'Completed'
        THEN price ELSE 0 END) as revenue,
    COUNT(DISTINCT customer_id) as customers,
```

```
    CASE
        WHEN SUM(CASE WHEN status = 'Completed'
           THEN price ELSE 0 END) > 80 THEN 'Strong'
        WHEN SUM(CASE WHEN status = 'Completed'
           THEN price ELSE 0 END) > 50 THEN 'Good'
        ELSE 'Needs Attention'
    END as performance_rating
FROM orders
GROUP BY DATE_FORMAT(order_date, '%Y-%m')
ORDER BY month;
```

This simple trend summary provides essential business metrics with AI-suggested performance ratings that make the data more actionable for business decision-making.

7.6 Maintaining Data Integrity During Reshaping

7.6.1 Understanding Data Integrity

Data integrity refers to maintaining the accuracy, consistency, and reliability of data throughout transformation processes. When reshaping data, it's crucial to ensure that no information is lost, corrupted, or misrepresented during the transformation.

Maintaining data integrity is essential because reshaping operations can introduce errors if not handled carefully. These errors can lead to incorrect business decisions, so understanding how to preserve data quality during transformations is a critical skill for any data analyst.

Data integrity involves several key principles: completeness (no data is lost), accuracy (calculations are correct), consistency (relationships are preserved), and validity (data remains meaningful). Each reshaping operation should be designed and validated to ensure these principles are maintained.

Understanding data integrity helps you build trust in your analysis results and ensures that business decisions based on your work are founded on reliable information. This trust is essential for effective data-driven decision-making.

7.6.2 Validating Transformation Results

Validation involves checking that your reshaping operations produce accurate and complete results. This process should include verifying row counts, checking calculations, and ensuring that important relationships in the data are preserved.

Effective validation catches errors early in the analysis process and provides confidence that your transformed data accurately represents the original information. This practice is essential for maintaining analytical credibility and ensuring reliable business insights.

Example: Validate a customer summary transformation

```sql
-- Original data counts
SELECT
    'Original Orders' as data_source,
    COUNT(*) as total_records,
    SUM(CASE WHEN status = 'Completed'
        THEN price ELSE 0 END) as total_revenue,
    COUNT(DISTINCT customer_id) as unique_customers
FROM orders

UNION ALL

-- Summarized data validation
SELECT
    'Customer Summary' as data_source,
    SUM(order_count) as total_records,
    SUM(completed_revenue) as total_revenue,
    COUNT(*) as unique_customers
FROM (
    SELECT
        c.customer_id,
        COUNT(o.order_id) as order_count,
        SUM(CASE WHEN o.status = 'Completed'
           THEN o.price ELSE 0 END) as completed_revenue
    FROM customers c
    LEFT JOIN orders o ON c.customer_id = o.customer_id
    GROUP BY c.customer_id
) customer_summary;
```

Result:

data_source	total_records	total_revenue	unique_customers
Original Orders	7	172.48	5
Customer Summary	7	172.48	5

This validation confirms that the summarization preserved all records and revenue totals, ensuring data integrity throughout the transformation.

7.7 Conclusion

Reshaping and reducing data are essential skills for transforming raw transactional records into formats that support analysis, reporting, and decision-making. In this chapter, you explored how SQL can be used to reorganize data through pivoting and unpivoting, summarize large datasets with grouping and aggregation, and simplify complex tables by focusing on business-relevant features.

You learned how CASE statements enable flexible pivot-style transformations even in databases without native PIVOT functions, and how unpivoting techniques restore normalized structures when needed for analysis. You also applied feature selection and derived variables to reduce dimensionality in a practical, business-oriented way—by emphasizing customer value, revenue drivers, and performance metrics rather than unnecessary detail.

Equally important, this chapter emphasized maintaining data integrity during reshaping operations. By validating totals, record counts, and relationships before and after transformations, you ensure that insights drawn from reshaped data remain accurate and trustworthy.

Together, these techniques form the foundation for effective business intelligence work. Mastering data reshaping and reduction allows you to adapt datasets to different analytical goals, communicate insights clearly, and support decision-making with confidence. As you continue building your SQL skills, these practices will remain central to producing reliable, meaningful, and actionable analysis.

7.8 Key Terms

Data Reshaping – Changing the structure of a dataset, such as converting rows to columns (pivot) or columns to rows (unpivot), to make it more suitable for analysis.

Pivot Tables – A method to summarize and reorganize data from long format to wide format, often to compare values across categories.

Unpivoting – The process of converting data from wide format back to long format, often to normalize it for analysis.

Long Format – A data layout where each observation or measurement is represented in a separate row.

Wide Format – A data layout where multiple measurements or categories are represented as separate columns.

CASE Statements – SQL conditional expressions used to create pivot-like transformations or derive new columns based on conditions.

Aggregation – The process of summarizing multiple rows of data into meaningful metrics, using functions like SUM, COUNT, or AVG.

Dimensionality Reduction – Simplifying a dataset by focusing on the most important variables while removing less relevant ones.

Feature Selection – Choosing the most relevant columns or variables in a dataset for analysis to reduce complexity.

Data Reduction – Reducing the size or complexity of a dataset while retaining essential information for analysis.

Simplified Data Views – Condensed representations of datasets that focus only on key metrics or variables.

Business-Critical Variables – Data elements that have the most impact on decision-making and business outcomes.

Grouping and Summarizing – Organizing data into categories and calculating summary statistics to reveal trends and patterns.

SQL Aggregate Functions – Functions like SUM, COUNT, AVG, MIN, and MAX used to summarize data in SQL queries.

Customer Segmentation – Dividing customers into groups based on shared characteristics, behavior, or value.

Revenue Analysis – Evaluating sales or income data to understand performance across customers, products, or regions.

Data Integrity – Ensuring that data remains accurate, complete, and consistent during transformations.

Validation Checks – Procedures to confirm that reshaped or summarized data matches the original dataset in key aspects.

Handling Missing Data – Techniques such as COALESCE or imputation to manage gaps in data without introducing errors.

Preserving Relationships – Maintaining the correct connections between related data elements during reshaping or summarization.

Quality Checks – Comprehensive reviews of transformed data to ensure accuracy, completeness, and business relevance.

AI-Assisted Summarization – Using AI tools to suggest grouping strategies, important metrics, or simplified views for datasets.

7.9 Review Questions

1. What is the difference between pivoting and unpivoting data, and when would you use each technique?
2. How can CASE statements be used in SQL to pivot data when a database lacks a PIVOT function?

3. Explain the concept of dimensionality reduction and why feature selection is important in analysis.
4. How does creating simplified data views help business decision-making?
5. What are business-critical variables, and how do you determine which to focus on during analysis?
6. Describe the process of grouping and summarizing large datasets. Why is it essential for business intelligence?
7. How can AI tools assist in summarizing and reshaping data, and what are the limitations of relying solely on AI?
8. What steps should you take to maintain data integrity during reshaping operations?
9. Why is it important to handle missing data carefully during pivoting, unpivoting, or reduction processes?
10. How can you validate that a reshaped dataset accurately preserves relationships and totals from the original data?
11. What is the purpose of quality checks on reshaped data, and what types of issues might they reveal?
12. Give an example of how a customer pivot or summary could be used to inform a business decision.

7.10 References

[1] W3Schools. (2024). SQL GROUP BY and Aggregate Functions Tutorial. https://www.w3schools.com/sql/sql_groupby.asp

[2] SQLBolt. (2024). Interactive SQL Tutorial - Queries with Aggregates and Groups. https://sqlbolt.com/lesson/select_queries_with_aggregates

[3] Mode Analytics. (2024). SQL Tutorial - Pivot Tables and Data Reshaping. https://mode.com/sql-tutorial/sql-pivot-table/

[4] Codecademy. (2024). Learn SQL - Advanced Aggregates and Data Summarization. https://www.codecademy.com/learn/learn-sql

[5] PostgreSQL Documentation. (2024). Aggregate Functions and Grouping Sets. https://www.postgresql.org/docs/current/functions-aggregate.html

7.11 Lab 7-1 Pivoting and Unpivoting

In business analytics, answering different questions often requires changing how data is structured. This process—pivoting and unpivoting—transforms data between formats to support reporting, analysis, and visualization.

As an analyst at *RetailMetrics*, you might need to create summary reports, build cross-tabulations, or convert aggregated tables back into detailed records. These tasks involve switching between wide format (pivoted data with more columns) and long format (unpivoted data with more rows), depending on the goal.

Pivoting and unpivoting are essential for organizing data for comparison, preparing it for statistical analysis, and ensuring it fits the requirements of different visualizations and business needs.

In this lab, you will learn how to pivot and unpivot data in R using both tidyverse functions such as pivot_wider() and pivot_longer(), as well as SQL-style techniques using CASE statements and aggregation. By the end, you will understand how and when to use each approach effectively.

7.11.1 Demonstration

7.11.1.1 Step 1: Setting Up R Environment and Sample Data

Let's create realistic sales data that demonstrates common pivoting scenarios. We'll work with RetailMetrics sales data to demonstrate various pivoting scenarios that reflect real business reporting needs.

```
# Load required packages
library(tidyverse)  # For pivot_wider, pivot_longer, and data
 ↪  manipulation
library(sqldf)      # For SQL-based pivoting
library(lubridate)  # For date handling

# Create sales transactions data (long format)
sales_data <- data.frame(
  transaction_id = 1:36,

  # Store IDs (36 rows total)
  store_id = rep(c("Store_A", "Store_B", "Store_C"), each = 12),

  # Product categories (36 rows total)
  product_category = rep(c("Electronics", "Clothing", "Home", "Books"),
   ↪  times = 9),

  # Sale months (36 rows total)
  sale_month = rep(c("January", "February", "March"), each = 12),

  sales_amount = c(
    # Store A
```

```
    15000, 12000, 8000, 5000,
    18000, 14000, 9500, 6000,
    20000, 16000, 11000, 7000,

    # Store B
    12000, 10000, 6000, 4000,
    14000, 11000, 7000, 4500,
    16000, 13000, 8000, 5500,

    # Store C
    8000, 6000, 4000, 2500,
    9000, 7000, 4500, 3000,
    10000, 8000, 5000, 3500
  ),

  units_sold = c(
    # Store A
    150, 80, 40, 100,
    180, 93, 48, 120,
    200, 107, 55, 140,

    # Store B
    120, 67, 30, 80,
    140, 73, 35, 90,
    160, 87, 40, 110,

    # Store C
    80, 40, 20, 50,
    90, 47, 23, 60,
    100, 53, 25, 70
  ),

  stringsAsFactors = FALSE
)

# Display the original data (long format)
cat("ORIGINAL SALES DATA (Long Format):\n")
```

```
ORIGINAL SALES DATA (Long Format):
```

```
print(head(sales_data[,1:4], 12))
```

```
  transaction_id store_id product_category sale_month
1              1  Store_A      Electronics    January
```

```
2              2  Store_A        Clothing    January
3              3  Store_A            Home    January
4              4  Store_A           Books    January
5              5  Store_A     Electronics    January
6              6  Store_A        Clothing    January
7              7  Store_A            Home    January
8              8  Store_A           Books    January
9              9  Store_A     Electronics    January
10            10  Store_A        Clothing    January
11            11  Store_A            Home    January
12            12  Store_A           Books    January
```

```
print(head(sales_data[,5:6], 12))
```

```
   sales_amount units_sold
1         15000        150
2         12000         80
3          8000         40
4          5000        100
5         18000        180
6         14000         93
7          9500         48
8          6000        120
9         20000        200
10        16000        107
11        11000         55
12         7000        140
```

```
cat("\nData Structure:\n")
```

```
Data Structure:
```

```
cat("Total transactions:", nrow(sales_data), "\n")
```

```
Total transactions: 36
```

```
cat("Stores:", length(unique(sales_data$store_id)), "\n")
```

```
Stores: 3
```

```
cat("Product categories:", length(unique(sales_data$product_category)),
↪  "\n")
```

```
Product categories: 4
```

```
cat("Months:", length(unique(sales_data$sale_month)), "\n")
```

```
Months: 3
```

7.11.1.2 Step 2: Pivoting with Tidyverse (Wide Format)

The tidyverse is a collection of R packages designed to make data manipulation more intuitive, consistent, and readable. It provides tools that allow analysts to transform and reshape data efficiently without relying on complex or hard-to-read syntax. One of its key strengths is handling data structure changes, such as pivoting. Pivoting refers to reorganizing data between "long" and "wide" formats depending on the analytical need. In a long format, each observation is stored in rows, which is ideal for analysis and modeling. In a wide format, values are spread across columns, making it easier to compare categories and create reports. The tidyverse is used in this context because its pivoting functions simplify this process, allowing analysts to quickly restructure data for reporting, visualization, and business decision-making.

```
# Scenario 1: Monthly sales comparison by store (pivot months to
↪ columns)
monthly_comparison <- sales_data %>%
  group_by(store_id, sale_month) %>%
  summarise(total_sales = sum(sales_amount), .groups = 'drop') %>%
  pivot_wider(names_from = sale_month,
              values_from = total_sales,
              names_prefix = "Sales_")

cat("MONTHLY SALES COMPARISON (Tidyverse):\n")
```

```
MONTHLY SALES COMPARISON (Tidyverse):
```

```
print(monthly_comparison)
```

```
# A tibble: 3 x 4
  store_id Sales_January Sales_February Sales_March
  <chr>            <dbl>          <dbl>       <dbl>
1 Store_A         141500             NA          NA
2 Store_B             NA         111000          NA
3 Store_C             NA             NA       70500
```

```
# Scenario 2: Product category performance by store (pivot
↪ categories to columns)
category_performance <- sales_data %>%
  group_by(store_id, product_category) %>%
  summarise(total_sales = sum(sales_amount), .groups = 'drop') %>%
  pivot_wider(names_from = product_category,
```

```
                values_from = total_sales)

cat("\nCATEGORY PERFORMANCE BY STORE (Tidyverse):\n")
```

```
CATEGORY PERFORMANCE BY STORE (Tidyverse):
```

```
print(category_performance)
```

```
# A tibble: 3 x 5
  store_id Books Clothing Electronics  Home
  <chr>    <dbl>    <dbl>       <dbl> <dbl>
1 Store_A  18000    42000       53000 28500
2 Store_B  14000    34000       42000 21000
3 Store_C   9000    21000       27000 13500
```

```
# Scenario 3: Store performance by month (pivot stores to columns)
store_performance <- sales_data %>%
  group_by(sale_month, store_id) %>%
  summarise(total_sales = sum(sales_amount), .groups = 'drop') %>%
  pivot_wider(names_from = store_id,
              values_from = total_sales)

cat("\nSTORE PERFORMANCE BY MONTH (Tidyverse):\n")
```

```
STORE PERFORMANCE BY MONTH (Tidyverse):
```

```
print(store_performance)
```

```
# A tibble: 3 x 4
  sale_month Store_B Store_A Store_C
  <chr>        <dbl>   <dbl>   <dbl>
1 February    111000      NA      NA
2 January         NA  141500      NA
3 March           NA      NA   70500
```

```
# Scenario 4: Multiple metrics pivot (both sales and units)
multi_metric_pivot <- sales_data %>%
  group_by(store_id, product_category) %>%
  summarise(
    total_sales = sum(sales_amount),
    total_units = sum(units_sold),
    .groups = 'drop'
  ) %>%
```

```
    pivot_wider(
      names_from = product_category,
      values_from = c(total_sales, total_units),
      names_sep = "_"
    )

  cat("\nMULTI-METRIC PIVOT (Tidyverse):\n")
```

```
MULTI-METRIC PIVOT (Tidyverse):
```

```
  print(multi_metric_pivot[,1:3])
```

```
# A tibble: 3 x 3
  store_id total_sales_Books total_sales_Clothing
  <chr>                <dbl>                <dbl>
1 Store_A              18000                42000
2 Store_B              14000                34000
3 Store_C               9000                21000
```

```
  print(multi_metric_pivot[,4])
```

```
# A tibble: 3 x 1
  total_sales_Electronics
                    <dbl>
1                   53000
2                   42000
3                   27000
```

```
  # Business insights using tidyverse
  cat("\n=== TIDYVERSE PIVOT INSIGHTS ===\n")
```

```
=== TIDYVERSE PIVOT INSIGHTS ===
```

```
  # Calculate month-over-month growth
  monthly_with_growth <- monthly_comparison %>%
    mutate(
      Jan_to_Feb_Growth = round((Sales_February - Sales_January) /
       ↪  Sales_January * 100, 1),
      Feb_to_Mar_Growth = round((Sales_March - Sales_February) /
       ↪  Sales_February * 100, 1)
    )

  cat("Month-over-month growth rates:\n")
```

```
Month-over-month growth rates:
```

```r
print(monthly_with_growth[, c("store_id", "Jan_to_Feb_Growth",
  ↪ "Feb_to_Mar_Growth")])
```

```
# A tibble: 3 x 3
  store_id Jan_to_Feb_Growth Feb_to_Mar_Growth
  <chr>                <dbl>             <dbl>
1 Store_A                 NA                NA
2 Store_B                 NA                NA
3 Store_C                 NA                NA
```

```r
# Find best performing category per store
best_categories <- category_performance %>%
  rowwise() %>%
  mutate(
    best_category = names(.)[which.max(c(Electronics, Clothing,
    ↪ Home, Books))],
    best_sales = max(c(Electronics, Clothing, Home, Books))
  ) %>%
  select(store_id, best_category, best_sales)

cat("Best performing category per store:\n")
```

```
Best performing category per store:
```

```r
print(best_categories)
```

```
# A tibble: 3 x 3
# Rowwise:
  store_id best_category best_sales
  <chr>    <chr>              <dbl>
1 Store_A  store_id           53000
2 Store_B  store_id           42000
3 Store_C  store_id           27000
```

7.11.1.3 Step 3: Pivoting with SQL in R

While the tidyverse provides an intuitive way to reshape data, SQL offers a more flexible and widely used approach, especially when working with large datasets or databases. Instead of using built-in pivoting functions, SQL achieves the same result through CASE statements combined with aggregation. This method allows you to explicitly control how values are grouped and transformed into columns, making it highly customizable and transparent. SQL-based pivoting is particularly valuable in real-world business environments where data is stored in relational databases and needs to be reshaped directly within queries. In this section, you will use SQL within R to replicate the same pivoting tasks, demonstrating how similar outcomes can be achieved using a more versatile and scalable approach.

```
# Scenario 1: Monthly sales comparison using SQL
monthly_sql <- sqldf("
  SELECT
    store_id,
    SUM(CASE WHEN sale_month = 'January' THEN sales_amount ELSE 0
↪ END) AS Sales_January,
    SUM(CASE WHEN sale_month = 'February' THEN sales_amount ELSE 0
↪ END) AS Sales_February,
    SUM(CASE WHEN sale_month = 'March' THEN sales_amount ELSE 0
↪ END) AS Sales_March
  FROM sales_data
  GROUP BY store_id
  ORDER BY store_id
")

cat("MONTHLY SALES COMPARISON (SQL):\n")
```

```
MONTHLY SALES COMPARISON (SQL):
```

```
print(monthly_sql)
```

```
  store_id Sales_January Sales_February Sales_March
1  Store_A        141500              0           0
2  Store_B             0         111000           0
3  Store_C             0              0       70500
```

```
# Scenario 2: Product category performance using SQL
category_sql <- sqldf("
  SELECT
    store_id,
    SUM(CASE WHEN product_category = 'Electronics' THEN
↪ sales_amount ELSE 0 END) AS Electronics,
    SUM(CASE WHEN product_category = 'Clothing' THEN sales_amount
↪ ELSE 0 END) AS Clothing,
    SUM(CASE WHEN product_category = 'Home' THEN sales_amount ELSE
↪ 0 END) AS Home,
    SUM(CASE WHEN product_category = 'Books' THEN sales_amount ELSE
↪ 0 END) AS Books
  FROM sales_data
  GROUP BY store_id
  ORDER BY store_id
```

```
")

cat("\nCATEGORY PERFORMANCE BY STORE (SQL):\n")
```

```
CATEGORY PERFORMANCE BY STORE (SQL):
```

```
print(category_sql)
```

```
  store_id Electronics Clothing  Home Books
1  Store_A       53000    42000 28500 18000
2  Store_B       42000    34000 21000 14000
3  Store_C       27000    21000 13500  9000
```

```
# Scenario 3: Store performance by month using SQL
store_sql <- sqldf("
  SELECT
    sale_month,
    SUM(CASE WHEN store_id = 'Store_A' THEN sales_amount ELSE 0
↪ END) AS Store_A,
    SUM(CASE WHEN store_id = 'Store_B' THEN sales_amount ELSE 0
↪ END) AS Store_B,
    SUM(CASE WHEN store_id = 'Store_C' THEN sales_amount ELSE 0
↪ END) AS Store_C
  FROM sales_data
  GROUP BY sale_month
  ORDER BY
    CASE sale_month
      WHEN 'January' THEN 1
      WHEN 'February' THEN 2
      WHEN 'March' THEN 3
    END
")

cat("\nSTORE PERFORMANCE BY MONTH (SQL):\n")
```

```
STORE PERFORMANCE BY MONTH (SQL):
```

```
print(store_sql)
```

```
  sale_month Store_A Store_B Store_C
1    January  141500       0       0
2   February       0  111000       0
3      March       0       0   70500
```

```
# Scenario 4: Complex pivot with calculations using SQL
complex_sql <- sqldf("
  SELECT
    store_id,
    SUM(CASE WHEN product_category = 'Electronics' THEN
↪ sales_amount ELSE 0 END) AS Electronics_Sales,
    SUM(CASE WHEN product_category = 'Electronics' THEN units_sold
↪ ELSE 0 END) AS Electronics_Units,
    SUM(CASE WHEN product_category = 'Clothing' THEN sales_amount
↪ ELSE 0 END) AS Clothing_Sales,
    SUM(CASE WHEN product_category = 'Clothing' THEN units_sold
↪ ELSE 0 END) AS Clothing_Units,
    ROUND(
      SUM(CASE WHEN product_category = 'Electronics' THEN
↪ sales_amount ELSE 0 END) /
      NULLIF(SUM(CASE WHEN product_category = 'Electronics' THEN
↪ units_sold ELSE 0 END), 0), 2
    ) AS Electronics_Avg_Price,
    ROUND(
      SUM(CASE WHEN product_category = 'Clothing' THEN sales_amount
↪ ELSE 0 END) /
      NULLIF(SUM(CASE WHEN product_category = 'Clothing' THEN
↪ units_sold ELSE 0 END), 0), 2
    ) AS Clothing_Avg_Price
  FROM sales_data
  GROUP BY store_id
  ORDER BY store_id
")

cat("\nCOMPLEX PIVOT WITH CALCULATIONS (SQL):\n")
```

```
COMPLEX PIVOT WITH CALCULATIONS (SQL):
```

```
print(complex_sql[,1:4])
```

```
  store_id Electronics_Sales Electronics_Units Clothing_Sales
1  Store_A             53000               530          42000
2  Store_B             42000               420          34000
3  Store_C             27000               270          21000
```

```
print(complex_sql[,5:7])
```

```
  Clothing_Units Electronics_Avg_Price Clothing_Avg_Price
```

```
1           280                    100             150.00
2           227                    100             149.78
3           140                    100             150.00
```

```
# Verify results match between tidyverse and SQL
cat("\n=== VERIFICATION: Tidyverse vs SQL Results ===\n")
```

```
=== VERIFICATION: Tidyverse vs SQL Results ===
```

```
cat("Monthly comparison - Tidyverse vs SQL match:",
    identical(as.data.frame(monthly_comparison), monthly_sql),
     ↪  "\n")
```

```
Monthly comparison - Tidyverse vs SQL match: FALSE
```

```
cat("Category performance - Tidyverse vs SQL match:",
    identical(as.data.frame(category_performance), category_sql),
     ↪  "\n")
```

```
Category performance - Tidyverse vs SQL match: FALSE
```

7.11.1.4 Step 4: Unpivoting (Long Format) with Tidyverse

While pivoting transforms data into a wide format for easier comparison and reporting, unpivoting reverses this process by converting data back into a long format. Long format organizes data into rows rather than columns, making it more suitable for analysis, statistical modeling, and many types of visualizations. In real-world workflows, analysts frequently move between wide and long formats depending on the task at hand.

The tidyverse provides the pivot_longer() function to simplify unpivoting by gathering multiple columns into key-value pairs. This allows you to take structured report-style data and convert it into a flexible format that is easier to analyze and manipulate. In this section, you will learn how to unpivot both simple and multi-metric datasets, preparing your data for deeper analysis and more advanced insights.

```
# Start with our pivoted monthly data
cat("STARTING WITH WIDE FORMAT:\n")
```

```
STARTING WITH WIDE FORMAT:
```

```
print(monthly_comparison)
```

```
# A tibble: 3 x 4
  store_id Sales_January Sales_February Sales_March
  <chr>            <dbl>          <dbl>       <dbl>
1 Store_A         141500             NA          NA
```

```
2 Store_B              NA         111000            NA
3 Store_C              NA             NA         70500
```

```
# Unpivot back to long format using pivot_longer
monthly_long <- monthly_comparison %>%
  pivot_longer(
    cols = starts_with("Sales_"),
    names_to = "month",
    values_to = "sales_amount",
    names_prefix = "Sales_"
  )

cat("\nUNPIVOTED TO LONG FORMAT (Tidyverse):\n")
```

```
UNPIVOTED TO LONG FORMAT (Tidyverse):
```

```
print(monthly_long)
```

```
# A tibble: 9 x 3
  store_id month    sales_amount
  <chr>    <chr>           <dbl>
1 Store_A  January        141500
2 Store_A  February           NA
3 Store_A  March              NA
4 Store_B  January            NA
5 Store_B  February       111000
6 Store_B  March              NA
7 Store_C  January            NA
8 Store_C  February           NA
9 Store_C  March           70500
```

```
# More complex unpivoting - multiple metrics
cat("\nSTARTING WITH MULTI-METRIC WIDE FORMAT:\n")
```

```
STARTING WITH MULTI-METRIC WIDE FORMAT:
```

```
print(multi_metric_pivot)
```

```
# A tibble: 3 x 9
  store_id total_sales_Books total_sales_Clothing total_sales_Electronics
  <chr>                <dbl>                <dbl>                   <dbl>
1 Store_A              18000                42000                   53000
2 Store_B              14000                34000                   42000
3 Store_C               9000                21000                   27000
```

```
# i 5 more variables: total_sales_Home <dbl>, total_units_Books <dbl>,
#   total_units_Clothing <dbl>, total_units_Electronics <dbl>,
#   total_units_Home <dbl>
```

```
# Unpivot the multi-metric data
# Unpivot the multi-metric data
multi_metric_long <- multi_metric_pivot %>%
  pivot_longer(
    cols = -store_id,
    names_to = c("prefix", "metric", "category"),
    names_sep = "_",
    values_to = "value"
  ) %>%
  select(-prefix) %>%  # drop "total"
  pivot_wider(
    names_from = metric,
    values_from = value
  )

cat("\nMULTI-METRIC UNPIVOTED (Tidyverse):\n")
```

```
MULTI-METRIC UNPIVOTED (Tidyverse):
```

```
print(multi_metric_long)
```

```
# A tibble: 12 x 4
   store_id category    sales units
   <chr>    <chr>       <dbl> <dbl>
 1 Store_A  Books       18000   360
 2 Store_A  Clothing    42000   280
 3 Store_A  Electronics 53000   530
 4 Store_A  Home        28500   143
 5 Store_B  Books       14000   280
 6 Store_B  Clothing    34000   227
 7 Store_B  Electronics 42000   420
 8 Store_B  Home        21000   105
 9 Store_C  Books        9000   180
10 Store_C  Clothing    21000   140
11 Store_C  Electronics 27000   270
12 Store_C  Home        13500    68
```

```
# Create a comprehensive long format for analysis
comprehensive_long <- sales_data %>%
  pivot_longer(
```

```
    cols = c(sales_amount, units_sold),
    names_to = "metric_type",
    values_to = "metric_value"
  )

cat("\nCOMPREHENSIVE LONG FORMAT:\n")
```

```
COMPREHENSIVE LONG FORMAT:
```

```
print(head(comprehensive_long[,1:5], 12))
```

```
# A tibble: 12 x 5
   transaction_id store_id product_category sale_month metric_type
            <int> <chr>    <chr>            <chr>      <chr>
 1              1 Store_A  Electronics      January    sales_amount
 2              1 Store_A  Electronics      January    units_sold
 3              2 Store_A  Clothing         January    sales_amount
 4              2 Store_A  Clothing         January    units_sold
 5              3 Store_A  Home             January    sales_amount
 6              3 Store_A  Home             January    units_sold
 7              4 Store_A  Books            January    sales_amount
 8              4 Store_A  Books            January    units_sold
 9              5 Store_A  Electronics      January    sales_amount
10              5 Store_A  Electronics      January    units_sold
11              6 Store_A  Clothing         January    sales_amount
12              6 Store_A  Clothing         January    units_sold
```

```
print(head(comprehensive_long[,6], 12))
```

```
# A tibble: 12 x 1
   metric_value
          <dbl>
 1        15000
 2          150
 3        12000
 4           80
 5         8000
 6           40
 7         5000
 8          100
 9        18000
10          180
11        14000
```

```
12          93
```

```
# Business analysis on long format data
cat("\n=== LONG FORMAT ANALYSIS ===\n")
```

```
=== LONG FORMAT ANALYSIS ===
```

```
# Calculate correlations between sales and units
correlation_analysis <- sales_data %>%
  group_by(product_category) %>%
  summarise(
    sales_units_correlation = round(cor(sales_amount, units_sold),
     ↪  3),
    avg_price_per_unit = round(mean(sales_amount / units_sold), 2),
    .groups = 'drop'
  )

cat("Sales-Units correlation by category:\n")
```

```
Sales-Units correlation by category:
```

```
print(correlation_analysis)
```

```
# A tibble: 4 x 3
  product_category sales_units_correlation avg_price_per_unit
  <chr>                              <dbl>              <dbl>
1 Books                                  1                 50
2 Clothing                               1                150.
3 Electronics                            1                100
4 Home                                   1                199.
```

7.11.1.5 Step 5: Unpivoting with SQL (UNION Approach)

Unpivoting in SQL is the reverse of pivoting, but unlike modern data tools, SQL does not have a dedicated unpivot function in many environments. Instead, analysts replicate this transformation using UNION ALL statements to stack columns back into rows. This approach manually reshapes data by selecting each column as a separate row-level output and combining the results into a single dataset.

Although more verbose than tidyverse methods, SQL unpivoting is widely used in real-world database systems because it is highly transparent and compatible with virtually all SQL platforms. It also gives analysts precise control over how data is reconstructed from wide formats. In this section, you will learn how to use UNION-based techniques to convert wide data back into long format and verify that the transformation preserves the original information correctly.

```
# Unpivot monthly data using SQL UNION
monthly_unpivot_sql <- sqldf("
  SELECT *
  FROM (
    SELECT store_id, 'January' AS month, Sales_January AS sales_amount
 ↪  FROM monthly_sql
    UNION ALL
    SELECT store_id, 'February' AS month, Sales_February AS
 ↪  sales_amount FROM monthly_sql
    UNION ALL
    SELECT store_id, 'March' AS month, Sales_March AS sales_amount FROM
 ↪  monthly_sql
  )
  ORDER BY
    store_id,
    CASE month
      WHEN 'January' THEN 1
      WHEN 'February' THEN 2
      WHEN 'March' THEN 3
    END
")

cat("UNPIVOTED MONTHLY DATA (SQL UNION):\n")
```

```
UNPIVOTED MONTHLY DATA (SQL UNION):
```

```
print(monthly_unpivot_sql)
```

```
  store_id    month sales_amount
1  Store_A  January       141500
2  Store_A February            0
3  Store_A    March            0
4  Store_B  January            0
5  Store_B February       111000
6  Store_B    March            0
7  Store_C  January            0
8  Store_C February            0
9  Store_C    March        70500
```

```
# More complex unpivoting with SQL
category_unpivot_sql <- sqldf("
  SELECT store_id, 'Electronics' AS category, Electronics AS
 ↪  sales_amount FROM category_sql
  UNION ALL
```

```
  SELECT store_id, 'Clothing' AS category, Clothing AS sales_amount
 ↪  FROM category_sql
  UNION ALL
  SELECT store_id, 'Home' AS category, Home AS sales_amount FROM
 ↪  category_sql
  UNION ALL
  SELECT store_id, 'Books' AS category, Books AS sales_amount FROM
 ↪  category_sql
  ORDER BY store_id, category
")

cat("\nUNPIVOTED CATEGORY DATA (SQL UNION):\n")
```

```
UNPIVOTED CATEGORY DATA (SQL UNION):
```

```
print(head(category_unpivot_sql, 12))
```

```
   store_id    category sales_amount
1   Store_A       Books        18000
2   Store_A    Clothing        42000
3   Store_A Electronics        53000
4   Store_A        Home        28500
5   Store_B       Books        14000
6   Store_B    Clothing        34000
7   Store_B Electronics        42000
8   Store_B        Home        21000
9   Store_C       Books         9000
10  Store_C    Clothing        21000
11  Store_C Electronics        27000
12  Store_C        Home        13500
```

```
# Verify unpivoting worked correctly
cat("\n=== UNPIVOT VERIFICATION ===\n")
```

```
=== UNPIVOT VERIFICATION ===
```

```
# Compare original totals with unpivoted totals
original_total <- sum(sales_data$sales_amount)
unpivoted_total <- sum(monthly_unpivot_sql$sales_amount)

cat("Original total sales:", original_total, "\n")
```

```
Original total sales: 323000
```

```
cat("Unpivoted total sales:", unpivoted_total, "\n")
```

```
Unpivoted total sales: 323000
```

```
cat("Totals match:", original_total == unpivoted_total, "\n")
```

```
Totals match: TRUE
```

7.11.2 Practice

You're working as a data analyst for "SalesForce Analytics," a company that tracks sales performance across regions, products, and time periods.

```
# Create comprehensive exercise dataset
salesforce_data <- data.frame(
  record_id = 1:36,
  region = rep(c('North', 'South', 'East', 'West'), each = 9),
  product_line = rep(c('Software', 'Hardware', 'Services'), 12),
  quarter = rep(c('Q1', 'Q2', 'Q3'), 12),
  revenue = c(
    # North region
    250000, 180000, 120000,  # Q1: Software, Hardware, Services
    280000, 200000, 140000,  # Q2
    320000, 220000, 160000,  # Q3
    # South region
    200000, 150000, 100000,  # Q1
    230000, 170000, 120000,  # Q2
    260000, 190000, 140000,  # Q3
    # East region
    300000, 220000, 150000,  # Q1
    340000, 250000, 170000,  # Q2
    380000, 280000, 190000,  # Q3
    # West region
    180000, 130000, 90000,   # Q1
    210000, 150000, 110000,  # Q2
    240000, 170000, 130000   # Q3
  ),
  units_sold = c(
    # North region
    500, 180, 60,   # Q1
    560, 200, 70,   # Q2
    640, 220, 80,   # Q3
    # South region
    400, 150, 50,   # Q1
    460, 170, 60,   # Q2
```

```
      520, 190, 70,   # Q3
      # East region
      600, 220, 75,   # Q1
      680, 250, 85,   # Q2
      760, 280, 95,   # Q3
      # West region
      360, 130, 45,   # Q1
      420, 150, 55,   # Q2
      480, 170, 65    # Q3
    ),
    stringsAsFactors = FALSE
  )

  # Display exercise data
  cat("SALESFORCE ANALYTICS DATASET:\n")
```

```
SALESFORCE ANALYTICS DATASET:
```

```
  print(head(salesforce_data, 12))
```

```
   record_id region product_line quarter revenue units_sold
1          1  North     Software      Q1  250000        500
2          2  North     Hardware      Q2  180000        180
3          3  North     Services      Q3  120000         60
4          4  North     Software      Q1  280000        560
5          5  North     Hardware      Q2  200000        200
6          6  North     Services      Q3  140000         70
7          7  North     Software      Q1  320000        640
8          8  North     Hardware      Q2  220000        220
9          9  North     Services      Q3  160000         80
10        10  South     Software      Q1  200000        400
11        11  South     Hardware      Q2  150000        150
12        12  South     Services      Q3  100000         50
```

```
  cat("\nDataset Overview:\n")
```

```

Dataset Overview:
```

```
  cat("Records:", nrow(salesforce_data), "\n")
```

```
Records: 36
```

```
  cat("Regions:", length(unique(salesforce_data$region)), "\n")
```

```
Regions: 4
```

```
cat("Product lines:", length(unique(salesforce_data$product_line)),
↪  "\n")
```

```
Product lines: 3
```

```
cat("Quarters:", length(unique(salesforce_data$quarter)), "\n")
```

```
Quarters: 3
```

7.11.2.1 Questions

1. Pivot the dataset so each region becomes a column and each row shows total revenue by quarter.
2. Create a pivot table showing total units sold for each product_line across all regions.
3. Pivot the data so product_line becomes columns and revenue is the value. Group by region.
4. Create a wide table showing revenue for each region by quarter, with quarters as columns.
5. Unpivot the revenue columns you created in Task 1 back into long format with columns: region, quarter, revenue.
6. Calculate total revenue per region and sort the results from highest to lowest.
7. Calculate average revenue per product_line across all regions and quarters.
8. Identify which region generated the highest total units_sold across all product lines.
9. Create a pivot showing both revenue and units_sold for each region and product_line (multi-metric pivot).
10. Using SQL (sqldf), create a pivot table showing revenue by quarter for each region using CASE statements.
11. Using SQL (sqldf), unpivot the SQL pivot you created in Task 10 back into long format.
12. Create a long-format version of the dataset where revenue and units_sold are combined into a single metric column with a metric_type column.

7.12 Lab 7-2: Feature Selection Techniques

Imagine working with a customer dataset containing 50 variables such as demographics, purchase history, website behavior, and support interactions. Your manager asks a key question: which of these factors actually predict customer churn, and what drives customer lifetime value?

This is where feature selection becomes important. Feature selection is the process of identifying the most relevant variables for prediction and business understanding while removing noise, redundancy, and unnecessary complexity. Instead of using every available variable, the goal is to focus on the ones that truly add value.

Feature selection matters because it improves predictive performance, simplifies models, and makes results easier to interpret. It also helps clarify which business factors are most important and reduces the cost and effort of working with large datasets.

In this lab, you will apply feature selection using statistical methods, model-based scoring, and business-driven filtering. You will learn how to reduce a high-dimensional dataset into a smaller set of meaningful predictors that improve interpretability and model performance.

7.12.1 Demonstration

We'll work with comprehensive customer data to demonstrate how feature selection transforms overwhelming datasets into focused, predictive models.

7.12.1.1 Step 1: Understanding the Full Dataset

Let's start with a realistic customer dataset with many potential features.

```
# Load required packages
library(tidyverse)  # For data manipulation
library(sqldf)      # For SQL queries in R
library(corrplot)   # For correlation visualization

# Create comprehensive customer dataset
set.seed(123)

customers_full <- data.frame(
  customer_id = 1:500,

  # Demographics
  age = sample(18:75, 500, replace = TRUE),
  income = round(rnorm(500, 55000, 20000)),
  education_years = sample(12:20, 500, replace = TRUE),
```

```
  # Geographic
  region = sample(c('North', 'South', 'East', 'West', 'Central'),
   ↪  500, replace = TRUE),
  urban_rural = sample(c('Urban', 'Suburban', 'Rural'), 500,
   ↪  replace = TRUE),

  # Behavioral
  years_customer = sample(1:15, 500, replace = TRUE),
  monthly_purchases = sample(0:20, 500, replace = TRUE),
  avg_order_value = round(runif(500, 25, 300), 2),
  website_visits_month = sample(0:50, 500, replace = TRUE),
  email_opens_month = sample(0:30, 500, replace = TRUE),

  # Engagement
  support_tickets_year = sample(0:12, 500, replace = TRUE),
  social_media_follower = sample(c(TRUE, FALSE), 500, replace =
   ↪  TRUE),
  newsletter_subscriber = sample(c(TRUE, FALSE), 500, replace =
   ↪  TRUE),
  mobile_app_user = sample(c(TRUE, FALSE), 500, replace = TRUE),

  # Financial
  credit_score = sample(300:850, 500, replace = TRUE),
  payment_method = sample(c('Credit', 'Debit', 'PayPal', 'Bank'),
   ↪  500, replace = TRUE),

  stringsAsFactors = FALSE
) %>%
  mutate(
    # Calculate key business metrics (our target variables)
    total_annual_spend = monthly_purchases * avg_order_value * 12,
    customer_lifetime_value = total_annual_spend * years_customer,
    engagement_score = website_visits_month + (email_opens_month *
     ↪  2) +
                       ifelse(social_media_follower, 10, 0) +
                       ifelse(newsletter_subscriber, 5, 0),

    # Create churn indicator (our prediction target)
    churn_risk = case_when(
      years_customer <= 1 & monthly_purchases <= 2 ~ 'High',
      years_customer <= 3 & monthly_purchases <= 5 ~ 'Medium',
      TRUE ~ 'Low'
    )
```

```
)

# Display the complex dataset
cat("FULL CUSTOMER DATASET:\n")
```

```
FULL CUSTOMER DATASET:
```

```
cat("Dimensions:", nrow(customers_full), "rows ×",
↪ ncol(customers_full), "columns\n")
```

```
Dimensions: 500 rows × 21 columns
```

```
#cat("Variables:", paste(names(customers_full)[1:10], collapse = ",
↪ "), "...\n")

# Show sample
print(head(customers_full[, 1:6]))
```

```
  customer_id age income education_years region urban_rural
1           1  48  43018              13  South       Rural
2           2  32  28386              15   West       Urban
3           3  68  43156              18  North    Suburban
4           4  31  91021              16  North       Rural
5           5  20  76107              15   West    Suburban
6           6  59  49162              19  North       Rural
```

```
# Show our target variables
cat("\nKEY BUSINESS METRICS (Target Variables):\n")
```

```

KEY BUSINESS METRICS (Target Variables):
```

```
target_summary <- customers_full %>%
  summarise(
    avg_annual_spend = round(mean(total_annual_spend), 2),
    avg_lifetime_value = round(mean(customer_lifetime_value), 2),
    avg_engagement = round(mean(engagement_score), 1),
    high_churn_risk = sum(churn_risk == 'High')
  )
print(target_summary)
```

```
  avg_annual_spend avg_lifetime_value avg_engagement high_churn_risk
1         19349.07           147040.9           62.7               2
```

7.12.1.2 Step 2: Correlation Analysis for Feature Selection

In this step, we use correlation analysis to identify which variables are most strongly related to key business outcomes in the dataset. Because not all features contribute equally to prediction or interpretation, correlation provides a systematic way to reduce the number of candidate variables by focusing on those with meaningful relationships to the targets. Correlation measures the strength and direction of a linear relationship between two numeric variables, where values close to $+1$ or -1 indicate a strong relationship and values near 0 suggest little or no linear association.

We start by isolating only the numeric variables in the dataset, since correlation is defined only for numerical data. The customer ID column is removed because it is purely an identifier and does not contain predictive information. After preparing the data, we compute a correlation matrix, which summarizes the pairwise relationships between all numeric variables.

From this matrix, we focus on three key business outcomes: total annual spend, customer lifetime value, and engagement score. For each outcome, we extract and rank all other variables based on the strength of their relationship with that specific target. We use absolute correlation values so that both strong positive and strong negative relationships are treated as equally informative.

Finally, we apply a correlation threshold to filter out weak relationships. This step reduces the feature space to a smaller set of variables that are more likely to be useful for predictive modeling and business decision-making.

```
# Extract numeric variables for correlation analysis
numeric_vars <- customers_full %>%
  select_if(is.numeric) %>%
  select(-customer_id)  # Remove ID column

# Calculate correlation matrix
correlation_matrix <- cor(numeric_vars, use = "complete.obs")

# Focus on correlations with our key business metrics
key_metrics <- c("total_annual_spend", "customer_lifetime_value",
↪ "engagement_score")

# Analyze correlations with total annual spend
spend_correlations <- correlation_matrix[, "total_annual_spend"]
spend_correlations <- spend_correlations[names(spend_correlations)
↪ != "total_annual_spend"]
spend_correlations <- sort(abs(spend_correlations), decreasing =
↪ TRUE)

cat("CORRELATION WITH ANNUAL SPEND:\n")
```

```
CORRELATION WITH ANNUAL SPEND:
```

```r
print(round(spend_correlations[1:10], 3))
```

```
   monthly_purchases customer_lifetime_value          avg_order_value
               0.751                   0.729                    0.566
                 age                  income             credit_score
               0.050                   0.050                    0.032
      years_customer       email_opens_month          education_years
               0.031                   0.029                    0.028
 support_tickets_year
               0.027
```

```r
# Analyze correlations with customer lifetime value
clv_correlations <- correlation_matrix[, "customer_lifetime_value"]
clv_correlations <- clv_correlations[names(clv_correlations) !=
↪ "customer_lifetime_value"]
clv_correlations <- sort(abs(clv_correlations), decreasing = TRUE)

cat("\nCORRELATION WITH CUSTOMER LIFETIME VALUE:\n")
```

```
CORRELATION WITH CUSTOMER LIFETIME VALUE:
```

```r
print(round(clv_correlations[1:10], 3))
```

```
  total_annual_spend    monthly_purchases       years_customer
               0.729                0.545                0.509
     avg_order_value    email_opens_month         credit_score
               0.422                0.095                0.084
    engagement_score               income website_visits_month
               0.074                0.063                0.012
support_tickets_year
               0.012
```

```r
# Analyze correlations with engagement score
engagement_correlations <- correlation_matrix[, "engagement_score"]
engagement_correlations <-
↪ engagement_correlations[names(engagement_correlations) !=
↪ "engagement_score"]
engagement_correlations <- sort(abs(engagement_correlations),
↪ decreasing = TRUE)

cat("\nCORRELATION WITH ENGAGEMENT SCORE:\n")
```

```
CORRELATION WITH ENGAGEMENT SCORE:
```

```
print(round(engagement_correlations[1:10], 3))
```

```
    email_opens_month    website_visits_month    support_tickets_year
                0.752                   0.683                   0.119
        years_customer                     age customer_lifetime_value
                0.106                   0.097                   0.074
     monthly_purchases            credit_score       total_annual_spend
                0.033                   0.029                   0.017
       avg_order_value
                0.010
```

```
# Identify top features based on correlation strength
correlation_threshold <- 0.3
top_spend_features <- names(spend_correlations[spend_correlations
↪ > correlation_threshold])
top_clv_features <- names(clv_correlations[clv_correlations >
↪ correlation_threshold])
top_engagement_features <-
↪ names(engagement_correlations[engagement_correlations >
↪ correlation_threshold])

cat("\n=== CORRELATION-BASED FEATURE SELECTION ===\n")
```

```
=== CORRELATION-BASED FEATURE SELECTION ===
```

```
cat("Features correlated with Annual Spend (>0.3):",
 ↪ length(top_spend_features), "\n")
```

```
Features correlated with Annual Spend (>0.3): 3
```

```
cat("Features:", paste(top_spend_features, collapse = ", "), "\n")
```

```
Features: monthly_purchases, customer_lifetime_value, avg_order_value
```

```
cat("\nFeatures correlated with CLV (>0.3):",
 ↪ length(top_clv_features), "\n")
```

```
Features correlated with CLV (>0.3): 4
```

```
#cat("Features:", paste(top_clv_features, collapse = ", "), "\n")
cat("\nFeatures correlated with Engagement (>0.3):",
 ↪ length(top_engagement_features), "\n")
```

```
Features correlated with Engagement (>0.3): 2
```

```
cat("Features:", paste(top_engagement_features, collapse = ", "),
↪ "\n")
```

```
Features: email_opens_month, website_visits_month
```

The output ranks variables by correlation strength, where values closer to 1 indicate stronger relationships. For annual spend, monthly_purchases (0.751), customer_lifetime_value (0.729), and avg_order_value (0.566) show the strongest associations, suggesting that purchase frequency and order size are key drivers of revenue. In contrast, age, income, and credit_score show weak relationships and add little explanatory power for spending behavior.

For customer lifetime value, the strongest predictors are total_annual_spend, monthly_purchases, and years_customer, highlighting the importance of long-term purchasing behavior. For engagement score, email_opens_month (0.752) and website_visits_month (0.683) dominate, reflecting direct digital activity as the main driver of engagement.

Overall, this step identifies statistically strong relationships with key outcomes, but it does not yet determine whether those variables are actionable or useful for business decision-making.

7.12.1.3 Step 3: Business-Driven Feature Selection

While correlation identifies statistical relationships, it does not reflect whether a variable is actually useful, controllable, or actionable in a business context. Some variables may be strongly correlated but not practically useful (such as age), while others may be slightly weaker statistically but far more valuable for decision-making (such as email engagement or website activity). Because of this, we shift from purely statistical selection to business-driven feature selection, focusing on variables that directly support marketing, retention, and revenue strategies.

In this step, we select features based on business purpose rather than correlation alone. Instead of asking what is correlated with the outcome, we ask what the business can actually act on.

We organize the variables into three strategy-based feature sets. The acquisition and retention model includes demographics, geographic factors, and early behavioral signals that help identify and retain customers. The value optimization model focuses on revenue drivers such as purchase behavior, engagement activity, and financial capacity to improve customer lifetime value. The churn prevention model uses risk and engagement indicators to identify customers who may be likely to leave.

Comparing these models highlights that feature selection is not only a statistical process but also a strategic one, where different variable sets serve different business goals.

```
# Business-driven feature selection based on strategic priorities
# Focus on actionable variables that business can influence

# Customer Acquisition & Retention Model
acquisition_features <- customers_full %>%
  select(
    customer_id,
    # Demographics (for targeting)
    age, income, education_years,
    # Geographic (for market strategy)
    region, urban_rural,
    # Early behavior indicators (for retention)
    years_customer, monthly_purchases, avg_order_value,
    # Engagement (actionable through marketing)
    website_visits_month, email_opens_month, engagement_score,
    # Target metrics
    total_annual_spend, customer_lifetime_value, churn_risk
  )

cat("BUSINESS-DRIVEN ACQUISITION MODEL:\n")
```

```
BUSINESS-DRIVEN ACQUISITION MODEL:
```

```
cat("Selected features:", ncol(acquisition_features) - 1, "out of",
 ↪  ncol(customers_full) - 1, "\n")
```

```
Selected features: 14 out of 20
```

```
print(names(acquisition_features))
```

```
 [1] "customer_id"              "age"
 [3] "income"                   "education_years"
 [5] "region"                   "urban_rural"
 [7] "years_customer"           "monthly_purchases"
 [9] "avg_order_value"          "website_visits_month"
[11] "email_opens_month"        "engagement_score"
[13] "total_annual_spend"       "customer_lifetime_value"
[15] "churn_risk"
```

```
# Customer Value Optimization Model
value_optimization_features <- customers_full %>%
  select(
    customer_id,
    # Value drivers
```

```
    monthly_purchases, avg_order_value, years_customer,
    # Engagement levers
    website_visits_month, email_opens_month,
    social_media_follower, newsletter_subscriber, mobile_app_user,
    # Financial capacity
    income, credit_score,
    # Target metrics
    total_annual_spend, customer_lifetime_value
  )

cat("\nBUSINESS-DRIVEN VALUE OPTIMIZATION MODEL:\n")
```

```
BUSINESS-DRIVEN VALUE OPTIMIZATION MODEL:
```

```
cat("Selected features:", ncol(value_optimization_features) - 1,
↪  "out of", ncol(customers_full) - 1, "\n")
```

```
Selected features: 12 out of 20
```

```
print(names(value_optimization_features))
```

```
 [1] "customer_id"             "monthly_purchases"
 [3] "avg_order_value"         "years_customer"
 [5] "website_visits_month"    "email_opens_month"
 [7] "social_media_follower"   "newsletter_subscriber"
 [9] "mobile_app_user"         "income"
[11] "credit_score"            "total_annual_spend"
[13] "customer_lifetime_value"
```

```
# Churn Prevention Model
churn_prevention_features <- customers_full %>%
  select(
    customer_id,
    # Risk indicators
    years_customer, monthly_purchases, support_tickets_year,
    # Engagement indicators
    website_visits_month, email_opens_month, engagement_score,
    # Loyalty indicators
    social_media_follower, newsletter_subscriber,
    # Target
    churn_risk
  )

cat("\nBUSINESS-DRIVEN CHURN PREVENTION MODEL:\n")
```

```
BUSINESS-DRIVEN CHURN PREVENTION MODEL:
```

```
cat("Selected features:", ncol(churn_prevention_features) - 1, "out
 ↪  of", ncol(customers_full) - 1, "\n")
```

```
Selected features: 9 out of 20
```

```
cat(names(churn_prevention_features), sep = "\n")
```

```
customer_id
years_customer
monthly_purchases
support_tickets_year
website_visits_month
email_opens_month
engagement_score
social_media_follower
newsletter_subscriber
churn_risk
```

```
# Compare business models
business_model_comparison <- data.frame(
  Model = c("Acquisition & Retention", "Value Optimization", "Churn
   ↪  Prevention"),
  Features = c(ncol(acquisition_features) - 1,
               ncol(value_optimization_features) - 1,
               ncol(churn_prevention_features) - 1),
  Focus = c("Customer targeting", "Revenue growth", "Risk
   ↪  management"),
  Business_Impact = c("Market expansion", "Profit maximization",
   ↪  "Customer retention")
)

cat("\n=== BUSINESS MODEL COMPARISON ===\n")
```

```
=== BUSINESS MODEL COMPARISON ===
```

```
print(business_model_comparison[,1:3])
```

```
                    Model Features              Focus
1 Acquisition & Retention       14 Customer targeting
2      Value Optimization       12     Revenue growth
```

```
3        Churn Prevention        9    Risk management
```

```r
print(business_model_comparison[,4])
```

```
[1] "Market expansion"    "Profit maximization" "Customer retention"
```

7.12.1.4 Step 4: Variable Importance Analysis

In this step, we extend feature selection by estimating the *predictive strength* of each variable for our key business outcomes. While correlation in Step 2 tells us whether two variables move together, it does not tell us how useful a variable would be for prediction. To address this, we approximate variable importance using a simple statistical method based on linear relationships.

For each predictor variable, we fit a simple relationship with the target outcome (such as total annual spend, customer lifetime value, or engagement score) and compute an R-squared value. R-squared represents the proportion of variation in the target variable that can be explained by a single feature. A higher R-squared means that the variable is more informative for predicting that outcome.

This function loops through all numeric variables, calculates their individual R-squared values with the target variable, and ranks them from most to least important. Unlike correlation, which only measures strength of association, this approach translates that relationship into an estimate of predictive power.

We then apply a threshold ($R^2 > 0.1$) to keep only variables that explain a meaningful amount of variation in the target outcome. This helps reduce the feature space further and focuses only on variables that are likely to contribute to a predictive model.

Finally, we combine importance scores across all three business outcomes to create an overall ranking of features. This allows us to identify variables that are consistently strong across multiple business objectives, rather than just one. The resulting ranking represents a transition from exploratory analysis toward model-ready feature selection.

```r
# Variable importance using simple linear relationships
# This simulates what more advanced ML algorithms would provide

calculate_variable_importance <- function(data, target_var) {
  numeric_cols <- data %>% select_if(is.numeric) %>% names()
  numeric_cols <- numeric_cols[numeric_cols != target_var &
↪ numeric_cols != "customer_id"]

  importance_scores <- sapply(numeric_cols, function(col) {
    if(col %in% names(data)) {
      # Calculate R-squared from simple linear regression
      model_data <- data[, c(col, target_var)]
      model_data <- model_data[complete.cases(model_data), ]
```

```
        if(nrow(model_data) > 10) {
          correlation <- cor(model_data[[col]],
↪   model_data[[target_var]])
          r_squared <- correlation^2
          return(r_squared)
        }
      }
      return(0)
    })

    return(sort(importance_scores, decreasing = TRUE))
  }

  # Calculate importance for annual spend
  spend_importance <- calculate_variable_importance(customers_full,
↪   "total_annual_spend")
  cat("VARIABLE IMPORTANCE FOR ANNUAL SPEND:\n")
```

```
VARIABLE IMPORTANCE FOR ANNUAL SPEND:
```

```
  print(round(spend_importance[1:8], 3))
```

```
      monthly_purchases customer_lifetime_value           avg_order_value
                  0.563                   0.532                     0.321
                    age                  income              credit_score
                  0.003                   0.002                     0.001
         years_customer       email_opens_month
                  0.001                   0.001
```

```
  # Calculate importance for customer lifetime value
  clv_importance <- calculate_variable_importance(customers_full,
↪   "customer_lifetime_value")
  cat("\nVARIABLE IMPORTANCE FOR CUSTOMER LIFETIME VALUE:\n")
```

```

VARIABLE IMPORTANCE FOR CUSTOMER LIFETIME VALUE:
```

```
  cat(round(clv_importance[1:8], 3), sep = "\n")
```

```
0.532
0.297
0.259
0.178
0.009
```

```
0.007
0.006
0.004
```

```
# Calculate importance for engagement score
engagement_importance <-
↪ calculate_variable_importance(customers_full, "engagement_score")
cat("\nVARIABLE IMPORTANCE FOR ENGAGEMENT SCORE:\n")
```

```
VARIABLE IMPORTANCE FOR ENGAGEMENT SCORE:
```

```
print(round(engagement_importance[1:8], 3))
```

```
    email_opens_month   website_visits_month    support_tickets_year
                0.565                  0.467                   0.014
       years_customer                    age customer_lifetime_value
                0.011                  0.009                   0.006
    monthly_purchases           credit_score
                0.001                  0.001
```

```
# Create importance-based feature sets
importance_threshold <- 0.1

spend_important_features <- names(spend_importance[spend_importance
↪ > importance_threshold])
clv_important_features <- names(clv_importance[clv_importance >
↪ importance_threshold])
engagement_important_features <-
↪ names(engagement_importance[engagement_importance >
↪ importance_threshold])

cat("\n=== IMPORTANCE-BASED FEATURE SELECTION ===\n")
```

```
=== IMPORTANCE-BASED FEATURE SELECTION ===
```

```
cat("Important for Annual Spend (R² > 0.1):",
  ↪ length(spend_important_features), "\n")
```

```
Important for Annual Spend (R² > 0.1): 3
```

```
cat("Features:", paste(spend_important_features, collapse = ", "),
  ↪ "\n")
```

```
Features: monthly_purchases, customer_lifetime_value, avg_order_value
```

```
cat("\nImportant for CLV (R² > 0.1):",
↪ length(clv_important_features), "\n")
```

```
Important for CLV (R² > 0.1): 4
```

```
cat("Features:\n")
```

```
Features:
```

```
cat(clv_important_features, sep = "\n")
```

```
total_annual_spend
monthly_purchases
years_customer
avg_order_value
```

```
cat("\nImportant for Engagement (R² > 0.1):",
↪ length(engagement_important_features), "\n")
```

```
Important for Engagement (R² > 0.1): 2
```

```
cat("Features:", paste(engagement_important_features, collapse = ",
↪ "), "\n")
```

```
Features: email_opens_month, website_visits_month
```

```
# Create comprehensive importance ranking
all_features <- unique(c(spend_important_features,
↪ clv_important_features, engagement_important_features))

feature_scores <- data.frame(
  feature = all_features,
  spend_importance = ifelse(all_features %in%
  ↪ names(spend_importance),
                            spend_importance[all_features], 0),
  clv_importance = ifelse(all_features %in% names(clv_importance),
                          clv_importance[all_features], 0),
  engagement_importance = ifelse(all_features %in%
  ↪ names(engagement_importance),

↪ engagement_importance[all_features], 0)
) %>%
  mutate(
```

```
    avg_importance = (spend_importance +
                      clv_importance +
                      engagement_importance) / 3
  ) %>%
  arrange(desc(avg_importance))

cat("\nTOP 10 FEATURES BY AVERAGE IMPORTANCE:\n")
```

```
TOP 10 FEATURES BY AVERAGE IMPORTANCE:
```

```
print(head(feature_scores[,1:3], 10))
```

```
                feature spend_importance clv_importance
1       monthly_purchases     0.5633351262    0.297072651
2       email_opens_month     0.0008428090    0.009072447
3 customer_lifetime_value     0.5318021637    0.000000000
4       total_annual_spend     0.0000000000    0.531802164
5          avg_order_value     0.3209218720    0.177690283
6     website_visits_month     0.0004071214    0.000153298
7           years_customer     0.0009575664    0.259125077
```

```
print(head(feature_scores[,4:5], 10))
```

```
  engagement_importance avg_importance
1          0.0011208978     0.28717623
2          0.5652283495     0.19171454
3          0.0055152704     0.17910581
4          0.0002941472     0.17736544
5          0.0001082967     0.16624015
6          0.4671104142     0.15589028
7          0.0113414801     0.09047471
```

This output summarizes the final step of the feature importance analysis, where each variable is evaluated across three business outcomes: annual spend, customer lifetime value, and engagement score. Instead of analyzing each outcome separately, the results are combined into a single table that shows the overall importance of each feature. The columns spend_importance, clv_importance, and engagement_importance represent how strongly each variable explains variation in each outcome using R-squared from simple linear relationships. The avg_importance column averages these values to produce a single ranking score.

From this ranking, monthly_purchases stands out as the most important overall feature due to its strong relationship with both spending and lifetime value. email_opens_month ranks highly as well, driven by its strong link to engagement, even though it contributes less to financial outcomes. Variables such as total_annual_spend and customer_lifetime_value also rank high because they are strongly tied to revenue behavior, though they are less informative for engagement. Features like avg_order_value and website_visits_month show moderate importance depending on the outcome, while years_customer mainly reflects long-term value rather than short-term behavior. Overall, this table highlights variables that are consistently useful across multiple business goals rather than those that matter for only a single outcome.

7.12.1.5 Step 5: Practical Feature Selection Workflow

In this final step, we bring together all the feature selection methods used so far into a single practical workflow. Up to this point, we have looked at correlation analysis, variable importance, and business-driven selection separately. However, in real data analytics work, these approaches are not used in isolation. Instead, they are combined into one structured process to decide which variables should actually be kept for modeling.

This workflow applies three filters to the data: a statistical filter based on correlation strength, a predictive filter based on importance scores, and a business filter based on domain knowledge and practical relevance. By merging these approaches, we reduce the feature set to only the variables that are statistically meaningful, useful for prediction, and relevant for business decision-making.

```
# Comprehensive feature selection workflow
feature_selection_workflow <- function(data, target_var,
↪ correlation_threshold = 0.3, importance_threshold = 0.1) {

  # Step 1: Correlation analysis
  numeric_data <- data %>% select_if(is.numeric)
  correlations <- cor(numeric_data, use = "complete.obs")[,
↪ target_var]
  correlations <- correlations[names(correlations) != target_var]
  correlation_features <- names(correlations[abs(correlations) >
↪ correlation_threshold])

  # Step 2: Variable importance
  importance_scores <- calculate_variable_importance(data,
↪ target_var)
  importance_features <- names(importance_scores[importance_scores
↪ > importance_threshold])

  # Step 3: Combine approaches
  statistical_features <- unique(c(correlation_features,
↪ importance_features))

  # Step 4: Business validation (simulate business expert input)
```

```
    business_critical <- c("monthly_purchases", "avg_order_value",
↪  "years_customer",
                              "engagement_score", "income", "age")
    business_features <- intersect(business_critical, names(data))

    # Step 5: Final feature set
    final_features <- unique(c(statistical_features,
↪  business_features))

    return(list(
      correlation_features = correlation_features,
      importance_features = importance_features,
      statistical_features = statistical_features,
      business_features = business_features,
      final_features = final_features,
      reduction_percent = round((1 - length(final_features) /
        ↪  (ncol(data) - 1)) * 100, 1)
    ))
  }

  # Apply workflow to our key business metrics
  spend_selection <- feature_selection_workflow(customers_full,
↪  "total_annual_spend")
  clv_selection <- feature_selection_workflow(customers_full,
↪  "customer_lifetime_value")
  engagement_selection <- feature_selection_workflow(customers_full,
↪  "engagement_score")

  cat("=== COMPREHENSIVE FEATURE SELECTION RESULTS ===\n")
```

```
=== COMPREHENSIVE FEATURE SELECTION RESULTS ===
```

```
  cat("\nANNUAL SPEND MODEL:\n")
```

```

ANNUAL SPEND MODEL:
```

```
  cat("Final features:", length(spend_selection$final_features),
   ↪  "\n")
```

```
Final features: 7
```

```
  cat("Reduction:", spend_selection$reduction_percent, "%\n")
```

```
Reduction: 65 %
```

```
cat("Features:\n")
```

```
Features:
```

```
cat(spend_selection$final_features, sep = "\n")
```

```
monthly_purchases
avg_order_value
customer_lifetime_value
years_customer
engagement_score
income
age
```

```
cat("\nCUSTOMER LIFETIME VALUE MODEL:\n")
```

```

CUSTOMER LIFETIME VALUE MODEL:
```

```
cat("Final features:", length(clv_selection$final_features), "\n")
```

```
Final features: 7
```

```
cat("Reduction:", clv_selection$reduction_percent, "%\n")
```

```
Reduction: 65 %
```

```
cat("Features:\n")
```

```
Features:
```

```
cat(clv_selection$final_features, sep = "\n")
```

```
years_customer
monthly_purchases
avg_order_value
total_annual_spend
engagement_score
income
age
```

```
cat("\nENGAGEMENT SCORE MODEL:\n")
```

```

ENGAGEMENT SCORE MODEL:
```

```
cat("Final features:", length(engagement_selection$final_features),
 ↪ "\n")
```

```
Final features: 8
```

```
cat("Reduction:", engagement_selection$reduction_percent, "%\n")
```

```
Reduction: 60 %
```

```
cat("Features:\n")
```

```
Features:
```

```
cat(engagement_selection$final_features, sep = "\n")
```

```
website_visits_month
email_opens_month
monthly_purchases
avg_order_value
years_customer
engagement_score
income
age
```

```
# Create final optimized datasets
spend_model_data <- customers_full %>%
  select(customer_id, all_of(spend_selection$final_features),
   ↪ total_annual_spend)

clv_model_data <- customers_full %>%
  select(customer_id, all_of(clv_selection$final_features),
   ↪ customer_lifetime_value)

engagement_model_data <- customers_full %>%
  select(customer_id, all_of(engagement_selection$final_features),
   ↪ engagement_score)

cat("\n=== OPTIMIZED DATASETS CREATED ===\n")
```

```

=== OPTIMIZED DATASETS CREATED ===
```

```
cat("Original dataset:", ncol(customers_full), "columns\n")
```

```
Original dataset: 21 columns
```

```
cat("Spend model:", ncol(spend_model_data), "columns\n")
```

```
Spend model: 9 columns
```

```
cat("CLV model:", ncol(clv_model_data), "columns\n")
```

```
CLV model: 9 columns
```

```
cat("Engagement model:", ncol(engagement_model_data), "columns\n")
```

```
Engagement model: 9 columns
```

The result is a simplified and optimized dataset for each business outcome (spend, lifetime value, and engagement), along with a clear measure of how much the feature space has been reduced. This represents the final stage of feature selection before model building, where the goal is no longer exploration, but preparing clean, efficient inputs for predictive analytics.

7.12.2 Practice

You're working with TechCorp's customer data to build predictive models for different business objectives.

```
# Create exercise dataset
set.seed(456)

techcorp_customers <- data.frame(
  customer_id = 1:300,

  # Demographics
  age = sample(25:65, 300, replace = TRUE),
  income = round(rnorm(300, 65000, 25000)),
  job_level = sample(c('Entry', 'Mid', 'Senior', 'Executive'), 300,
  ↪  replace = TRUE),

  # Company characteristics
  company_size = sample(c('Small', 'Medium', 'Large',
  ↪  'Enterprise'), 300, replace = TRUE),
  industry = sample(c('Tech', 'Finance', 'Healthcare',
  ↪  'Manufacturing', 'Other'), 300, replace = TRUE),

  # Product usage
  products_used = sample(1:5, 300, replace = TRUE),
  usage_hours_week = sample(1:40, 300, replace = TRUE),
  feature_adoption_score = sample(1:100, 300, replace = TRUE),
```

```
    # Engagement
    training_sessions = sample(0:20, 300, replace = TRUE),
    support_tickets = sample(0:15, 300, replace = TRUE),
    community_posts = sample(0:50, 300, replace = TRUE),

    # Financial
    contract_value = round(runif(300, 5000, 100000), 2),
    payment_terms = sample(c('Monthly', 'Quarterly', 'Annual'), 300,
     ↪  replace = TRUE),

    # Satisfaction
    nps_score = sample(-100:100, 300, replace = TRUE),
    satisfaction_rating = sample(1:10, 300, replace = TRUE),

    stringsAsFactors = FALSE
  ) %>%
    mutate(
      # Calculate target variables
      annual_revenue = contract_value,
      renewal_probability = pmax(0, pmin(1, (nps_score + 100) / 200 +
       ↪  runif(300, -0.2, 0.2))),
      expansion_potential = case_when(
        feature_adoption_score >= 80 & usage_hours_week >= 20 ~
↪  'High',
        feature_adoption_score >= 60 & usage_hours_week >= 10 ~
↪  'Medium',
        TRUE ~ 'Low'
      )
    )

  cat("TECHCORP CUSTOMER DATASET:\n")
```

```
TECHCORP CUSTOMER DATASET:
```

```
  cat("Dimensions:", nrow(techcorp_customers), "rows ×",
   ↪  ncol(techcorp_customers), "columns\n")
```

```
Dimensions: 300 rows × 19 columns
```

```
  print(head(techcorp_customers[, 1:5]))
```

```
  customer_id age income job_level company_size
1           1  61  81749    Senior        Large
```

```
2              2  59 106444     Senior       Medium
3              3  62  48002 Executive   Enterprise
4              4  45  87219        Mid   Enterprise
5              5  51  67047 Executive   Enterprise
6              6  49  60603      Entry       Medium
```

7.12.2.1 Questions

1. Identify all numeric variables in the TechCorp dataset and list them.
2. Calculate the correlation between usage_hours_week and annual_revenue. Is the relationship strong or weak?
3. Rank all numeric variables by their absolute correlation with annual_revenue. Which three variables are most strongly related?
4. Using a correlation threshold of 0.3, list all variables that meet the threshold for predicting annual_revenue.
5. Compute the correlation between feature_adoption_score and renewal_probability. What does the value suggest?
6. For the target variable renewal_probability, identify the top five correlated predictors.
7. Fit a simple linear relationship between usage_hours_week and annual_revenue. Report the R-squared value.
8. Calculate R-squared values for all numeric predictors of annual_revenue. Which variables exceed an R-squared of 0.1?
9. Compare the top correlated features and the top R-squared features for annual_revenue. Which variables appear in both lists?
10. Identify which variables would be considered business-actionable for improving renewal_probability. Explain your choices.
11. Create a feature set for a customer expansion model using only product usage and engagement variables. List the variables you selected.
12. Based on the dataset, which variables would you include in a churn-prevention model focused on customer dissatisfaction? Explain your reasoning.
13. Apply a combined feature selection approach (correlation + importance + business relevance) for predicting annual_revenue. List your final selected features.
14. Using the expansion_potential variable, identify which predictors differ the most between High and Low groups. Which features might be useful for classification?

7.13 Lab 7-3 Summarization and Aggregation

Imagine working with a database containing more than 100,000 individual sales transactions. On their own, these rows tell you what happened—but not what it *means*. When your CEO asks, "How are we performing by region this quarter?" or "Which product categories are driving the most revenue," raw transaction-level data can't answer those questions directly. To move from information to insight, you need summarization and aggregation.

Data summarization is the process of transforming detailed records into meaningful business metrics. By grouping data—whether by region, product category, or time period—and calculating totals, averages, and counts, you reveal patterns that support real decision-making. These summaries power business intelligence dashboards, help track KPIs over time, and make it possible to identify trends across markets, customers, and product lines.

Aggregation is the engine behind this transformation. Grouping organizes your data into logical segments; aggregation computes the metrics that matter; summarization turns those metrics into business-ready insights. Together, they allow analysts to convert large, messy datasets into clear, actionable information.

In this lab, you'll learn how to perform these essential summarization and aggregation tasks using both R and SQL—skills that form the foundation of modern analytics work.

7.13.1 Demonstration

7.13.1.1 Step 1: Understanding Detailed Transaction Data

We'll work with a comprehensive sales dataset to demonstrate how summarization transforms detailed transactions into business intelligence.

Let's start with realistic sales transaction data that needs summarization.

```
# Load required packages
library(tidyverse)  # For data manipulation
library(sqldf)      # For SQL queries in R

# Create detailed sales transaction data
set.seed(123)

# Generate realistic sales transactions
sales_transactions <- data.frame(
  transaction_id = 1:1000,
  customer_id = sample(1:200, 1000, replace = TRUE),
  product_category = sample(c('Electronics', 'Clothing', 'Home',
  ↪ 'Books', 'Sports'), 1000, replace = TRUE),
  product_name = paste("Product", sample(1:50, 1000, replace =
  ↪ TRUE)),
```

```
  region = sample(c('North', 'South', 'East', 'West', 'Central'),
  ↪ 1000, replace = TRUE),
  sales_rep = sample(paste("Rep", 1:20), 1000, replace = TRUE),
  transaction_date = sample(seq(as.Date('2024-01-01'),
  ↪ as.Date('2024-12-31'), by="day"), 1000, replace = TRUE),
  quantity = sample(1:10, 1000, replace = TRUE),
  unit_price = round(runif(1000, 10, 500), 2),
  discount_percent = sample(c(0, 5, 10, 15, 20), 1000, replace =
  ↪ TRUE, prob = c(0.5, 0.2, 0.15, 0.1, 0.05)),
  stringsAsFactors = FALSE
) %>%
  mutate(
    # Calculate derived fields
    gross_amount = quantity * unit_price,
    discount_amount = gross_amount * (discount_percent / 100),
    net_amount = gross_amount - discount_amount,
    month = format(transaction_date, "%Y-%m"),
    quarter = paste0("Q",
    ↪ ceiling(as.numeric(format(transaction_date, "%m")) / 3))
  )

# Display the detailed data
cat("DETAILED SALES TRANSACTIONS:\n")
```

```
DETAILED SALES TRANSACTIONS:
```

```
cat("Total transactions:", nrow(sales_transactions), "\n")
```

```
Total transactions: 1000
```

```
cat("Columns:", ncol(sales_transactions), "\n")
```

```
Columns: 15
```

```
print(head(sales_transactions[, 1:5]))
```

```
  transaction_id customer_id product_category product_name  region
1              1         159            Books   Product 41   South
2              2         179           Sports   Product 44   South
3              3          14         Clothing   Product 17 Central
4              4         195             Home   Product 45   South
5              5         170      Electronics   Product 48    East
6              6          50            Books   Product 33 Central
```

```r
print(head(sales_transactions[, 6:8]))
```

```
  sales_rep transaction_date quantity
1     Rep 5       2024-12-06        4
2    Rep 10       2024-03-31        1
3    Rep 20       2024-12-22        6
4     Rep 4       2024-06-10        3
5    Rep 18       2024-11-10        8
6     Rep 3       2024-11-13        5
```

```r
# Show the challenge - too much detail for business insights
cat("\nSample of detailed data (first 5 transactions):\n")
```

```
Sample of detailed data (first 5 transactions):
```

```r
print(sales_transactions[1:5, c("transaction_id",
↪  "product_category", "region", "net_amount", "month")])
```

```
  transaction_id product_category  region net_amount   month
1              1            Books   South    270.878 2024-12
2              2           Sports   South    343.660 2024-03
3              3         Clothing Central   2727.165 2024-12
4              4             Home   South    661.713 2024-06
5              5      Electronics    East    919.296 2024-11
```

7.13.1.2 Step 2: Basic Grouping and Aggregation

Once you understand *why* summarization matters, the next step is learning *how* to produce these summaries from raw transactional data. Basic grouping and aggregation is the foundation of almost every analytical workflow: it's how you move from thousands of individual records to clear, business-ready metrics.

In this step, you'll practice grouping data by meaningful dimensions—such as region and month—and calculating core summary statistics like counts, totals, averages, and units sold. These operations reveal performance patterns that would be impossible to see in row-level data.

To reinforce the concepts, you'll implement the same summary using both SQL and the tidyverse. Seeing the two side by side helps you understand not just the syntax, but the shared logic behind all aggregation tools: define your groups, compute your metrics, and return a compact dataset that tells a clear story.

```r
# Following section 7.4.2: Basic Grouping and Aggregation
# Example: Summarize sales by region and month
```

```
# Using SQL approach (following the material pattern)
regional_monthly_sql <- sqldf("
  SELECT
    region,
    month,
    COUNT(transaction_id) as transaction_count,
    SUM(net_amount) as total_revenue,
    AVG(net_amount) as avg_transaction_value,
    SUM(quantity) as total_units_sold
  FROM sales_transactions
  GROUP BY region, month
  ORDER BY region, month
")

cat("REGIONAL MONTHLY SUMMARY (SQL approach):\n")
```

```
REGIONAL MONTHLY SUMMARY (SQL approach):
```

```
print(head(regional_monthly_sql, 10))
```

```
    region   month transaction_count total_revenue avg_transaction_value
1  Central 2024-01                19      24919.11             1311.5319
2  Central 2024-02                14      14230.67             1016.4762
3  Central 2024-03                12      10836.96              903.0801
4  Central 2024-04                14      12049.80              860.7003
5  Central 2024-05                17      24394.41             1434.9654
6  Central 2024-06                18      22234.16             1235.2312
7  Central 2024-07                18      33298.18             1849.8991
8  Central 2024-08                11      12221.24             1111.0216
9  Central 2024-09                 7      12472.12             1781.7311
10 Central 2024-10                11      13412.05             1219.2775
   total_units_sold
1               107
2                91
3                60
4                66
5                98
6                93
7               124
8                56
9                45
10               67
```

```r
# Using tidyverse approach for comparison
regional_monthly_tidy <- sales_transactions %>%
  group_by(region, month) %>%
  summarise(
    transaction_count = n(),
    total_revenue = sum(net_amount),
    avg_transaction_value = round(mean(net_amount), 2),
    total_units_sold = sum(quantity),
    .groups = 'drop'
  ) %>%
  arrange(region, month)

cat("\nREGIONAL MONTHLY SUMMARY (tidyverse approach):\n")
```

```
REGIONAL MONTHLY SUMMARY (tidyverse approach):
```

```r
print(head(regional_monthly_tidy, 10))
```

```
# A tibble: 10 x 6
   region  month   transaction_count total_revenue avg_transaction_value
   <chr>   <chr>               <int>         <dbl>                 <dbl>
 1 Central 2024-01                19        24919.                 1312.
 2 Central 2024-02                14        14231.                 1016.
 3 Central 2024-03                12        10837.                  903.
 4 Central 2024-04                14        12050.                  861.
 5 Central 2024-05                17        24394.                 1435.
 6 Central 2024-06                18        22234.                 1235.
 7 Central 2024-07                18        33298.                 1850.
 8 Central 2024-08                11        12221.                 1111.
 9 Central 2024-09                 7        12472.                 1782.
10 Central 2024-10                11        13412.                 1219.
# i 1 more variable: total_units_sold <int>
```

```r
# Demonstrate the power of summarization
cat("\n=== SUMMARIZATION IMPACT ===\n")
```

```
=== SUMMARIZATION IMPACT ===
```

```r
cat("Original detail records:", nrow(sales_transactions), "\n")
```

```
Original detail records: 1000
```

```
cat("Summarized records:", nrow(regional_monthly_sql), "\n")
```

```
Summarized records: 60
```

```
cat("Data reduction:", round((1 -
↪   nrow(regional_monthly_sql)/nrow(sales_transactions)) * 100, 1),
↪   "%\n")
```

```
Data reduction: 94 %
```

7.13.1.3 Step 3: Creating Business Summaries

After learning how to group and aggregate data, the next step is turning those summaries into *business-ready insights*. Executives don't want raw counts or long tables—they want clear indicators of performance, customer activity, product strength, and sales effectiveness. This step focuses on building exactly those kinds of summaries.

Business summaries combine multiple aggregated metrics into concise, decision-support views. Instead of looking at thousands of transactions, leaders can see quarterly revenue, customer activity, discount behavior, category performance, and sales-rep productivity in just a few rows. These summaries highlight what's working, what's lagging, and where attention is needed.

In this section, you'll generate three essential business views:

- a quarterly executive performance summary,
- a product category revenue analysis,
- and a ranked list of top-performing sales representatives.

```
# Following section 7.4.3: Creating Business Summaries
# Focus on metrics that support business decision-making

# Executive-level business performance summary
executive_summary <- sqldf("
  SELECT
    quarter,
    COUNT(DISTINCT customer_id) as active_customers,
    COUNT(transaction_id) as total_transactions,
    SUM(net_amount) as total_revenue,
    AVG(net_amount) as avg_transaction_value,
    SUM(quantity) as total_units,
    ROUND(SUM(discount_amount) * 100.0 / SUM(gross_amount), 1) as
↪   avg_discount_percent
  FROM sales_transactions
  GROUP BY quarter
```

```
  ORDER BY quarter
")

cat("EXECUTIVE BUSINESS SUMMARY:\n")
```

```
EXECUTIVE BUSINESS SUMMARY:
```

```
print(executive_summary)
```

```
  quarter active_customers total_transactions total_revenue
1      Q1              135                236      278529.0
2      Q2              147                242      314024.1
3      Q3              134                259      362737.2
4      Q4              150                263      328755.6
  avg_transaction_value total_units avg_discount_percent
1              1180.207        1244                  6.3
2              1297.620        1310                  4.5
3              1400.530        1500                  5.7
4              1250.021        1399                  4.9
```

```
# Product category performance analysis
category_performance <- sqldf("
  SELECT
    product_category,
    COUNT(transaction_id) as transactions,
    SUM(net_amount) as revenue,
    AVG(net_amount) as avg_transaction,
    SUM(quantity) as units_sold,
    ROUND(SUM(net_amount) * 100.0 / (SELECT SUM(net_amount) FROM
↪ sales_transactions), 1) as revenue_share_percent
  FROM sales_transactions
  GROUP BY product_category
  ORDER BY revenue DESC
")

cat("\nPRODUCT CATEGORY PERFORMANCE:\n")
```

```
PRODUCT CATEGORY PERFORMANCE:
```

```
print(category_performance)
```

```
  product_category transactions  revenue avg_transaction units_sold
1             Home          217 284108.9        1309.258       1165
2           Sports          203 267243.1        1316.468       1111
```

```
3       Electronics          215 260445.8        1211.376        1182
4             Books          184 244435.4        1328.453         997
5          Clothing          181 227812.6        1258.633         998
  revenue_share_percent
1                  22.1
2                  20.8
3                  20.3
4                  19.0
5                  17.7
```

```
# Sales representative performance
rep_performance <- sqldf("
  SELECT
    sales_rep,
    COUNT(DISTINCT customer_id) as customers_served,
    COUNT(transaction_id) as transactions,
    SUM(net_amount) as total_sales,
    ROUND(AVG(net_amount), 2) as avg_transaction,
    ROUND(SUM(net_amount) / COUNT(DISTINCT customer_id), 2) as
↪ revenue_per_customer
  FROM sales_transactions
  GROUP BY sales_rep
  ORDER BY total_sales DESC
  LIMIT 10
")

cat("\nTOP 10 SALES REPRESENTATIVES:\n")
```

```
TOP 10 SALES REPRESENTATIVES:
```

```
print(rep_performance)
```

```
   sales_rep customers_served transactions total_sales avg_transaction
1     Rep 17               50           59    89025.90         1508.91
2     Rep 14               52           61    83638.76         1371.13
3     Rep 15               47           55    79616.82         1447.58
4     Rep 18               51           61    74582.83         1222.67
5     Rep 12               47           52    72082.12         1386.19
6     Rep 16               52           56    71292.35         1273.08
7      Rep 1               50           59    70965.23         1202.80
8      Rep 8               42           48    67893.74         1414.45
9      Rep 4               44           51    67643.54         1326.34
10    Rep 19               47           50    64085.19         1281.70
   revenue_per_customer
```

```
1               1780.52
2               1608.44
3               1693.97
4               1462.41
5               1533.66
6               1371.01
7               1419.30
8               1616.52
9               1537.35
10              1363.51
```

7.13.1.4 Step 4: Advanced Aggregation Techniques

Once you can produce basic grouped summaries, the next level of analysis is learning how to extract deeper patterns from your data. Advanced aggregation techniques allow you to move beyond simple totals and averages and begin answering richer business questions—questions about trends, customer value, regional competitiveness, and performance rankings.

In this step, you'll explore three powerful analytical patterns commonly used in real business environments. First, you'll analyze time-based trends and calculate month-over-month growth to understand how performance is shifting over time. Next, you'll segment customers based on their total spending to identify high-value groups and revenue concentration. Finally, you'll evaluate regional performance using ranking metrics that highlight which areas lead or lag across key indicators.

These techniques transform your dataset into a multidimensional view of business performance, enabling more strategic insights and more informed decision-making. They're the kinds of analyses analysts and data teams produce every day to support marketing, finance, operations, and executive leadership.

```
# Time-based trend analysis
monthly_trends <- sales_transactions %>%
  group_by(month) %>%
  summarise(
    revenue = sum(net_amount),
    transactions = n(),
    avg_transaction = round(mean(net_amount), 2),
    customers = n_distinct(customer_id),
    .groups = 'drop'
  ) %>%
  arrange(month) %>%
  mutate(
    # Calculate month-over-month growth
    revenue_growth = round((revenue / lag(revenue) - 1) * 100, 1),
```

```
    transaction_growth = round((transactions / lag(transactions) -
    ↪ 1) * 100, 1)
  )

cat("MONTHLY TRENDS WITH GROWTH RATES:\n")
```

```
MONTHLY TRENDS WITH GROWTH RATES:
```

```
print(head(monthly_trends, 8))
```

```
# A tibble: 8 x 7
  month    revenue transactions avg_transaction customers revenue_growth
  <chr>      <dbl>        <int>           <dbl>     <int>          <dbl>
1 2024-01  81921.            70           1170.        54           NA
2 2024-02 102384.            80           1280.        69           25
3 2024-03  94224.            86           1096.        71           -8
4 2024-04  80866.            72           1123.        56          -14.2
5 2024-05 115056.            81           1420.        62           42.3
6 2024-06 118102.            89           1327.        82            2.6
7 2024-07 149615.           100           1496.        76           26.7
8 2024-08  98670.            81           1218.        70          -34.1
# i 1 more variable: transaction_growth <dbl>
```

```
# Customer segmentation analysis
customer_segments <- sqldf("
  SELECT
    CASE
      WHEN total_spent >= 5000 THEN 'High Value'
      WHEN total_spent >= 2000 THEN 'Medium Value'
      WHEN total_spent >= 500 THEN 'Regular'
      ELSE 'Low Value'
    END as customer_segment,
    COUNT(*) as customer_count,
    AVG(total_spent) as avg_customer_value,
    SUM(total_spent) as segment_revenue,
    AVG(transaction_count) as avg_transactions_per_customer
  FROM (
    SELECT
      customer_id,
      SUM(net_amount) as total_spent,
      COUNT(transaction_id) as transaction_count
    FROM sales_transactions
    GROUP BY customer_id
  ) customer_totals
```

```
  GROUP BY customer_segment
  ORDER BY avg_customer_value DESC
")

cat("\nCUSTOMER SEGMENTATION ANALYSIS:\n")
```

```
CUSTOMER SEGMENTATION ANALYSIS:
```

```
print(customer_segments)
```

```
  customer_segment customer_count avg_customer_value segment_revenue
1       High Value            117           8803.598      1030020.91
2     Medium Value             59           3729.168       220020.91
3          Regular             22           1536.413        33801.09
4        Low Value              1            202.920          202.92
  avg_transactions_per_customer
1                      6.094017
2                      3.847458
3                      2.681818
4                      1.000000
```

```
# Regional performance with rankings
regional_performance <- sales_transactions %>%
  group_by(region) %>%
  summarise(
    revenue = sum(net_amount),
    transactions = n(),
    customers = n_distinct(customer_id),
    avg_transaction = round(mean(net_amount), 2),
    .groups = 'drop'
  ) %>%
  mutate(
    revenue_rank = rank(desc(revenue)),
    transaction_rank = rank(desc(transactions)),
    customer_rank = rank(desc(customers))
  ) %>%
  arrange(revenue_rank)

cat("\nREGIONAL PERFORMANCE WITH RANKINGS:\n")
```

```
REGIONAL PERFORMANCE WITH RANKINGS:
```

```
print(regional_performance)
```

```
# A tibble: 5 x 8
  region  revenue transactions customers avg_transaction revenue_rank
  <chr>     <dbl>        <int>     <int>           <dbl>        <dbl>
1 North   282039.          202       124           1396.            1
2 South   278787.          232       137           1202.            2
3 West    262372.          211       132           1243.            3
4 East    233376.          174       111           1341.            4
5 Central 227472.          181       120           1257.            5
# i 2 more variables: transaction_rank <dbl>, customer_rank <dbl>
```

7.13.2 Practice

You're analyzing RetailCorp's sales data to create business summaries for different stakeholders.

```
# Create exercise dataset
set.seed(789)

retailcorp_sales <- data.frame(
  order_id = 1:800,
  customer_id = sample(1:150, 800, replace = TRUE),
  store_location = sample(c('Downtown', 'Mall', 'Suburban',
  ↪  'Online'), 800, replace = TRUE),
  product_line = sample(c('Fashion', 'Electronics', 'Home &
  ↪  Garden', 'Beauty', 'Sports'), 800, replace = TRUE),
  brand = sample(paste("Brand", LETTERS[1:10]), 800, replace =
  ↪  TRUE),
  order_date = sample(seq(as.Date('2024-01-01'),
  ↪  as.Date('2024-12-31'), by="day"), 800, replace = TRUE),
  order_value = round(runif(800, 25, 800), 2),
  cost_of_goods = round(runif(800, 10, 400), 2),
  shipping_cost = round(runif(800, 0, 25), 2),
  customer_type = sample(c('New', 'Returning', 'VIP'), 800, replace
  ↪  = TRUE, prob = c(0.3, 0.5, 0.2)),
  stringsAsFactors = FALSE
) %>%
  mutate(
    profit = order_value - cost_of_goods - shipping_cost,
    profit_margin = round((profit / order_value) * 100, 1),
    month = format(order_date, "%Y-%m"),
    quarter = paste0("Q", ceiling(as.numeric(format(order_date,
    ↪  "%m")) / 3))
```

```r
)

cat("RETAILCORP SALES DATASET:\n")
```

```
RETAILCORP SALES DATASET:
```

```r
cat("Total orders:", nrow(retailcorp_sales), "\n")
```

```
Total orders: 800
```

```r
print(head(retailcorp_sales[, 1:8]))
```

```
  order_id customer_id store_location  product_line   brand order_date
1        1          45         Online        Beauty Brand B 2024-03-26
2        2          12         Online        Sports Brand I 2024-04-11
3        3         116           Mall       Fashion Brand G 2024-02-21
4        4          42           Mall        Sports Brand F 2024-02-02
5        5         112           Mall   Electronics Brand J 2024-10-26
6        6         100       Downtown Home & Garden Brand A 2024-05-18
  order_value cost_of_goods
1      126.98        231.74
2      158.96         36.37
3      715.62        347.46
4      765.20        375.74
5       73.48        178.12
6      119.21        139.42
```

7.13.2.1 Questions

1. Calculate the total number of orders for each store_location.
2. Find the average order_value for each product_line.
3. Determine which brand generated the highest total revenue (sum of order_value).
4. Summarize total profit by month.
5. Count how many customers are New, Returning, and VIP.
6. Calculate the average profit_margin for each store_location.
7. Identify the top 5 customers based on total spending (sum of order_value).
8. Create a quarterly summary showing total revenue, total profit, and number of orders for each quarter.
9. Determine which product_line has the highest average profit per order.

10. Group orders by customer_type and calculate the average order_value and average profit for each group.

www.ingramcontent.com/pod-product-compliance
Lightning Source LLC
Chambersburg PA
CBHW061353240926
51846CB00007B/1388
9781969233425